Dance and Music

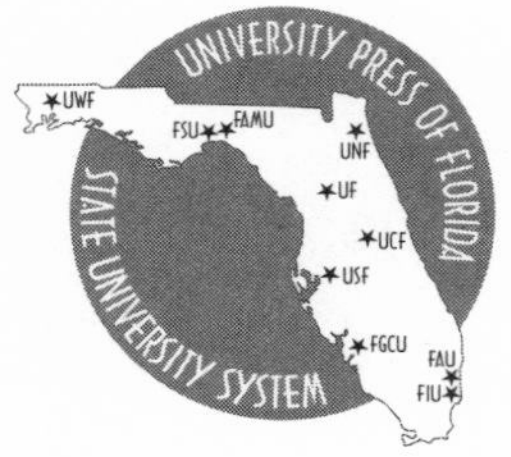

Florida A&M University, Tallahassee
Florida Atlantic University, Boca Raton
Florida Gulf Coast University, Ft. Myers
Florida International University, Miami
Florida State University, Tallahassee
University of Central Florida, Orlando
University of Florida, Gainesville
University of North Florida, Jacksonville
University of South Florida, Tampa
University of West Florida, Pensacola

~ *Dance and Music*

A Guide to Dance Accompaniment
for Musicians and Dance Teachers

Harriet Cavalli

University Press of Florida
Gainesville · Tallahassee · Tampa · Boca Raton
Pensacola · Orlando · Miami · Jacksonville · Ft. Myers

Printed in the United States of America on acid-free paper

First printing in German as *Tanz und Musik:* March 1998, to commemorate the 25th anniversary of the Swiss Ballet Teachers' Association (SBLV), Armin Wild, president.
German translation by Barbara Hesse, Binz, Switzerland
Illustrations by Thomas Ziegler, Bern, Switzerland

06 05 04 03 02 01 6 5 4 3 2 1

ISBN 0-8130-1887-0
CIP data available.
The University Press of Florida is the scholarly publishing agency for the State University System of Florida, comprising Florida A&M University, Florida Atlantic University, Florida Gulf Coast University, Florida International University, Florida State University, University of Central Florida, University of Florida, University of North Florida, University of South Florida, and University of West Florida.

University Press of Florida
15 Northwest 15th Street
Gainesville, FL 32611–2079
http://www.upf.com

To my family, the Weymouths, and especially my daughters, Celia and Beth.

To the memory—and in honor—of three people who still have a profound effect on my professional life:

- Maxine Cushing Gray, editor and publisher of *Northwest Arts* (Seattle), who gave me my first professional writing opportunity, and whose commitment to quality is still an inspiration;
- Vera Volkova, a tiny dynamo with a monumental knowledge of dance, dancers, and psychology, who challenged me to break bad habits; and
- Perry Brunson, who taught me most of what I know about dance accompaniment, ballet technique, discipline, and commitment.

And never-ending thanks to

- Donna Silva, for keeping Perry Brunson's legacy alive; and
- Martin Schläpfer, for his trust, respect, integrity, and honesty.

Contents

Foreword

In 1969, while appearing with the Stuttgart Ballet in their first New York season, I followed the suggestion of some of my colleagues to take classes with the latest ballet guru whose studio was located in one of those rickety old warehouse buildings sandwiched between skyscrapers and discount stores in midtown Manhattan.

I hadn't seen the class pianist enter the studio that day because I was flat on my back on the floor, exhausted from the rigors of the heavy performance the night before, slowly stretching the aches out of my tired feet and generally feeling extremely virtuous for having dragged myself to an early-morning class in the first place. Meanwhile the studio had filled to overflowing with an array of aspiring young dancers—some students, some unemployed professionals—who, fresh as a lark in springtime, were anything but prostrate on the floor, including many who were engaged in that traditional ballet-jungle occupation of demonstrating their supposedly considerable but as yet undiscovered talents.

At first the music started softly, like a gentle massage on the temples. It was a theme from Tchaikovsky's Piano Concerto no. 1, and coming so early on this particular morning, it couldn't have been more soothing. As the pianist modulated into Satie's *Gymnopédie no. 1*, my muscles relaxed in response; I rolled my head and, releasing a huge sigh of relief, half mumbled, "Who-o-o is that pianist?" "Oh, that's our Harriet," the girl next to me replied, her voice warm with affection.

Like the beckoning call of a snake charmer's flute, Harriet's preclass music, so perceptively chosen, played upon our tired muscles as it drifted from classical to contemporary—even some show tunes. In all it took perhaps only fifteen minutes, but at the end of that time, I had forgotten my fatigue and late hours from the night before. As if by hypnosis her music had wooed my weary body back into another day of work but with a feeling of freshness that was almost eerie. As our teacher entered the room and we all placed ourselves at the barre for the endless ritual of class, I of course looked over to see who this musical magician was who had so miraculously prepared us for our lesson. It was then that I finally saw this gently rounded figure of a woman sitting at her upright piano and grinning like a Cheshire cat. So this was the "music" called Harriet!

But Harriet is not just good. She is uniquely attuned to her class, the teacher, and the dancers through her being and through her music. She gives her total involvement to each exercise through her understanding of how the music can assist and energize every aspect of the lesson. She literally feels the mood of the dancers even before the class begins. She knows how to calm tension, to animate certain dancers who are lethargic, or to bring a special lightness into the atmosphere of a class that may have struck upon a lull.

Harriet is foremost among those classroom pianists who regard their profession as special and necessary—a unique element, if you wish—rather than as the final stop on the thwarted career of a once-aspiring concert pianist. Hers is a special talent, refined by years of hard work, keen observation, an unswerving dedication to improving her profession, and all this mixed with a good dash of homespun humor. Lucky are the ones who can learn from what she has to say, for, as this book will show, she feels a deep need to express and, in my opinion, possesses an unsurpassed ability to communicate her personal musical philosophy, which she has developed over many decades.

Harriet Cavalli should feel proud of her book. The dance community certainly will be grateful for her contribution to our profession.

Richard Cragun
Former international guest artist of the Stuttgart Ballet
and director of the Deutsche Oper Berlin Ballet; currently director
of De Anima—Ballet Contempôraneo do Paraná (Brazil)

Preface

There were four reasons for writing this book: to encourage more musicians to explore the field of dance accompaniment; to offer helpful suggestions to those already in the field; to provide musical assistance to dance teachers; and to promote clear and productive communication between dance teachers and accompanists.

Dance accompaniment is an art that seems to defy verbalization and systemization. However, there are certain principles and approaches that can be described. It is hoped that this book will provide a reference source for musicians and aspiring accompanists, and for teachers who want to improve their classes through a more creative approach to music. Conductors for dance and, of course, dancers will also find helpful information.

The majority of references to music in dance books is related to music for stage performance. That is a vitally important area, but so is the daily, often grueling work a dancer must go through during his training period. This area deserves broader coverage in relation to music. There is an ever-increasing need for effective and motivating accompaniment, and it is obvious that there would be more and better accompanists if musicians knew that such a profession existed.

One of my purposes is to show—through personal experience when necessary—that many facets of playing for dance can be learned from a book. The trial-and-error method of learning is not an efficient one. Since certain dance accompaniment skills, such as the adaptation of music to fit the needs of dance, are so individual, it made sense to state my approaches in certain areas, rather than to give the impression that there is only one way to do it. These approaches will serve to demonstrate one means to an end, and can be used as guidelines. There is no single right way, so there will be many suggestions and illustrations, but very few invariable rules.

The technical discussions in the area of dance throughout this book are based on my own personal experiences during my years of studying and teaching dance. They may not necessarily jibe with a dance pedagogue's experience or knowledge and, if they do nothing more than make someone question her own or my approach to a particular idea, they will have served their purpose.

The American term *combination* has been chosen instead of the (primarily) British *enchaînement.*

I have arbitrarily chosen to refer to teachers as she and to accompanists and dancers as he throughout the text, in order to facilitate reading. The terms *student* and *dancer,* as well as *introduction* and *preparation,* are usually interchangeable. The terms *bar* and *measure, adage* and *adagio,* and *big waltz* and *grand allegro waltz* are always interchangeable.

The use of the word *count* instead of *bar* or *measure* will be emphasized throughout the text—for example, a 4-*count* introduction, instead of a 4-*bar* introduction. See page 65 for a detailed explanation. (One of my editors said that I repeat myself too much. My response was, "Yes, I do, when the subject is really important." And I feel that this differentiation between *count* and *bar* for beginning accompanists is really important.)

Examples of counting within the text are very carefully written. A dash (-) takes the same amount of time as the other words in the sentence, but is silent. Therefore, "ONE - and two - and THREE - and . . ." is a typical way to count a waltz. The upper- and lowercase words reflect the peaks-and-valleys effect found in a great deal of music for dance.

Since chapter 5 has been written primarily for accompanists, most information for teachers in that chapter has been placed in the notes.

Acknowledgments

Steve Heck, a former teacher at Cornish College of the Arts in Seattle, gave me the initial push to write this book in 1978.

Olga Maynard, one of the dance world's finest journalists, was the first person (and one of the few) in my career who acknowledged that dance accompanists are much more knowledgeable than we are ever given credit for.

The following people took the time and trouble to wade through the first draft several years ago and point out its weaknesses:

- Kathryn Daniels, Dance Department Chair, Cornish College of the Arts;
- Patrick Stults, holder of master's degrees in conducting and teaching;
- Hannah Wiley, Director of the Dance Program, University of Washington (Seattle); and
- especially Gretchen Ward Warren, Professor of Dance, University of South Florida (Tampa), who took time away from her own book to do a very detailed editing job on this one, as well as providing constant and invaluable assistance during the preparation of the book in English.

This book first appeared in German, under the title *Tanz und Musik,* in March 1998 through the sponsorship of the Swiss Ballet Teachers' Association (Schweizerische Ballett-Lehrer Verband, SBLV). Its publication would have been impossible without the contributions of the following people:

- Armin Wild, immediate past president of the SBLV, may not have been the first to see the value of improving communication between teacher and accompanist, but he was the first to take the initiative and sponsor the translation of this publication;
- Suzanne Nicks, a fellow accompanist and good friend, waded through the second draft and made countless invaluable suggestions, as well as standing by with instant information and help with the English version;
- Anne Marchand was always willing to help with meticulous proofreading and cross-checking;
- Angèle and Fritz Köhler generously loaned me their electronic keyboard;
- Sasha and Dieter Thommen gave me much moral and technological support during the preparation of both the German and English versions;
- Hasan Koru was always ready to help me understand computerese, and painstakingly cleaned up all the musical examples and printed them, as well as working his usual magic on the titles and text in English; his patience and good humor know no bounds;
- Markus Imhoof did the cutting and pasting of the original musical examples;
- Simone Cavin patiently held her arms in second position to ensure an accurate rendering of Thomas Ziegler's drawing on page 165.
- Barbara Hesse somehow managed to make sense out of all the endnotes, rewrites, inserts, and detours that I sent her along with the original manuscript in English;
- Martha Kalt typed the original manuscript in German;
- Patrizia Landgraf Maurer edited the book, transcribed it to another computer system, did the lay-out, and shepherded it through the printing process—an indescribably huge amount of work.

To all of you: merci, danke schön, and THANK YOU!

And a special thank you to Bob Furnish, the copy editor of this version, whose corrections always enhanced my words without ever changing the meaning, as well as to Gillian Hillis, the project editor, whose patience with my last-minute additions and corrections was above and beyond the call of duty.

1 ~ *What Is Dance Accompaniment?*

Music must move a dancer emotionally, literally, and figuratively. It must give the dancer a reason to dance.

The purpose of music for dance is different from music for the concert hall. Unlike music to be listened to, music for dance complements, reflects, motivates, and enhances movement. An accompanist's classroom repertoire must therefore be geared toward helping dancers learn movement through music.

Dance is movement. That is obvious. A series of pretty poses does not impress an audience. How a dancer moves into and out of those positions makes an audience sit up and take notice. The flow of the movement—the physical peaks and valleys in relation to the music—is a large part of the visual stimuli to which an audience reacts.

By now, thanks to television and movies, almost everyone has seen some form of dance. Fred Astaire and Gene Kelly, Mikhail Baryshnikov and Martha Graham are household words. These artists, along with myriad others, prove one thing that is common to all styles of dance: It looks easy. That may be one reason why "easy," insubstantial music seems acceptable in the dance classroom. Nothing could be further from the truth.

The following are a few misconceptions about music for dance:

- Many non-dance-oriented musicians say, "Music has to be distorted for adaptation to the dance classroom." While I understand and sympathize with the reasons behind this pronouncement, I hope to show how distortion can be avoided. This topic will be discussed at length, especially throughout the information for accompanists.
- "Music for dance has no substance." Some of the music composed specifically for dance is, indeed, insubstantial. Toward the end of the nineteenth century, composers such as Ludwig Minkus and Riccardo Drigo were accused of writing "yard music." They would be given detailed instructions concerning stage action, meter, and—in many cases—even the number of bars needed by the choreographer. They would then retire to write music by the yard to these exacting and restricting specifications. While some of this music may be inconsequential, it served the needs of the choreogra-

phers at that time, and much of it remains in the international dance repertoire. And there is an abundance of music by Tchaikovsky, Prokofiev, Ravel, Bartók, Debussy, and Stravinsky—to name but a few respected composers—which certainly holds its own on the "serious" concert stage as well as in the pit at a dance performance.

- "All you have to do is keep the beat." While rhythm is a motivating constant behind most dance music, there is a good deal more to music than rhythm, just as there is more to dancing than legs and feet. The "keeping the beat" misconception may also stem from the fact that one may often see no reaction to music from some dancers, especially students. The demands of technical execution may sometimes leave a look of grim concentration on all but those rare dancers who are truly musical. But they *are* hearing the music—certainly not in the way a person sits down and listens to a piece of music on the radio—and not even in the way the teacher is hearing it. A dancer absorbs music almost through the fibers of his body; it seeps into him by osmosis, providing guidelines for the beginner and inspiration to the advanced dancer.

Music for dance is not elevator music. It is not just a thudding beat for maintaining rhythm. It is not background music, and it is not frippery. It is *almost* not accompaniment, for it should be as organic a part of the dance as the dancer's body. The only sense in which it is literally accompaniment is that it accompanies the music that is already inside every true dancer's body.

While there are some schools of thought that believe that music should not always reflect the dynamics of the movement, this book is written on the premise that dancers (including students) need and deserve all the support they can get. I have taken dance classes on and off for decades, and the technical improvement and spiritual liberation I've felt in a class with a truly fine, supportive accompanist is an unmatchable high.

Aside from the inspiration music should provide for dancers, music is the only guide a dancer has onstage. (There are dances done to silence, such as Jerome Robbins's masterpiece, "Moves," but they are rare.) Teachers, ballet masters, and choreographers do not stand in the wings yelling, "Tendu! Fourth position! Seventeen pirouettes!" The music tells the dancers where they should be and when—and how.

Cues for curtains, lighting, and scenery changes are very often written into the musical score which a stage manager may use for his cue sheet. If a dancer stops dancing during a piece, the performance will usually continue, but if the music stops during a piece, there is chaos.

Music is a dancer's only temporal link to the audience. He must learn to be responsive to its structure, complexities, and nuances, not just to the rhythm.

This process begins in the classroom, so classroom accompaniment must reflect the myriad genres of music to which dancers dance.

The most difficult aspect of dance accompaniment is that it is impossible to categorize. How easy (but, ultimately, how boring) it would be if "You *always* play a march for grands battements," or "You *always* play a 3/4 for ronds de jambe à terre." One of the reasons it cannot be categorized is because there are as many ways of teaching dance as there are dance teachers. The learning and teaching of dance is done primarily by handing it down from generation to generation. There are some codified systems of teaching ballet, such as the Vaganova, Cecchetti, Bournonville, and Royal Academy of Dancing methods, as well as Graham, Limón, and Cunningham techniques in the area of modern/contemporary dance. But each of these systems takes on the personality of each individual teacher. Dance is a purely physical art; the essence and nuances of movement will probably never be captured in the written word.

Another reason that dance accompaniment can't be standardized is that some teachers feel the dancer must do most of the work unaided by supportive music, while others feel the music should match the quality of the movement and provide a reason for moving. For the purposes of this book, I shall concentrate on the second approach.

Dance is perhaps the most difficult art form to master. It requires total control of almost every muscle in the body. Sadly, many students, as they work to gain this control, lose both the essence of what dance truly is and the motivation that made them want to dance in the first place. Music is the constant reminder that tells the student that he is not involved in a series of calisthenic exercises. It must provide a constant impetus and energy source for his movement; it should almost impose itself on his consciousness (or even his subconscious) in order to enable him to express himself through movement.

One of the main reasons for the scarcity of good accompanists is the communication problem between dance teachers and musicians. (While the following true story is amusing, it illustrates perfectly the problems of a novice accompanist. An accompanist once came to me for help, saying, "I don't have the slightest idea of what that teacher is talking about. Yesterday it sounded like he wanted two frappés, three Grand Marniers, and four croissants with camembert.") This book is intended to help bridge the communication gap, emphasizing above all the productive and pleasurable interaction between the two driving forces of the classroom.

2 ~ *Essential Elements of Music for Dance*

Music evokes images. Walt Disney's *Fantasia* is a perfect example of how certain music can be translated into complementary images. Disney in a sense choreographed *Fantasia* in direct response to the feelings and visions that the music suggested to him. That is how choreographers often work: A piece of music suggests a story, a mood, or a quality of movement that they develop into a dance. Usually, classroom accompanists are asked to reverse this process: We see a phrase of movement and are required to match its physical qualities with corresponding musical ones. No matter which way the process goes—music inspiring movement or movement inspiring music—our task is to evoke images and help dancers want to embody our music.

An accompanist must realize the effect music has on a moving human body. If you've ever done any sort of physical exercise such as calisthenics, isometrics, jogging, or weight lifting, you've felt the rhythm inherent in the execution. And exercise takes on a different feeling and added dimensions when melody is added; even more with the addition of harmony, and so on.

The musical elements which follow are arranged in order from the most obvious to the most subtle.

Rhythm

Rhythm is the prime moving force for a dancer. It must be as constant as his pulse, and just as vital. It sets the pace for his dance and must never be vague. For dancers in a professional company, the music for stage performance will become a part of them during the many hours of rehearsal. In the classroom, however, dancers will not always hear the music before they execute combinations, so the rhythm must be instantly obvious in order to provide a firm foundation for the movement.

As an accompanist, you want to re-create the lower register of an orchestra with your left hand. The rhythm of a symphonic composition is generally carried in the percussion section and—for richness of tone—in the low strings and brass. Be sure to take advantage of the piano's properties as a percussion instrument with a full range of tones, and strive for a lush, full sound (when appropriate) while maintaining the inexorable momentum and energy of the rhythm.

Syncopation is something that all dance people need to understand, partly because it defines some ballet steps, such as temps de cuisse and contretemps, and mostly because it is an ear-catching, enjoyable ingredient of music. *The Concise Oxford Dictionary of Music* defines it thus: "A device used by composers in order to vary position of the stress on notes so as to avoid regular rhythm. Syncopation is achieved by accenting a weak instead of a strong beat, by putting rests on strong beats, and by introducing a sudden change of time signature." Listen to a tango or a rag, and you are listening to pieces built on syncopation.

If any reader has a problem identifying the rhythm or meter of a particular piece, listen to the low notes of the music; in an orchestra, the low strings and brasses, as well as the percussion section, are usually responsible for the rhythm, and a pianist's left hand re-creates these tones. Or ask the pianist to play just the left hand for you, until you can identify the difference between the rhythm and the melody. For those readers who don't read music: On each page of the musical examples you will see five sets of two connected staves, each of which has five lines. The melody—what you would sing—is written on the upper staff, and the rhythm—what your feet would tap—is written on the bottom staff.

Meter/time signature

I don't think of meter as an element of music in the same way that I do of rhythm and melody. But meter is vital to everyone involved in dance, because meter is reflected in how one counts a piece of music that will eventually be danced to.

Meter is the way in which rhythm is organized. The meter of a piece is also called the time signature—the fraction appearing near the beginning of nearly every written piece of music. The top number represents the number of beats in one measure of music, and the bottom number denotes the value of each beat. Therefore, 3/4 means there are three beats in one measure of music, and each beat is a quarter note; 5/16 means there are five beats in one measure of music, and each beat is a 16th note.

Very simply put, 99 percent of the music in dance classrooms is counted either, "ONE and two and THREE and four and . . ." (duple meter) or, "ONE and uh two and uh THREE and uh four and uh . . ." (triple meter) in the appropriate tempo, and in phrases of either six or eight.[1] A two is counted in duple meter and is arranged in maxi-phrases of eight. A three is counted in triple meter and is arranged in maxi-phrases of eight. A six is subdivided in either duple or triple meter, and is arranged in mini-phrases of six. I have been hearing these terms ever since I started playing for dance and, while they are not as incisive as we accompanists might like, they are certainly better than nothing.

I purposely don't use time signatures to identify pieces of music because they can be misleading to someone without training in music theory. For example, say "3/4" to most dance teachers and they will probably think waltz and nothing else. Polonaises, boleros, minuets, and example 55 (a 3/4 adagio) are but a few examples of pieces throughout the world of music that bear no relationship to what most dance teachers think of as a 3/4.

The words in a movement phrase can change:

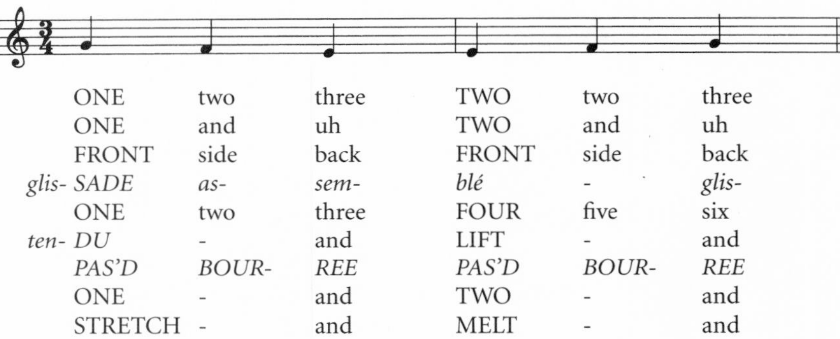

but the meter will not change.

Melody

Rhythm is such a powerful element of dance movement that it is possible, though not recommended, to teach most of a ballet class to drum accompaniment. (Can you imagine an adage done to the beat of a drum?) The addition of melody can soften the rigidity of the percussive rhythm without detracting from it.

Singing a melody is a more natural form of expression than voicing a rhythm, and a well-trained dancer should ultimately dance to a melodic phrase instead of to metronomic beats. If a pianist hears a dancer humming something he has played in class, the dancer will probably be humming the melody, not the rhythm. When this happens, it means the pianist has made himself truly heard, not just felt.

The sensitive use of melody can contribute a great deal to a dancer's progress through improved breathing. Surprisingly, dancers sometimes forget about breathing because of the art form's rigorous technical demands, but a truly musical dancer will often sing along with the music, breathing with the melodic phrase, which often corresponds with the movement phrase.

Melody can often mirror the choreography in frappé, petit battement, and petit allegro combinations. While this one-to-one correspondence is less often used in choreography, it can be a helpful device for students learning a new step in the classroom. This will be illustrated more fully in the section on qualities of steps and movements.

In this book, I purposely do not delve into the fine points of how music is put together because I feel that teachers are already too insecure about their knowledge of music, and theoretical discussions could easily make them even more uncomfortable. But there are two points to be made about music that will hopefully clear up some long-standing misunderstandings, and they are both about melody.

- Hemiola is a device that composers use. (Interesting: Do they actually use it, or does the flow of their creative impulses result in hemiola?) Anyway, hemiola is what you hear when the melody is in two and the rhythm stays in three (or vice versa). (It is possible for hemiola to occur in other time signatures, also.) Tchaikovsky was very fond of it; maybe it was just a relief for him to get away from the waltz feeling in the huge number of waltzes he wrote. Hemiola is very much in evidence at the ends of the Waltz of the Flowers and the waltz Finale from *Nutcracker.* Dancers who have to count can be confused by this change in the melody; if they are told that the basic underlying waltz rhythm is still there, they will know what to listen for and be more secure.

- Most nonmusicians think that the first note of a melody they hear must be "1." In probably 90 percent of the cases it is, but if you are having trouble counting a piece organically, it is probably because it is one of the other 10 percent. For instance, in the famous female variation from the last-act pas de deux of *Nutcracker* (better known as the Dance of the Sugar-Plum Fairy), the first note one hears in the melody is actually the "and" after "1." This is such a well-known piece that it doesn't need to be counted, but there are other less well-known pieces that can cause counting confusion. (See examples 2 and 60.) And melodies can occasionally start before "1," as in example 3. (One teacher I know won't let me play this piece because she can't count it. It's so famous that it's not necessary to count it unless one is totally unmusical.)

Tempo

The tempo of a piece of music is as intrinsic to its particular personality as its rhythm and melody. The easiest way to understand this is by playing or listening to any well-known piece twice as fast and then twice as slowly as what you are used to hearing.

Because so much music from the traditional ballet repertoire is unfamiliar to a beginning accompanist, he will often not know the tempo of a piece, and will play what may sound totally wrong to a dance teacher. It is up to the teacher to help the accompanist understand the correct tempo—rather, the proportion of tempo variance.

There is not just one single tempo in which a piece may be played, but rather a range of slightly slower and slightly faster tempos in which it still retains its special character. This same variability of speed is also present, to a lesser degree, in the way a dancer dances a variation from day to day. A sensitive dance conductor knows the proportion of tempos not only of his music but also of the dancers' movements, and will try to adjust his tempos according to how he sees a dancer moving onstage.

Because of the importance of this proportion of tempo, MMs (Maelzel metronomes markings) should be used solely for the purpose of establishing the median tempo—the tempo in between the slowest and the fastest proportional limits—of unfamiliar music. Metronomes operate inflexibly, but music must reflect the variability of humanity. This is especially true in the marriage of music and dance.

It is impossible to state the exact tempo of a given piece of music because tempo depends on the composer's directions and on the conductor's interpretation, as well as on each piece's particular personality. The needs of a dancer, as well as an accompanist's own personal taste and technical ability, are two more factors affecting the tempo. Therefore, each MM in this book represents a median of the proportionate range of tempo.

Tempo is one of the main communication problems between dance teacher and accompanist, and will be dealt with in detail throughout this book.

Harmony

Harmony provides music with additional texture. This added richness helps a dancer to feel more breadth in his movement.

Tonality

The subject of tonality often elicits interesting opinions, branching off into esoteric discussions of the color of E-flat major, the emotional content of g minor, and so forth. I will confine my comments to very pragmatic considerations.

Pieces in minor keys should be given as much consideration as those in major keys, but accompanists will eventually realize that a musical pall can descend subconsciously on the dancers if they hear too many pieces in minor keys.

As accompanists become more experienced, they will become aware of the necessity of changing keys from combination to combination. There are too many other things to think about at first, but after a while, accompanists usually hear for themselves why it is wise to avoid playing more than two pieces in a row in the same key.

Transposing and the changing of registers are extremely effective ways of adding a lift and a renewal of energy for dancers. In both cases, a dancer will more than likely not be able to describe what has happened musically, but almost invariably he will say something like, "That new section really picked me up when I was getting tired!"

Changing from a minor to a major key within a combination also gives dancers an extra surge of strength, although—again—they will rarely be able to define it, or even to remember it after class.

Phrasing

Basic phrasing is often difficult for a beginning accompanist to put into practice. Mere execution of the notes may seem to have the highest priority, but ignoring phrasing, whether the composer has written it in or not, produces wooden music. The result is much like omitting breathing when you speak, or omitting punctuation when you write. A helpful way to keep phrasing uppermost in your mind is by actually singing. The human voice naturally phrases and uses dynamics because it depends on breathing for execution, so phrasing and dynamics are inextricably linked.

Phrasing is to dance and music what syntax is to language: the arrangement of words for effective communication. Just as you would not communicate with a friend in blunt, clipped sentences, neither should you ignore the inherent phrasing—the ebb and flow—the peaks and valleys—of any piece you play.

All combinations of movement have peaks and valleys in varying altitudes. A series of eight tendus is an example of a movement phrase having barely discernible peaks and valleys. On the other end of the spectrum, grand allegro and pirouette combinations are full of peaks and valleys, and the peaks normally fall on odd-numbered counts, which a sensitive accompanist will want to accent with more volume. (It is a moot point whether the music we use is actually written with these peaks on the odd-numbered counts, or whether we just subconsciously react to them that way in our playing.)

Peaks occur on the odd-numbered counts in the maxi-phrases of twos and threes. Peaks occur on "1" and "4" of the mini-phrases of sixes.

~

Over the years I have felt the need to use the terms *mini-phrase* and *maxi-phrase* to help clarify some matters of phrasing. The proper terms are *phrase* and *period;* I have found, however, that most nonmusicians have a hard time remembering that the "phrase" is mini and the "period" is maxi.

Tchaikovsky's Waltz of the Flowers from *Nutcracker* (example 1) will serve to demonstrate these terms. This piece was chosen because it is one that almost everyone connected with dance can sing.

The first sixteen bars—a maxi-phrase—are made up of two mini-phrases of four counts each, then two mini-phrases of two counts each, then a final mini-phrase of four counts. (Not all musicians' bars are equal to dancers' counts, but in this instance they are. Please refer to page 65 for a detailed description of this common misunderstanding.) This maxi-phrase repeats, and is followed by another sixteen-bar maxi-phrase which is made up of four mini-phrases of four counts each. These four mini-phrases have identical rhythmic patterns in the melody (hereafter referred to as melodic rhythm), a device common to almost every form of pre-"contemporary" music.

Tchaikovsky wrote this music to be danced to, and musically sensitive choreographers can't help but observe the phrasing as they create movement. The more experienced an accompanist becomes, and the more varied his repertoire and/or improvisational abilities become, the better he will be able to reverse this process: to see mini-phrases of movement within maxi-phrases of dance combinations, and to play selections that correspond to them. This will remind the dancers that there are indeed phrases of movement, not just long strings of steps—and it will remind them to breathe.

The terms *peaks and valleys, maxi-phrase, mini-phrase,* and *melodic rhythm* will be used throughout this book.

Dynamics

Just as you would not speak to someone in a monotone, neither should you ignore the dynamics (whether written or implied) in a piece. As variety is said to be the spice of life, so are dynamics the spice of music, and their markings are self-explanatory. There are instances, however, when we accompanists must tamper with these markings, and these will be described and justified in their appropriate places throughout the book.

Music for performance is always executed according to the composers' wishes. Music for the classroom, however, must be executed according to the dancers' needs. It makes no sense to observe a composer's "subito pp" when the dancers have reached a point in a combination requiring maximum output of energy.

Accompanists gradually learn to associate particular dynamic levels with particular movement combinations. For example, grand battement and grand allegro combinations are always loud. Teachers may request different dynamics for very legitimate reasons, and they should be quick to point out these wishes to their accompanists before they start demonstrating their combinations, so that the accompanists will not waste time looking for a piece with the usual dynamic quality.

If you come across a piece of music that has no dynamic markings, think of lines and of peaks and valleys. Ascending and descending melodic lines are going somewhere, so let the dancers know where the departure and arrival points are dynamically. Awareness of the peaks and valleys will help prevent the movement of both the music and the dancers from becoming static and colorless.

Music builds up momentum too, just as movement does. This is especially true in music for dance, and is reflected in the classroom not necessarily by an increase in tempo but by an increase in dynamic intensity.

Line

Line is found everywhere in the performing arts: A dancer works to perfect his body line; a singer or musician practices the lines of scales endlessly; an actor studies his lines; and so on. Sadly, during the rigors of accomplishing these lines, performers often forget that *how* one gets to the peak of a line can often be of more artistic value than the final point of the line. The end of every line is usually the end of a phrase; this is indicated in punctuation by a semicolon or period, and in speaking by a breath. Lines in music for dance are a helpful way to show a dancer how to move effectively from one step or phrase to another.

The composer Aleksandr Glazunov was a master of line. An excerpt from his Grand Adagio in the first act of *Raymonda* (example 2) is used here to illustrate line in music.

The soprano, or melodic, line is the most obvious, as is true with most adagios. Note, however, the subtle line of the rhythm in the bass—the dotted half, half, and quarter notes in the left hand. They make up a kind of melody also. Then notice the running 16th-note figure in the first half of the excerpt. This is a fairly standard rhythmic structure that adds underlying substance to music, assuring flow and energy. Notice that, in the second half, the 16th-note figure sometimes changes to a scale that leads very definitely from one point to the next. A sensitive dancer will be led by that sound, and will make movements grow with the ascent of each scale. Lines such as these, whether in the melody, harmony, or rhythm, are hereafter referred to as leading lines.

Style

Of all the elements in music for dance, style is surely the most difficult to understand or to define. And so it is with dance: One of the most fundamental visual lines in classical dance, the arabesque, must be executed in a variety of different ways appropriate to the style and emotional content of each dance work, but the basic form rarely changes.

Style is the realm in which an accompanist can become an educator. By providing himself with an ever-expanding repertoire of music in all styles, he can help the dance students become aware of all those styles. If one plays Satie's *Gymnopédie no. 1* for an adagio combination one day and a Verdi aria for the same combination the next, the difference should be reflected in the movement quality of the dancers. (The dance teacher, of course, must help less advanced students to become aware of the difference in styles.)

One can broaden one's stylistic education through exposure and experience (always the best teacher). Every person involved in dance owes it to herself and her art (whether it be music or dance) to experience as much dance as possible: live, on film, on videocassette, on record or tape, or on television. See the various styles of dance. Compare Marius Petipa's formal grandeur with the lightheartedness of Auguste Bournonville, for instance, or effusive, lush Michel Fokine choreography with the starkness of some George Balanchine pieces. Hear the many styles of music in their original instrumental forms. And begin to form your own judgments about good taste with the help of people whose opinions you trust. (Just because something is presented on a stage does not necessarily mean that it is good or tasteful or artistic.)

Dance accompanists cannot afford the self-indulgence of being "Chopin specialists" or "schmaltz specialists" or "Impressionists." We must be conversant in many styles of music, and must have a keen eye for judging not only what music would be stylistically appropriate for any given combination, but also when to play it. The element of top-notch dance accompaniment that is probably the most difficult to grasp, especially by accompanists who have never taken a dance class, is assessing the mood of a class and knowing how to deal with it.

The atmosphere in class is so often governed by what accompanists play, and a first-class accompanist will play what he senses, from the teacher's mood and/or the dancers' vibes, would be appropriate. An experienced accompanist plays certain styles of music at certain times according to what he feels would help the class: an uplifting group waltz from *Swan Lake* for pliés on a particularly dreary day, or a sarabande for pliés after a particularly strenuous performance the night before. And for the first combination after each of these choices, a contrasting musical style is called for. An experienced accompanist has learned that there can be as many as ten different musical styles for, say, one dégagé combination.

The style of each piece an accompanist plays must be appropriate not only to the quality of each individual movement combination but also to its place within the context of the class. For example, many teachers find the group waltz from *Swan Lake* stylistically inappropriate for pliés; they prefer music with a less driving emotional motor for the first combination of the class. There is no right or wrong here; it is purely a matter of taste. As another example, a Sousa march is a wonderful choice for grands battements at the barre or a pirouette combination in the center, but totally inappropriate for tendu combinations at the barre, which are often counted in exactly the same rhythm and tempo as grands battements. As a last example, I remember being in one of Perry Brunson's classes with a very fine pianist who was just beginning to play for dance. The last combination at the barre in a Brunson class was always a simple one facing the barre: either finding our balance or just four grands pliés in second position—four counts down and four counts up. The mood was always very inner-directed. The accompanist played a legato waltz in exactly the right tempo, but it was mezzo-forte (medium-loud) and very dissonant, and my attention was thoroughly distracted from my body by this atonal intrusion.

Most teachers, especially those who have danced professionally, understand stylistic differentiation, and—instead of refusing an accompanist's choice of music with, "No, I don't like that" or "It doesn't work"—will probably have to explain their musical needs to novice accompanists.

~

A dance accompanist's sense of responsibility grows according to his understanding and involvement. It is unreasonable to expect a beginning accompanist to be able to incorporate all the necessary elements of music for dance into his work at first. He may make stylistically inappropriate choices, misjudge tempos, lose energy, play wrong notes, or sacrifice certain musical components in order to accomplish the basics of skeletal rhythm and melody. It is up to the dance teacher to help him become aware of the dancers' needs. If she senses that he is on the right track, she can alter her teaching methods temporarily to suit his capabilities. If he makes the same mistake(s) repeatedly, she should speak to him after class, telling him not only what is wrong, but why it is wrong and suggesting, if possible, how to fix it.

An accompanist, it seems, should strive for a happy balance between being a computer and a free spirit. No competent classical musician—and especially no dance accompanist—ever sacrifices the inexorable rhythm of music. However, the emotional and evocative qualities of music—the basic uplifting purpose of music—are equally important. A cohesive, artistic whole is impossible to achieve if any one factor is left out. This achievement is quite an undertaking, but I can think of worse ways to spend a lifetime.

3 ~ *Musical Forms for Dance and How to Count Them*

If a pianist is classically trained, his knowledge of dance forms is usually restricted to those forms found in the classical piano repertoire, such as in Bach's Keyboard Suites (minuet, gavotte, sarabande, bourrée, etc.) or in Chopin's music (waltz, polonaise, mazurka). Descriptions of most of these forms can be found in any music encyclopedia. This chapter will include those forms that enjoy widespread use in the dance classrooms of today, with the purpose of acquainting musicians and dance teachers with the personalities of the most common "nameable" forms, as well as those equally unnameable. Each of the forms has certain characteristics which define it. These characteristics are within the areas of rhythmic structure, median tempo, and quality (legato, happy, elegant, etc.).

When I teach Music for Dance Teachers, I use this chapter as a starting point, and we always study adagios of all meters in separate sessions. (Adagios are usually the most troublesome part of class for the sole reason of the uncertainty of tempo.) That practice is continued here.

The forms are arranged by meter in an ascending scale of tempo: the slowest 3/4 first, the fastest 3/4 last; the slowest 6/8 first, the fastest 6/8 last; and so forth. The median tempos of these forms are arranged from a musician's point of view. Most musicians think of a bolero, for instance, as being quite slow, because there is so much time between the "1" of one bar and the "1" of the next. But a dancer may think of it as fast because his steps correspond to each beat or count (three beats/counts in one bar of a bolero).

Throughout this book, easily accessible music (such as Johann Strauss waltzes and polkas) and "pieces every beginning accompanist plays" (such as Schubert waltzes) are purposely omitted; one can find these anywhere. The musical contents here are intended to be new, refreshing, and challenging to every accompanist.

While a thorough knowledge of musical dance forms is vital for an accompanist and helpful for a teacher, the most productive way for a teacher to communicate her musical needs is by the way she moves and speaks and sings or hums. There are many musical forms for dance that don't have convenient labels like *rag* or *polacca*, and a dance teacher cannot be expected to put a label on every piece of music she uses. She will get the best out of her accompanist—and her students—if she counts clearly and infuses her demonstrations with the appropriate spirit of each combination.

Time signatures should not be considered infallible. Some slow 3/4s are more accurately described as 9/8s. Many fast 3/4s can be used interchangeably with many 6/8s. 3/2s, 6/4s, and 12/8s are mathematically the same; a composer may choose to write in 3/2 because his piece has very few quarter or eighth notes—or simply because he likes the look of 3/2 better than 6/4 or 12/8.

When people are asked to count a piece they are listening to, they will count the melody, that is, put syllables on the melodic notes. All the musical examples in this book are counted in this way. During a classroom demonstration, a teacher won't always have a specific piece in mind but she will know the meter, and will count the rhythm. Therefore, the counting you see after each of the forms may be different from the counts that appear in the corresponding examples, because the former refers to how the rhythm of a piece within that form is counted, while the latter refers to the melody of that specific example. (A detailed description of how to learn to count correctly appears in the chapter for dance teachers.)

There are often stylistic differences within each form of music (see *polonaise*, for example). I have noted in the text when there is not a difference. For example, if a teacher requests a tarantella, almost any tarantella will work because almost every one has both a median tempo and a quality that rarely vary. This is most definitely not the case with waltzes.

When applicable, steps and movements that are often given to a particular form of music are included.

I did not invent the different ways of counting included herein. I have been listening to dance teachers for over forty years, and what you see for counting is a distillation of what I have been hearing from the smartest teachers. Good teachers (one cannot be a good teacher without some instinctive connection to music) almost always count like this (with the exceptions of pieces like boleros and polaccas, which they usually muddle through—if they use them at all). I have also included the terms *two, three*, and *six,* because they are terms that many musical teachers use, instead of asking for particular musical forms for their combinations. (A reminder: Twos and threes are always in maxi-phrases of eight; sixes are always in mini-phrases of six.)

As with all things artistic, there are no infallible rules, so consider this chapter a guideline, not an edict. It is intended to facilitate the identification of music, providing a common ground for communication between teacher and accompanist.

2/4 or ¢ - examples 3–12: all are twos

In the 2/4 meter there are two quarter notes (or the equivalent thereof) in each measure.

Except for the tango family, all 2/4 forms are counted: "ONE and two and THREE and . . . ," up through "eight (and)."

Tango (habañera, beguine, zapote, samba, rumba) - examples 3 and 3a

These Spanish pieces in duple meter have many different names, many different median tempos, and varying qualities. In order to simplify reading and understanding, they will be referred to throughout the text as tangos, since tangos usually comprise the majority of pieces within the general group.

Tangos have a Spanish flavor, are usually sensuous, and are always syncopated in both the melody and the rhythm. Following the tango example you will find a "de-syncopated" version of the first four measures, so you can hear the difference.

Tangos have wide ranges of both median tempos and personalities, so they must be used judiciously. Some very legato tangos can be a welcome change for rond de jambe à terre and fondu combinations for more advanced dancers. (Less advanced dancers must hear the fluidity of a waltz until they understand that these important movements are always legato.) Other kinds of tangos work well occasionally for tendus, dégagés, and frappés; I have sometimes been asked for a tango for grands battements; and I recently chose—almost by accident—a tango for a beginner piqué turn combination, and it worked extremely well.

Most dance teachers count the syncopation in the melody (actually, most dance teachers sing example 3) as they demonstrate, making it very clear to the pianist that he should play a tango, as in: "ONE AND - uh TWO - AND - THREE AND - uh FOUR - AND - . . . ," up through "EIGHT - AND - ."

March (to be discussed under 4/4s)

Rag - example 4

Rags are sometimes written in 4/4, are usually happy, and are always syncopated; normally, the right hand—the melody—is syncopated and the left hand—the rhythm—maintains a steady beat. (There are very usable ragtime waltzes too, but when a teacher asks for "a rag," she almost invariably wants one in duple meter. By the time I realized how much I rely on ragtime waltzes in certain situations—for some reason, especially for fondus—I no longer had the electronic keyboard at my disposal, so I am unable to include one in the musical examples. Scott Joplin wrote at least two great ones: *Bethena* and *Pleasant Moments.*) Rags go well with almost all petit allegro steps in duple meter, as well as with many tendu and dégagé-family combinations.

Polka - example 5

Polkas usually have a "heel-and-toe" stepping rhythm incorporated into their melodic structure; this motif is apparent in the melody of bars 4 and 6, as well as the first three notes of bars 17, 18, 19, 21, 22, and 23 in example 5. I have yet to meet an unhappy polka. Polkas and rags can usually be used interchangeably, as their personalities are very similar.

The median tempo and quality of polkas seldom vary.

~

So far, the basic rhythmic structure in the left hand of all the 2/4s we have discussed has half as many beats per count as the next three examples. (Please remember that we are discussing beats per count, not counts per measure; different notation produces different numbers of counts per bar, and most dance teachers don't know a lot about bar lines.) These three are counted in exactly the same way, but they have a driving energy that is missing from the previous 2/4s.

Coda, galop, can-can (sometimes even "circus music") - examples 6 and 7

To a musician, *coda* means the ending section of a piece. To most dance teachers, *coda* means a piece with a specific rhythmic structure, because codas of classical grands pas de deux—almost without exception—are built on this particular structure, as in the following two examples. Codas, galops, and can-cans are structurally the same in the left hand.

Example 6 is a standard, garden-variety coda which could support the famous "thirty-two fouettés" from the Black Swan pas de deux from *Swan Lake.*

Example 7 (as well as the structurally similar "Stars and Stripes Forever") is a prime example of why it can be dangerous to ask a beginning accompanist for a "march." Sousa's fame resulted mainly from his marches, yet the rhythmic structure of this selection differs radically from not only that of the first section of the piece, a 6/8 march (example 41), but also a "typical" duple-meter march, such as example 35.

Oddly enough, the step called galop cannot be done organically to a musical galop.

Czardas-friszka - example 8

A czardas always has two sections. The first, the lassú, is described in the 4/4 category. The second section, the friszka, often has the rhythmic structure of a coda, as in example 8. This form has a Hungarian flavor.

~

Codas, galops, can-cans, and friszkas are usually interchangeable. They are generally used for some virtuoso grand allegro steps; for combinations of turns in succession (fouetté turns, piqué turns, etc.); and, if the accompanist is technically advanced, often for dégagé-family, frappé, and petit battement combinations at the barre.

Miscellaneous – examples 9–12

There is a huge number of 2/4s that cannot be labeled. Four examples follow, arranged in an ascending scale of tempo.

Although example 9 is quite slow, it doesn't feel like a dancer's adagio, since the abundance of melodic accents and lack of rhythmic flow lessen the smoothness that is characteristic of most adagios. I call pieces like this moderato twos, and they are also often written in 4/4. They are especially good for rond de jambe à terre combinations if the teacher doesn't specify a three, and for tendus with demi-plié.

Example 10 is typical of the music for many male variations in the classical ballet repertoire. They can also be written in 4/4. They are suitable for grand battement combinations, and for grand allegro combinations for which the teacher doesn't want a waltz.

Example 11 is one of those rare and wonderful pieces that doesn't lose too much personality when played a lot more slowly than the composer intended. It is particularly suitable for "and" tendu or dégagé combinations. (See page 196 for a description of "ands.")

Example 12 is labeled "one of those" in my mental computer. ("One of those" is a useless term for teachers to use if they have accompanists who haven't read this book.) I think of this one as a ¢, but not all ¢s have this particular median tempo and personality; that's why I don't have a ¢ category. I used to try to turn this kind of piece into a coda before I knew better. I find such pieces to be the fastest and lightest of the 2/4s, and they are suitable for some barre combinations in the dégagé family that include piqués/pointés, and for quick, light, Bournonville-esque jumps across the floor. I think of them as being temperamentally between polkas and codas.

3/4 - examples 13–29: sixes and threes

In the 3/4 meter there are three quarter notes (or the equivalent thereof) in each bar.

Sarabande - example 13: six or three

This form is seldom used in dance class, but one is included here because some teachers occasionally want an especially soothing quality for their plié music and will request a sarabande. It has a subdued, somber quality, and is very often in a minor key.

A sarabande can produce a very special atmosphere for the adagio in the center. The combination that follows it, as well as its musical accompaniment, must have a radically different quality, in order to get the dancers back into a more physically energetic mood.

How to count a sarabande: either "ONE two three four five six, TWO two three four five six, THREE two three four five six, FOUR two three four five six"; or "ONE two three, TWO two three, THREE two three, . . ." up through "EIGHT two three."

Polonaise/Polacca - examples 14 and 15: six

Example 14 evokes images of elegance, grandeur, nobility, and huge, flowing costumes. It represents what most teachers think of when they think of a polonaise.

Example 15 is bouncier and more lighthearted. It was labeled polacca by its composer, *polacca* being the Italian word for polonaise.

Chopin invented the "heroic" polonaise, which is similar to the first example. Most polonaises/polaccas written before Chopin are similar in quality to the second example. The rhythmic structure in the first measure of example 14 is found in almost all polonaises/polaccas.

Another distinguishing feature of the polonaise/polacca is that, while the primary emphasis is always on the "1" of every bar, the second and third beats are almost as prominent as the first. This makes them invaluable forms for the dance teacher who is giving beginning students such three-part steps as pas de basque. Instead of slowing a waltz down to a tempo suitable for a beginner, the accompanist can play a piece that was written in that particular tempo. If your accompanist tries to play a polonaise for beginner balancés, praise him for the logic of his thinking, but explain that a polonaise is stylistically wrong for a balancé.

A polonaise is what a teacher wants—even though she may request a mazurka—when she demonstrates a grand battement combination in the following way: grand battement up on "1," tendu on "2," and close on "3." This is a very common mistake.

Polonaises are almost never used for small jump/petit allegro combinations (they are too heavy), while polaccas almost always are.

The median tempo of polonaises rarely changes; the median tempo of polaccas is slightly faster than that of polonaises, and also rarely changes within the form.

How to count polonaises/polaccas: "ONE and uh two - three - four - five - six, TWO and uh two - three - four - five - six, . . ." up through "FOUR and uh two - three - four - five - six, . . ." often with additional "ands," depending upon each piece's melody.

Bolero - example 16: six

Say the word *bolero* and most people think of the famous one by Ravel. I don't know whether it could be considered a truly Spanish bolero, but its legato sensuousness prevents it from being part of my personal bolero category. Many of my boleros aren't truly Spanish, either, but my mental computer needed a label for storing bouncy sixes, and *bolero* came the closest to being reasonably accurate. *Bolero* may not be the pedagogic word for this category, but if it establishes a common ground of understanding for teacher, accompanist, and dancer, I feel its use is justified. I must admit that, if I had known about polaccas when I was first exposed to bouncy sixes, I would have named them polaccas instead of boleros. These days my polacca and bolero categories are gradually merging into one group.

I recently played for an exceptionally musical teacher whose ability to count was practically nonexistent. He demonstrated a combination using rhythmic grunts, which I finally deciphered into a bolero; then he managed to count it in mini-phrases of eight instead of its actual sixes. Needless to say, the students were confused, so I asked if we could mark it, whereupon it all made sense. After class I explained my theory about boleros, and he said, "I'm so happy to know what to call that weird thing! Up till now, I never had a pianist who could figure it out." I gently explained that, if he had dared to count it clearly in sixes, he wouldn't have needed a name.

Boleros share a distinguishing feature with polonaises/polaccas: almost equal emphasis on each of the three beats within one bar. Boleros are a welcome change from the traditional 2/4 for dégagé-family and petit allegro combinations, as movement phrases of six counts are just as valid as phrases of four or eight. Madame Volkova loved to use boleros for the first jump combination on Mondays, because she felt that twenty-four little jumps were better than thirty-two on the first day of the week.

The median tempo and quality of boleros rarely change.

How to count a bolero: "ONE and two and three and four and five and six and, TWO and two and three and four and five and six and, THREE and two and three and four and five and six and, FOUR and two and three and four and five and six and." (Teachers: If you can't hear a bolero in your head, you can feel it in your body by doing two phrases of the following: four changements and don't move for two counts.)

Minuet - example 17: six or three

Minuets are also elegant, but much more delicate and smooth than polonaises. They, too, have almost equal emphasis on each beat in a bar, and can also be used for three-part steps, such as pas de basque, balancé, and pas de bourrée. A beneficial experiment for the teacher is to have her students do the following: eight pas de bourrée or eight pas de basque or eight balancés to eight bars of a heroic polonaise, then to eight bars of a bolero, then to eight bars of a minuet. The quality of movement should change according to the quality of the music.

The median tempo and quality of minuets seldom vary.

How to count a minuet: in three: "ONE two three, TWO two three, THREE two three, FOUR two three, . . ." up through "EIGHT two three"; or in six: "ONE two three FOUR five six, TWO two three FOUR five six, . . ." up through "FOUR two three FOUR five six."

Ländler - example 18: three (sometimes six)

There are at least two recognizably different types of ländler. One is the type you might imagine hearing in a Bavarian beer parlor, and the other, like example 18, is more lyrical. The median tempo of ländlers is fairly slow, which makes them ideal for the transition between, for instance, beginner-tempo and intermediate-tempo pas de bourrée. They are also recommended for balancés for beginners. The first type of ländler is usually too heavy for ballet classes.

The median tempo of ländlers seldom changes.

How to count a ländler: either in three or in six (see the counting of minuets).

Mazurka - examples 19–21: three (occasionally six)

Another form with a wide stylistic range is the mazurka. Most of Chopin's mazurkas are relatively light and delicate. I would never play one in response to a request for a mazurka by a dance teacher; they are usually expecting something like one of the following three selections.

Example 19 is bouncier and less legato than Chopin mazurkas, but less robust than the following two examples.

Example 20 embodies what I feel are a mazurka's normal qualities: broad, robust, pesante, and gutsy. (Those sound like adjectives for "heavy" music. I think there is a fine but definite line between substantial/full and heavy/ponderous.)

Mazurkas are full of unique accents. The most common is reflected in the right hand of the introductions to all the mazurka examples in this book; whenever I hear a teacher counting like that, I know she's singing a mazurka in her head.

Some distinguished musicians insist that a mazurka always has a stressed accent on the second beat of every bar. Other equally distinguished musicians insist that a mazurka always has this accent on the third beat of every bar. (Strong accents on "1" are invariable.) Then there are mazurkas with almost equal melodic accents on all three beats, such as example 21. An accompanist's decision about which kind of mazurka to play is usually dictated by the quality of the movement, and by where the movement accents fall.

Teachers must realize that, for their purposes, one of the main differences between a mazurka and a polonaise or bolero is the speed at which each is intended to be played. This is a common misunderstanding of teachers, who often ask for a mazurka when what they really need is a polonaise or bolero. A beginning accompanist will almost always play what a teacher asks for, since he is not yet experienced enough to read movement and judge for himself. And the teacher probably feels and hears that the mazurka is not suitable, but has no idea of what *is* suitable.

Some of the difference between a mazurka and a polonaise or bolero can be understood by comparing the rhythmic structures of the three forms: There are twice as many notes in the left hand of polonaises and boleros as there are in mazurkas. Another way of understanding the difference is by slowing down a mazurka to the median polonaise/bolero tempo. Notice how ponderous and heavy it becomes. Then reverse the process: Speed up a polonaise or bolero to a common mazurka tempo. If a pianist can accomplish that, he has sufficient technique for Carnegie Hall, but the quality of the music has been completely sacrificed. And it will not feel right to a dancer. After all, one of our main objectives is to provide appropriate music for a dancer so that he can accomplish his tasks as easily and enjoyably as possible.

Mazurkas enjoy great popularity, and work especially well for pirouette combinations. Mazurkas are almost never used for small jump/petit allegro combinations.

How to count a mazurka: in three is the norm, but in six is certainly possible (see the counting under minuets).

Waltz - examples 22–28: three

While the basic rhythmic structure of waltzes ("OOM pah pah") rarely changes, this form comes in a huge variety of sizes. The many melodies and wide range of median tempos produce a broad range of styles. Because waltzes are so versatile, they are generally the predominant musical form in every accompanist's repertoire.

Slow waltz - example 22

What makes a slow waltz slow and a fast waltz fast? It would be so convenient to be able to say, "The more notes in the melody, the slower it is." Chopin's "Minute Waltz" (op. 64, no. 1) refutes that. The only way to figure out what any piece is, is by looking at the composer's intentions, and then discovering its tempo and personality for oneself.

Example 22 has a very special quality; its fluidity and inherent slow tempo, combined with a subtle melodic stress on the "1" of many of the bars, make it particularly useful for rond de jambe à terre, temps lié, and port de bras combinations. (A surprising number of dance people say this particular piece is a six. There is no doubt that its phrasing is in mini-phrases of six, but if a dance teacher requested a six while hearing this piece in her head, her accompanist would never play this piece.)

Medium-tempo waltz - example 23

There is no typical medium-tempo waltz. They can be loud, soft, happy, sad, staccato, legato, and any combination thereof. The example I have chosen is a substantial, full, legato waltz.

Spanish waltz - example 24

Because the melodies of Spanish waltzes are almost always syncopated, they are especially useful for steps that are by nature syncopated, such as temps de cuisse and contretemps. This does not, however, preclude their being used for other combinations.

Spanish waltzes come in a wide spectrum of median tempos, so they must be carefully chosen. Example 24 is suitable for many petit allegro and medium allegro combinations, among others.

Viennese waltz

A Viennese waltz's unique character can be traced directly to the slightly altered rhythm of the left hand. The second of the three beats is anticipated slightly—not enough to be reflected in the music notation, but certainly enough to be heard in the ear and felt in the body. I once asked Mr. Brunson when I should use that device, and he replied, "Unfortunately, I can't tell you, but if you watch long enough, you'll know." He was right; I saw eventually that it is appropriate for certain jumping combinations that are on the lighter side.

I have decided to omit a Viennese waltz example because its identifying characteristic is never reflected in music notation. When called for, this Viennese feeling can be tastefully applied to many waltzes.

The most famous Viennese waltz is probably "On the Beautiful Blue Danube."

Fast waltz - example 25

Fast waltzes can often be substituted for 2/4s in petit battement serré/battu combinations if the teacher doesn't have a specific reason for using a 2/4. They are also widely used for petit allegro and chaîné/déboulé combinations.

Example 25 is one of everybody's favorites, mine included.

Since there seems to be so much confusion about the difference between waltzes and 6/8s, here is a very short course in music theory that may help. Everyone knows (I hope) that a waltz always has the following rhythmic figure: "OOM pah pah, OOM pah pah." Think of a 6/8 as having the following rhythmic figure: "OOM - pah, OOM - pah." Those two missing beats radically change the quality of the music. Another way that has helped my students to understand the difference is: the three beats of a waltz correspond to the three steps of a balancé, and the rhythm of a 6/8 is the rhythm of a skip. (On the same subject, there are people who have a hard time differentiating between twos and threes; I tell them to march to a two and waltz to a three. And patting these rhythmic figures on the shoulders of musically insecure dance people is a great way to clarify the differences; many people can't count and move at the same time, but they can feel.)

"Big waltz" or "grand allegro waltz" - examples 26–28

You will not find these two terms in a music encyclopedia. They are used by dance teachers who want a very specific kind of waltz. Big waltzes (this term will be used throughout the text) are never "piddly" (actually, no music for a dance class should be piddly, especially not big waltzes—sometimes light, yes, but *never* piddly); they are broad, loud, more orchestral than usual in scope, rich in texture, grandiose, and uplifting in every sense of the word, since they have to motivate the energy for lifting a leg (in a grand battement combination) or a whole body (in a grand allegro combination).

There is no concrete rule for differentiating grand allegro waltzes from other kinds of waltzes except by feeling or, often, by the fact that they are used for male variations in the traditional ballets. However, the following factors are worth mentioning. The peaks-and-valleys effect is very evident in big waltzes that are used to support combinations of grand allegro movement (as opposed to consecutive leaps across the floor, which need 3/8s without peaks and valleys). These combinations almost always have the highlighted steps occurring on every odd-numbered count (i.e., on counts 1, 3, 5, 7, and so on). Therefore, those odd-numbered counts must be more accented than the even-numbered ones. What is also extremely important is the lead-ins to those odd-numbered counts. How well a dancer does the preparatory steps determines the quality of the jump, so those steps must be reflected musically.

I have found that a large majority of my big waltzes have no melodic sound on the second beat of the odd-numbered bars—possibly to emphasize the airborne quality of the jumps. (See example 31 for an exception.) And the first note in every odd-numbered bar is never a half note, and rarely a quarter note, for exactly the same reason.

Pedaling is discussed extensively beginning on page 168, but the correct use of the pedal in grand allegro combinations (actually, in all jump combinations) is so vital that it is touched upon briefly here. The pedal must not be depressed on the odd-numbered counts—where the highlights (no pun intended) occur. Otherwise, the waltz will feel very heavy. The pedal should be depressed on the preparatory steps, in order to emphasize the richness and strength of the plié, and there should be a crescendo into every odd-numbered count's forte.

Big waltzes come in a surprisingly wide variety of tempos, and can also be written in 3/8 or 6/8.

Example 26 has the peaks-and-valleys effect all the way through until counts 5 through 8 of the second phrase of eight. Its median tempo (I find) is on the slow side of medium.

Example 27, in a medium tempo, alternates four counts of peaks and valleys with four counts of stress on each count (what I think of as the 3/8 effect).

Example 28 is a fast big waltz. One can see by its structure (each of the first four bars has a silent second beat in both the rhythm and the melody) that it would lose its rhythmic drive if played much more slowly than allegro. This piece, like most fast big waltzes I know, consists almost entirely of stress on each count—on the "1" of every bar (again, the 3/8 effect), therefore lending itself especially well to consecutive steps across the floor (such as arabesques sautées), rather than to phrases of movement. I have yet to find a fast big waltz that is technically easy.

How to count a waltz: "ONE and uh two . . ."; "ONE - and two . . ."; "ONE two three two, . . ." up through "eight and uh"; "eight - and"; "eight two three." Any combination of these words is possible. Rarely: "ONE two three FOUR five six. . . ." (See also the diagram on page 6.)

Miscellaneous - example 29: six

It is possible that you will never need a piece like example 29, but I have included it here because it and others like it solved a big problem for me in Mr. Brunson's class. Its median tempo is in the "pol-bo-min" (polonaise-bolero-minuet [which also includes allegro 9/8s]) range, but it has a very different quality from these forms.

How to count this piece: like a bolero, in phrases of six.

3/8 - examples 30–33: all are threes

In the 3/8 meter there are three eighth notes (or the equivalent thereof) in every measure.

I have found that the distinguishing factor of the 3/8 meter seems to be more stress on the "1" of every bar than occurs in a 3/4. However, this is even less of a fixed rule than some of the others we have discussed, primarily due to the fact that composers are not absolutely consistent about the meter labels they apply to their music.

The 3/8 family has no nameable forms, such as *waltz* or *rag*; however, I have a 3/8 category in my mental computer that pops up when I hear or see combinations in triple meter with stress on the "1" of every bar.

Medium-tempo - examples 30 and 31

I find two distinct divisions in this group.

Example 30 is representative of what I call a cross between a waltz and a mazurka. It has the emphasis on the "1" of every bar like a mazurka, but has more of a flowing quality like a waltz. It is suitable for pirouette combinations that also include balancés.

How to count this piece: like a waltz but with more emphasis on the even-numbered counts.

Example 31 is essentially a big waltz. It is particularly well-suited for fouettés sautés (not to be confused with the well-known consecutive fouetté turns) because of the definite melodic accent on the second beat of every odd-numbered bar (where the height and greatest difficulty of that movement occur).

How to count this piece: I would say, "ONE AND - two and uh THREE

AND - four and uh . . . ," up through "eight and - ." Counting this way signals to the accompanist that he should choose or improvise a piece with this melodic rhythm.

Allegro - examples 32 and 33

Example 32 is part of the finale of the exciting ballet *Etudes,* choreographed by Harald Lander to Czerny piano exercises arranged and orchestrated by Knůdage Riisager. (By now, you may have noticed a preponderance of Czerny excerpts. They are included for the enlightenment of poor souls who consider Czerny a bore. More on that subject in the "Repertoire" section in chapter 5.)

While the initial stress on the "1" of every measure becomes less apparent after the first 16 bars, the forceful and demanding rhythm of those first 16 counts sets the pace for the whole piece. Like a fast big waltz, it lends itself especially well to consecutive grand allegro steps across the floor, and is also as technically difficult, since it combines speed with the orchestral fullness necessary to support strenuous (albeit fun) movement.

Example 33 is the first section of Moritz Moszkowski's third Spanish Dance. The second section of the piece undergoes a distinct change in character, becoming very legato, so the two sections are not compatible when played for the same combination.

While this section shares the same median tempo with the Czerny example above, it is much lighter and bouncier, and is particularly adaptable for petit battement and petit allegro (especially brisé) combinations.

How to count these pieces: in three, like a 6/8: "ONE - and TWO - and THREE - and . . . ," up through "EIGHT - and."

4/4 or C - examples 34–39: all are twos

In the 4/4 meter there are four quarter notes (or the equivalent thereof) in each bar.

I have found that the major distinguishing factor of the 4/4 meter relevant to dance is that 4/4s rarely go fast. Musicologists may disagree heartily with that statement, but the subtle differences between a 4/4 and a non-coda 2/4 of the same median tempo are indistinguishable to a moving body. And I think it is much more productive for teachers, students, and accompanists to find a common ground in the terms *duple meter* and *two* than to nitpick over whether it is a 4/4 or a 2/4, especially since so many duple-meter forms can be written in either 2/4 or 4/4.

All 4/4s are counted exactly like 2/4s: "ONE and two and THREE and . . . ," up through "eight and."

Czardas-lassú - examples 34a and 34b

The lassú, or slow section, of the czardas is sometimes written in 2/4. This form is very broad and grand. However, each czardas has one of two distinctly different qualities. Examples 34a and 34b demonstrate both.

Example 34a is processional, grand, and heroic in feeling, making it ideal for a grand battement combination. It is one of those rare pieces that can be used for either an "and" grand battement combination or one in which the leg goes up on the count: because of its accents and also because its character doesn't suffer too much from being played as slowly as necessary for the "and" combination.

Example 34b is lush and sensuous; it is an appropriate complement to an advanced fondu combination.

When a teacher asks for, "A czardas, please," she almost always means a piece with the quality of example 34a.

March - example 35

Marches are another staple of the dance accompanist's repertoire. They are used extensively in children's classes, are widely used for grand battement combinations, can often be used for pirouette and grand allegro combinations when a triple meter is not required, and can also be written in 2/4 and 6/8.

Example 35 has a melodic line that lends itself to grands battements when the leg goes up on a count (not on an "and"), because its melody often keeps leading to the peak of each mini-phrase, which corresponds to the peak of each battement.

Accompanists will often hear teachers count "ONE TWO THREE FOUR . . ." in children's classes when they are demonstrating marching combinations instead of "ONE and two and" for the same amount of time. It just means to the accompanist that he can play a normal march but with more stress on every beat—less of the peaks-and-valleys effect—than he would normally play; each of these beats will be a child's step.

Gavotte - example 36

Gavottes are also written in C, 2/4, and ¢. They are mostly courtly and elegant, with a distinct but indescribable, slightly subdued quality—but you may occasionally find one that will work for petit allegro combinations. Gavottes always have an anacrusis, so musicians must be very clear about where the phrases begin; sometimes the anacrusis is "eight and" and sometimes it is "ONE and." In example 36, the anacrusis is "eight and."

Stop time - example 37

One can play stop time in all meters, but it is usually used in duple meter, and is a staple of old vaudeville soft-shoe routines. I used to resist using stop time, because I felt that dancers of all levels needed constant musical support. But I eventually came to realize that dancers enjoy the challenge of sharpening their own internal sense of rhythm (it challenges ours too), and it forces lazy, self-indulgent, and/or unmusical dancers to obey the music; when something is missing, they absolutely have to count. And it is not unheard of for a solo instrument in an orchestra to forget to come in; such an occurrence will be slightly less frightening for a dancer who has been exposed to stop time.

If a teacher or an accompanist has trouble keeping perfect time during the silent parts of stop time, try sniffing quietly at the rests. This will maintain the pulse without taking away the challenge for the dancers by counting out loud.

Miscellaneous - examples 38 and 39

Tchaikovsky didn't label example 38 a march, but I certainly would. It is well suited to non-"and" grands battements, and for some grand allegro combinations.

There are a large number of pieces (Czerny wrote many) which have a fairly continuous melodic structure of dotted rhythm. They are mentioned here because they are almost always reliable for "and" combinations of tendus and the dégagé family, as well as for duple-meter assemblé combinations. They can also be written in 2/4. (See example 39.)

6/8 - examples 40–48: all are threes except the 6/8 march (two)

In the 6/8 meter there are six eighth notes (or the equivalent thereof) in each measure.

The major distinguishing factor of 6/8s is that there are usually rests instead of sounds on the second and fifth beats of each measure, either in the melody or in the rhythm, or in both. (Refer back, if necessary, to the comments under Fast Waltz for clarification.) This produces a lilting or rocking rhythm, which is especially noticeable in barcarolles.

Pieces in 6/8 are never counted in six. This is discussed in the "Learning to count correctly" section of chapter 4.

Barcarolle - example 40: three

Originally songs of the Venetian gondoliers, barcarolles are especially obvious examples of the lilting rhythm described above because they almost always lack the second and fifth notes in both the melody and the rhythm. They are particularly useful for fondu combinations in triple meter; fondus generally follow ronds de jambe à terre in the barre order and, since ronds de jambe are usually done to a waltz, another waltz for fondus could be less stimulating than a barcarolle, if a three is requested. Their gentle flow mirrors a beginning dancer's glissade, and is also a pleasant change for port de bras and temps lié combinations. Pieces labeled "sicilienne" are often barcarolle-ish in feeling.

The median tempo and personality of barcarolles seldom vary.

How to count a barcarolle: "ONE - and two - and THREE - and . . . ," up through "eight - and."

March - example 41: two

A 6/8 march is counted in exactly the same way as a duple-meter march, and for all intents and purposes may seem to sound exactly the same. I think this is the reason accompanists get stuck in the "duple-meter march" rut: Nothing in a dance teacher's counting suggests anything different. The 6/8 factor is constant in the rhythm and often in the melody, and is extremely difficult for nonmusicians to identify.

I will never forget the day I discovered the best thing about 6/8 marches: They will always work for "and" grand battement combinations. Duple-meter marches with accents helpful to this kind of combination are not so easy to find. 6/8 marches are also suitable for duple-meter pirouette combinations, and for walking and marching in children's classes.

The quality of 6/8 marches seldom varies, but there is a wide range of median tempos.

How to count a 6/8 march: like duple meter marches: "ONE and two and THREE and . . . ," up through "eight and." (Please refer to the last paragraph under 4/4 marches for a variation.)

"Big waltz" or "grand allegro waltz" - examples 42 and 43: three

There may be musicians who insist that a 6/8 can never be called a waltz. But most dancers and many musicians find it difficult to tell the difference between 3/4 big waltzes and 6/8 big waltzes.

There are two distinctly different categories of 6/8 big waltzes. The first group is comprised of peaks-and-valleys waltzes, as in example 42. The second group has the 3/8 factor, as in example 43. To add further to the confusion, some 6/8 big waltzes are written using the waltz bass, as in example 42, and others are "genuine" 6/8s, as in example 43.

How to count 6/8 big waltzes: exactly like 3/4 big waltzes: "ONE - and two - and THREE - and . . . ," up through "eight - and."

Just as I feel it is unnecessary for a teacher or dancer to be able to differentiate between 2/4 and 4/4, so I feel it is unnecessary that they must know the difference between peaks-and-valleys 6/8 and 3/4 waltzes. Likewise between 3/8 and 6/8 big waltzes. (I don't recall any teacher in my career being able to define correctly why she specifically wanted a 6/8; I mention that not as a criticism, but as an emphasis on the communication problems between teacher and—especially beginning—accompanist.) What *is* necessary is that a teacher learn to demonstrate clearly—both verbally and physically—so that the accompanist can read the movement well enough to choose between a peaks-and-valleys waltz and one with stress on the "1" of every bar.

Tarantella - example 44: three

Tarantellas are written with a running eighth-note figure in the left hand, as in

or with single chords on the first and fourth beat of each bar, as in

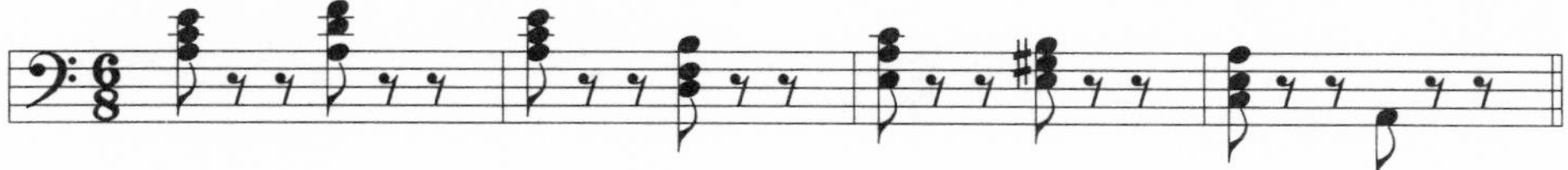

or with a stride piano bass, as in example 44. They have a unique flavor, and are often in a minor key.

The median tempo of tarantellas is so fast that the 6/8 factor ("OOM - pah OOM - pah") is not always readily discernible, except in those shaped like example 44.

Counting tarantellas can often be a bone of contention between accompanists on the one hand, and choreographers and teachers on the other. Most tarantellas have an anacrusis (as in example 44), which always feels like an "eight - and" to me. Many dance people, however, will count it as "ONE - and," probably because their first step begins on it. It is one of the few "dancerly" ways of counting that I have been unable to adapt to because, to me, it goes completely against the grain of the phrasing.

Tarantellas are especially useful for quick, small, Bournonville-esque jumps across the floor that go from one leg to the other (such as emboîtés), and for petit battement combinations. (Recently a creative teacher requested a tarantella for the Royal Academy of Dancing [RAD] combination of galops and spring points.)

The median tempo and quality of tarantellas seldom vary.

How to count a tarantella: "ONE - - two - - THREE - - . . ." or "ONE - and two - and THREE - and . . . ," up through "eight - - " or "eight - and."

Miscellaneous - examples 45–48: all are threes

These unlabeled 6/8s share fairly similar median tempos, yet their personalities are distinctly different.

Example 45 is Giselle's first-act entrance music from the ballet of the same name, and is probably the most famous 6/8 in the dance world. Contrary to what I said about avoiding the use of easily accessible music in this book, I have included this particular piece because it is so typical of what teachers usually want if they ask for a 6/8 for small jumps: light, bouncy, and happy.

Example 46 is more legato and lyrical than the previous example, and often unconsciously becomes a waltz when I play it. (I play it for assemblé combinations, but never the other two.)

Example 47 loses very little when played more slowly than Czerny's tempo marking ("Molto Allegro [MM=112]"), and is more robust than the previous examples.

All three examples are very useful for varying kinds of petit allegro combinations in triple meter.

Example 48 is a full, lush, orchestral kind of 6/8, and it almost demands a sissonne or cabriole combination. Its median tempo is a hairsbreadth slower than the three previous examples.

9/8 - example 49: six

In the 9/8 meter there are nine eighth notes (or the equivalent thereof) in each bar.

The 9/8 meter is relatively obscure in the world of music, and is almost unheard of in the world of dance. There are not many 9/8s in any tempo, but they are extremely useful—especially adagios, as we shall see.

Allegro 9/8s are very similar to boleros but, to a dancer, the triplet feeling between beats in the 9/8 feels quite different from the couplet feeling in a bolero. Allegro 9/8s are very suitable for combinations of the dégagé family and of petit allegro. (The Royal Academy of Dancing calls them triple jigs.) And teachers should remember that children can hop and skip and galop in phrases of six just as productively as in phrases of eight. I am convinced that, if children were exposed to phrases of six earlier in their training, they wouldn't have so much trouble with them later on. But this will never happen until the teachers themselves know how to use them—and how to ask for them from their accompanists.

How to count an allegro 9/8: in mini-phrases of six: "ONE - and two - and three - and FOUR - and five - and six - and, TWO - and two - and three - and FOUR - and five - and six - and . . . ," up through "FOUR - and two - and three - and FOUR - and five - and six - and."

12/8 - example 50: three

In the 12/8 meter there are twelve eighth notes (or the equivalent thereof) in each measure.

The 12/8 meter is only slightly less obscure than the 9/8, and has no distinguishing factor other than its ability to be counted in several different ways. Adagio 12/8s are extremely useful—again, as we shall see.

The only allegro 12/8 I am familiar with is example 50, a favorite of every dancer. (It is possible that Mr. Czerny wrote it in 12/8 only so it would legitimately fit into his collection of eight-measure exercises.) A dance teacher would be hard put to define it as an allegro 12/8; I am almost positive that the only way a teacher could request this piece is by singing it.

How to count an allegro 12/8: in three: "ONE - and two - and THREE - and four . . . ," up through "eight - and."

The adagio - examples 51–64

To a musician, *adagio* is a word that means slow(ly). In the dance world, *adagio* (or *adage*—both terms are used) is a noun that refers to either a section of a grand pas de deux (see "The grand pas de deux" section in chapter 5) or a classroom combination of slow steps and movements. An adagio is not a form in the same way a rag or bolero is, because it doesn't come in only a single meter or quality (a tarantella, for example, is always a fast 6/8). But it will be referred to hereafter as a form. The adagio is the most difficult form a dance accompanist must deal with. It is one form that proves conclusively, if proof were necessary, that the meter alone cannot be the deciding factor in selecting appropriate music for a given combination.

What I call a normal adagio is what 98 percent of the teachers in the dance world count as a medium-slow 3/4, even when they say, "I would like a 4/4 adagio, please." After about fifteen years of playing only this kind of adagio, I asked some of the teachers for whom I was playing if they could sometimes count an adagio in two, so I could play something new. However, dance teachers seem to be constitutionally unable to count adagios in anything but three—possibly because they sound so martial in two. (If you are a teacher like this, you can solve the problem by asking your accompanist to play a bit of an "abnormal" adagio for you, so you have the rhythm in your ear and your body before you start to set the combination.)

Eventually I began to recognize movement combinations that would benefit from a slower tempo than that of a normal adagio; at around the same time I realized that the median tempos of 4/4 and 12/8 adagios are slower than those of normal adagios. I will never forget the day that I first dared to substitute a 12/8 adage (a two) for a normal one (a three); it felt like a real liberation from the medium-slow-three rut. The difference in counting doesn't seem to confuse anyone (maybe I should be depressed about that): "ONE and uh two - and THREE - and . . ." for a normal adagio, as opposed to "ONE and two and THREE and . . ." for 4/4s and 12/8s.

If a teacher has difficulty finding music slow enough for an adagio or plié combination, or if an accompanist finds he has to slow down and distort an adage to suit the tempo needs of the teacher, a 9/8, a 4/4, or a 12/8 will usually solve the problem.

Substituting a 9/8 to slow down a normal 3/4 adagio would seem like a very logical approach. But I think the main reason I never do it is because it is really difficult for most people to grasp the highly unusual 9/8 meter from the introduction unless one is expecting it—and is familiar with it. (I learned this the hard way. I would try to use the 9/8 when I knew that teachers would slow down their demonstrated normal adagios, and invariably they would say, "No, I'd like something else, please"; they would never say, "That's nice, but I can't count it; could you help me, please?" I always thought that nobody liked my 9/8s until I realized that it was just a question of not being able to count them.)

The following diagram shows the rhythmic structures of two bars of music that can be used for a demi-plié in two counts (or a mini-phrase of adagio movement in two counts). The slow 3/4 has more notes—more substance—than the rhythmic structure of a waltz, and the 9/8 has even more, and so on. These additional notes and the increased substance allow more time for the execution of the movement, because the tempo is slower. I encourage teachers to get together with their accompanists and decide on the median tempo that they feel is the best for their plié combinations. This is certainly not to say that it can never be changed, but rather that the accompanist has an idea of the tempo parameter within which he can choose plié music—certainly one of the most important musical choices he will make in every class.

A) Slow waltz
MM: ♩ = 104

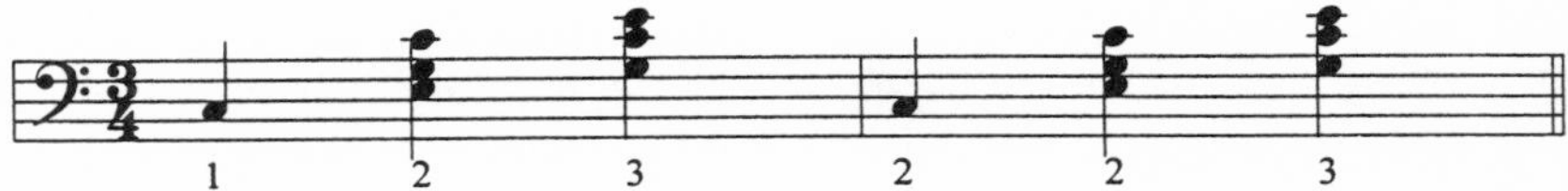

B) Slow 3/4
MM: ♩ = 96

C) Slow 9/8
MM: ♩ = 80

D) *Very* slow 3/4
MM: ♩ = 69

I have never been asked for what I call the *very* slow 3/4 for pliés; it is too slow. I can't think of a better term than *very* slow 3/4, but it is a dangerous one; most teachers unwittingly say they want a very slow adage, thinking—probably—that if their movement is slow, the music should be correspondingly slow. *Wrong*—it's just the opposite. The following discussion will hopefully clarify this prevalent misunderstanding.

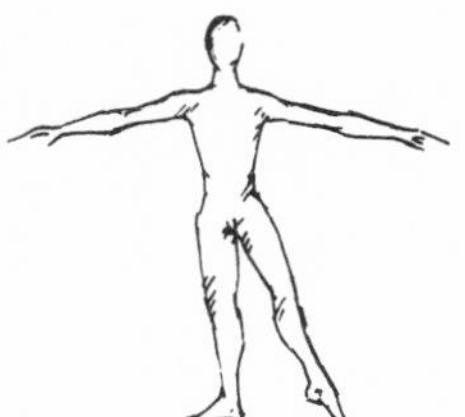

Since a développé—a staple of adagio movement—normally goes through four visually identifiable positions, we will use it as an example. Most développés à la seconde look like the following: (a) passé, (b) développé à la seconde, (c) tendu à la seconde, and (d) close. If each position is attained in two counts in a tempo like A in the preceding music diagram, they will all constitute an 8-count développé in a reasonable tempo for the body. If each position is attained in two counts in a tempo like D in the preceding music diagram, they will all constitute an 8-count développé in an absolutely murderous tempo for the body. However, there is no reason for not doing a 2-count développé in a tempo like D—or C. This would, of course, require the teacher to be aware that her entire adage combination has to be counted in and adjusted to an unusual tempo. (Remember that 98 percent of dance teachers count adagios like B.)

Most teachers count développés in four counts; tempo A would produce a rather speedy 4-count développé, tempo B a normal one, tempo C a slower-than-normal one, and tempo D a grueling one. From another point of view, it will take 12 seconds to produce a 4-count développé in tempo A, 14 seconds in tempo B, 17 seconds in tempo C, and 20 seconds in tempo D. A three-second difference in holding one's leg extended in the air may not seem like much to the uninitiated, but in certain situations it can feel like three hours.

2/4 adagio - example 51: two

The prevailing quality of an adagio is slow, smooth, and lyrical. Most adagio 2/4s have a nonflowing rhythmic structure; they are usually built similarly to what I call moderato twos, like example 51, and they are not well suited to sustained movement. They are very useful for tendu combinations with demi-plié, for some fondu combinations, for ronds de jambe à terre in duple meter, and for "adagios" in beginning children's classes. Some teachers always give a pre-plié warm-up for the feet which they always count in three; I like to vary the musical choice by using one of these moderato twos sometimes—with their permission, of course.

Time signatures don't always mean what we expect them to mean: Mendelssohn wrote his op. 85, no. 14 in 2/4, but it sounds to me like a 12/8.

How to count 2/4 adagios/moderato twos: "ONE and two and THREE and . . . ," up through "eight and."

3/4 adagio - examples 52–55: threes and sixes

Adagios in 3/4 exhibit several different rhythmic structures, as well as an endless variety of dynamic ranges. The following adages are arranged in a descending scale of tempo: the fastest first, the slowest last.

Example 52 has **six notes per bar** in the rhythmic structure. It is typical of what I call a normal adagio. (This example is analogous to Tempo B in the preceding tempo diagram.)

The six chords per bar, instead of single notes, in example 53 slow the tempo down a shade from the previous example's rhythmic structure.

How to count examples 52 and 53: in three: "ONE - and two - and THREE and uh four - and . . . ," up through "eight and uh."

Nine notes per bar in example 54 slow the tempo down even more from the previous two examples. This rhythmic structure will be referred to hereafter as a 9/8, because of the nine consecutive triplets in the left hand. (This example is analogous to Tempo C in the preceding tempo diagram.)

How to count a 9/8 adagio appears after the 9/8 adagio information.

Twelve notes per bar, subdivided in three sets of four eighth notes each, make example 55 slower still. (This example is analogous to Tempo D in the preceding tempo diagram.)

How to count example 55: in six, also, but with a difference: "ONE and two and three and FOUR and five and six and, TWO and two and three and FOUR and five and six and . . . ," up through "FOUR and two and three and FOUR and five and six and." The six counts per mini-phrase in example 54 were subdivided into triplets; example 55 is subdivided into quadruplets. To *see* the theory behind this, compare the second bar of example 55 with the second-to-last bar of example 54; then, if you can't play them yourself, get someone to play the two different bars for you (preferably the two different pieces in their entirety), so you can *hear* the difference.

3/8 adagio - example 56: three

Example 56 is a simple, lovely adagio that I find very similar to the normal adagio (example 52) in the areas of tempo and dynamic range. The so-called 3/8 factor is present in 3/8 adagios but, because of the inherent quality of adagios, is less pronounced.

How to count this 3/8 adagio (for some reason, I hesitate to say, "all 3/8 adagios"; there may be some renegade 3/8 out there that defies normalcy): in three, like a normal adagio: "ONE - and two - and THREE - and . . . ," up through "eight - and."

4/4 or C adagio - examples 57–60: twos

There is a variety of underlying rhythmic structures for 4/4 adagios. I shall deal with the three most common ones here in, again, a descending scale of tempo.

The consecutive **eight notes/chords per bar** in example 57 doesn't produce the flowing feeling necessary for most adagio movement, so it is a more appropriate selection for tendus with demi-plié and ronds de jambe à terre in duple meter. It is in my moderato two category.

Example 58 has an undercurrent of **twelve notes/chords per bar,** subdivided in four sets of three 8th notes each. Pieces structured like this will henceforth be called 12/8s.

Example 59 has **sixteen notes per bar,** subdivided in four sets of four 16th notes each, to maintain the flow and energy.

Example 60 is a highly unusual piece, in that it contains **all three above-mentioned rhythmic structures.** It is advisable to play the first three bars slightly more slowly than might feel natural, in order to leave room for the 16th notes that begin in measure nine, thereby maintaining the same tempo throughout.

Teachers who want to be able to count this piece should know that the first note one hears in the melody is not "1." I'm not sure it's so important to be able to count this piece; one could become so caught up in the unusual counting that one misses the beauty of the music. The phrasing is not at all difficult to grasp.

How to count all 4/4, C, and 12/8 adagios: in two: "ONE and two and THREE and . . . ," up through "eight and."

6/8 adagio - example 61: three

The median tempo of most 6/8 adagios is approximately the same as that of barcarolles, but the consecutive 16th-note figure produces more smoothness. (If there are consecutive 16th notes in a slow 6/8 piece, I put it into my adagio category; if there is the previously discussed 6/8 factor—OOM - pah, OOM - pah—it goes into my barcarolle file.) This 6/8 median tempo, like the one belonging to example 61, is usually the same as the normal adagio tempo.

How to count a 6/8 adagio: in three, like a normal adagio: "ONE - and two and uh THREE - and . . . ," up through "eight and uh."

9/8 adagio - example 62: six

Not once in more than forty years of playing for dance has a teacher asked me for an allegro or adagio 9/8 (except for my students). And not until I met Vera Volkova did 9/8s become an extremely useful category for me. Madame Volkova, like most teachers, could not explain in musical terms what she wanted, but she was adamant, like all good teachers, about having the proper accompaniment for each combination. At the beginning of our working together, she was not happy with my plié music. "Too heavy—too plodding," she grumbled. One day I played one of my favorite adagios, and she literally bounded over to the piano and exclaimed, "That's what I want for pliés!" It was a 9/8—example 62—and I have treasured all 9/8s ever since.

Many adagio 9/8s are labeled 3/4; if the left hand has triplet 8th notes throughout, I always put it in my 9/8 file. Here is another instance of realizing that the meter is not the sole factor in determining the suitability of a particular piece of music; the composer may not have labeled it as carefully as we dance accompanists would like.

How to count a 9/8 adagio (it may be written in 3/4, but it neither sounds nor feels like a 3/4 adagio): in six: "ONE - and two - and three - and FOUR - and five - and six - and, TWO - and two - and three - and FOUR - and five - and six - and, . . ." up through "FOUR - and two - and three - and FOUR - and five - and six - and."

12/8 adagio - examples 63 and 64: two (rarely, three)

Adagios in 12/8 exhibit a variety of rhythmic structures, and the three most common are shown here.

I have chosen to include as an illustration only a small part of this Chopin Nocturne (in E-flat, op. 9, no. 2). It is played to death—and often badly—in dance classrooms, and is probably the most famous 12/8 in the world. It is definitely not a waltz, but its rhythmic structure is fairly similar to a waltz, and produces a choppier, less flowing feeling than the rest of the 12/8 examples.

How to count this 12/8: in three: "ONE - - two - and THREE - - . . . ," up through "eight - - ."

Example 63 has consecutive 8th notes throughout, and does not have a wide dynamic range.

Example 64 has consecutive 8th-note chords throughout, and has a huge dynamic range.

How to count examples 63 and 64: in two: "ONE and two and THREE and . . . ," up through "eight and."

FOR MUSICIANS ONLY: Just to be absolutely clear, the *very* slow 3/4, the 6/8, and the 12/8 adagios all have twelve units of sound in each bar of the rhythmic structures—twelve 16th notes in the first two cases, and twelve 8th notes in the last. The key, of course, is the subdivision: In the *very* slow 3/4, we have three beats of four units each (a six); in the 6/8, we have six beats of two units each (a three); and in the 12/8, we have four beats of three units each (a two).

The following is an example of something that really complicates the counting and understanding of adagios.

Martin Schläpfer—the best music-for-dance-teachers student I have ever had and currently my boss—was observing class yesterday. He was listening to me play a normal 3/4 adage and said, "That's a 12/8, isn't it?" I said, "No, it's a three." "But I hear twelve things in the left hand." And of course he's absolutely right: there are twelve eighth notes in two bars of many adages in three. He studied both the violin and the piano, but what he hears and what I see on the printed page can have two completely different labels. I think it is a grave mistake, in cases like this, for musicians to tell dance teachers that their thinking is wrong. Granted, it is hard for us musicians to explain why it is not a 12/8, but the fact of the matter is, his ears *are* hearing twelve eighth notes. It is not realistic to expect dance teachers to understand music notation (most pianists are not conversant in dance technique, either), and I am almost at the point of discouraging them from delving deeply into music theory. If further attempts at understanding this foreign language called music produce only confusion, it seems to make no sense for dance teachers to try to digest any more than the fact that adagios in 9/8, 12/8, and 4/4 will give a slower tempo than normal adagios in three.

It is important for teachers and essential for accompanists to remember that the majority of 12/8 adagios can be more productively counted in duple meter.

~

The importance of each adagio's median tempo cannot be stressed strongly enough, if the respect for music is to be maintained and fostered.

~

The meters and forms that have been discussed in this chapter comprise the majority of all dance accompanists' repertoires. But there are pieces in many other meters that are suitable for the dance classroom: 5/4, 3/2, 12/16, 6/4, 4/8, etc. And there are many other forms—often folk-dance forms—which are just as suitable for dance but less well known: jota, trepak, hopak, krakowiak, redowa, jig, hornpipe, schottische, reel, and so on.

It saves time when a teacher can say, "I'd like a polonaise, please" instead of, "I need a piece that is broad and majestic and grand . . . maybe in 6/8 or 3/4. . . ." As we have already discussed, an understanding of musical forms and meters is very helpful. But if a teacher is not absolutely sure about the name of the form or meter she wants, she must rely on clear body language or an accurate verbal rendering of her combination. Recently I played for a very musical teacher who demonstrated a "normal" pirouette combination, and I played one of my "normal" pirouette waltzes. He came over to the piano and said, "Maybe it would be better with a 6/8." Despite many years of experience, I was totally confused—first, because I didn't see anything wrong with my selection and, second, because I didn't understand how a 6/8 (as I understand 6/8s) would improve the situation. Because I knew it would take a lot of time to decipher what he really wanted, and also because I didn't want to undermine his authority in front of the students, I changed to another kind of waltz (which he fortunately accepted) and said, "Let's talk about this after class." During our discussion, he said, "I wanted something that sounded like, 'ONE two three FOUR five six,'" which in my mental computer is not a 6/8. I would call it a 3/8, but I neither expect nor suggest that dance teachers try to figure out what a 3/8 is. This teacher would have been better off humming or singing what he spoke to me after the class. A less experienced pianist would have played a 6/8 of heaven knows what kind—probably one for a petit allegro combination, since he is probably not yet familiar with 6/8 waltzes (many of which are grand allegros)—and a lot of time would have been wasted trying to make sense out of this unclear communication.

It would be most helpful for all teachers and accompanists to be familiar with the musical forms contained herein, but this is rarely the case. Often the accompanist's knowledge of musical forms for dance is as limited (if not more so) as the teacher's. So the fact remains that the most prevalent method of communication by teachers is body language, augmented by vocal inflections.

4 ~ *For Dance Teachers*

Dance teachers, you have my undying admiration! You have chosen to teach an art form that is most difficult to master, and you strive toward your goals under the most trying circumstances: daily classes (for, often, the same students) which involve the ceaseless repetition of basically the "same old steps." This process demands that you create an atmosphere charged with energy and the love of dance, and that you find new sources of inspiration and an infinite number of fresh ways to give corrections while coming up with combinations that continually challenge your students. This mind-boggling responsibility deserves as much help as possible. One source of inspiration that accompanies you to every class is music—whether live or mechanically reproduced.

Music and you

Music will help you to show your students that you are teaching them how to move, not just to execute technical feats. One of the main inspirations that turns a phrase of movement into a fulfilled and fulfilling experience—into dancing—is music. This should be stressed from the beginning plié combination to the révérence, and at every level of technical achievement. A professional dancer will be taking a class every day of his dancing career, and he will have to look in every nook and cranny for sources of inspiration for this daily devotion. Music fills those nooks and crannies, and the sooner a student can learn to use it and to appreciate it, the better and happier dancer he will be. A dancer who really absorbs the music progresses faster than a merely rhythmic dancer who only manages to get to the right place at the right time.

If I had my druthers, I would strike the word *exercise* from the dance classroom's vocabulary. It implies drudgery. Too often I see dancers who plod through the barre and only start to dance in the center. Dancing begins with the introductory arm positions before pliés. I feel this probably comes from a few teachers' subconscious attitude toward and treatment of the barre as simply a necessary evil that is part of classical dance.

The development of a feeling for music does not have to go hand in hand with playing an instrument. (There are many dancers who play musical instruments quite well, but somehow manage to be glaringly unmusical.) Musicality in a dancer is evidenced by an instinctive understanding of phrasing, style, and emotional content. These qualities usually show themselves from the very beginning phases of training. I feel that true musicality is also a kind of integrity. I have known maybe six infallibly musical dancers during my career (some of whom are still dancing or teaching), and they could no more have been off the music than they could have refused to breathe; they had no other choice than to do what the music says. (Unfortunately, I know a lot of dancers who think they are one of those six.) If forced to choose between, for instance, an extra pirouette and staying with the music, they unquestionably chose to ignore the superfluous pirouette. They were driven by the music, not by their own personal body tempos.

I have mixed opinions concerning the use of tapes. (For the sake of brevity throughout the text, the word *tape[s]* is used to encompass all mechanically reproduced music—i.e., records, cassettes, reel-to-reel tapes, and CDs.) Tapes are often the only source of music for dance teachers in small towns. But it is sad to see, for a number of reasons, how extensive their use has become in larger cities. The slight but discernible tempo differences between music for a preschool and a children's class, for instance, are of the utmost importance to a teacher; tempos on tapes are unchanging constants (unless you distort the music through tempo-varying devices). You are restricted in every combination by the number of counts in the corresponding selection on the tape, which severely limits spontaneity. And you waste so much valuable class time running back and forth to the tape machine.

Students whose daily classes are done to the inflexibility of tapes often have a difficult time adjusting to the flexibility of live music because of slight variations in tempo of the accompanist from day to day. Also, many teachers tend to give almost the same combinations every day when restricted by tapes. This leads to students' impaired ability to pick up combinations and choreography.

Therefore, I encourage you—with the help of this book—to use live accompaniment, if you are not already doing so. It seems grossly unfair that, along with the other functions you must fulfill, you are usually stuck with training a pianist if you want live music. *But the importance of live music for class cannot be overemphasized.*

Local high school music students and teachers, students in the music departments of universities, and church organists are a few of the people who may have the necessary requisites for accompanying your classes. You need someone with a basic technique and a willingness to learn; the all-important infallible sense of rhythm, a feeling for movement, and respect for dance are qualities that, unfortunately, do not always show up during an audition. When you hire a new pianist, I strongly recommend a three- or six-month trial period, so that he can decide if he likes this kind of work, and you can see whether he improves and really works at understanding this new milieu. Establishing a trial period makes it easier for each of you to sever the relationship, should you so desire.

Working with a new pianist may be difficult for you at first, as you may have to put up with a lot of wrong notes, inappropriate tempos which you will have to correct incessantly, and a lack of understanding of the musical and movement qualities that vary so much from combination to combination. It will be worth your time and trouble, though, if for no other reason than the fact that *you,* not a machine, will be able to control the tempo and length of every combination, which gives you much more control over the class in general.

Some dance teachers say they prefer to teach to tapes due to their ease or predictability. But dance itself is not always predictable (how boring that would be), and such an attitude is counterproductive.

Also, many a dance teacher may, understandably, not want to bother with the added difficulties of teaching a pianist how to accompany for class when she already has her hands full with teaching her students how to dance. But as a teacher becomes aware of why the pianist can't yet produce what she wants to hear, she will be able to handle the problems more easily.

The following are three areas in which our training as pianists does not correspond to the needs of dance teachers.

- A classically trained musician is taught to revere the printed page. Therefore, beginning accompanists who do not improvise almost invariably play exactly what is written—no less and especially no more (like preparations, clean finishes, etc.). This is why a beginning accompanist so often plays pieces that not only aren't "squared off" (into 8-, 16-, and 32-measure phrases), but also are sparse in texture (music is not always written with octaves on every count, which add richness and support to music for dance). Additionally, there are pedaling techniques helpful to dancers that are in direct opposition not only to what pianists are taught in their classical training, but also to what is written on the printed page.

  I rarely encourage accompanists to deviate from the composer's intent. What I do try to foster in every accompanist is the ability to play a piano reduction of a symphony the way the Vienna Philharmonic would play it, a Joplin rag the way Joplin would have played it, a Sousa march sounding like a ninety-piece marching band, one of Satie's *Gymnopédies* as if the piano keys were eggshells—in other words, to respect the composer's intent. This may be done by augmenting the existing notes with octaves and inner harmonies, thereby producing the breadth, fullness, and support you want for your dancers—or by knowing when not to tamper with the printed page.

The piano allows the possibility to produce the scope of an orchestra, from the crashing tympani to the sweet tones of the flute, although it cannot produce the wide variety of timbres and colors of each instrument. This awareness of the full range of the piano is what I try to promote in accompanists. Since dancers use their entire bodies when they dance, it doesn't make sense for an accompanist to use any less than the full range of the keyboard.

- A pianist is rarely trained to follow another person's directions during the performance of a piece. All of a sudden he finds himself in a situation in which someone is telling him what to play, how to play it, and at what speed. And most pianists rarely have the distractions of loud talking and moving bodies during the performance of their music. I am thoroughly convinced that a lot of potentially fine accompanists quit because they feel their artistic output is both distorted by the needs of dancers and dictated solely by the whims of dance teachers.

  If a pianist can be helped through the difficult beginning stages, he will soon be able to see that, despite certain parameters necessary for the qualities of movement he is required to match, he has a great deal of artistic freedom.

  It is up to you to make him realize that he is an extremely important part of the dance process. If you gently guide him into learning to follow you, he will eventually (first through force of habit, and then through true understanding) develop his kinesthetic sense until you will seldom have to say a word to him.

- Musicians, from their very first lessons, are taught to count but—as I'm sure you've discovered—they don't count like dancers. A musician counts a waltz, "ONE two three ONE two three ONE two three. . . ." A knowledgeable dance teacher usually counts a waltz, "ONE two three two two three THREE two three, . . ." up through "eight two three." Musicians don't count the number of bars in a phrase because there is no need to. Dance teachers do count them because the teaching of dance requires movement to be organized into phrases. Dance teachers also sometimes count the number of steps they do, which often jibes with neither dancers' counts nor musicians' counts.

Although counting is discussed in detail starting on page 63, it must be mentioned here. Counting is *vital.* The more clearly you count, the more exactly your students will do the combinations, and the better chance your accompanist will have to choose suitable music. There are many aspects of teaching (for example, how and when to give effective corrections) that will become apparent only through the daily, monthly, and yearly accumulation of experience. Counting is *not* one of them. You must learn to do it correctly from the beginning.

Most teachers who can't (or won't) count, or who are verbally illiterate about music, are often quite musical; they instinctively feel musical phrasing, and don't understand why everybody doesn't. (I cringe when I hear a teacher berate a student for having been unmusical when the teacher herself has been very vague in her musical demands.) We all aren't born with a sublime musical instinct, and those who don't have it and want to dance, *have* to develop it. If students have to guess what counts their movements are supposed to be executed on, their energies are focused on the guesswork, instead of on proper physical (and hopefully artistic) execution. After a while, they may even ignore the music; since it doesn't seem to matter to the teacher, why should they expend any brain power on it? This makes for sloppy dancing.

There isn't a ballet company in the world that doesn't emphasize the need for counting. Which makes more sense: "That arabesque is on '3,' people!" or "I'm not sure where that arabesque happens, but you'll know when you get there"? (Do not confuse executing that arabesque on "3" with being musical. A choreographer or teacher, not the music, tells a dancer to do an arabesque on "3.")

For the past three weeks (autumn of 2000) I have had the incredibly good fortune to work with Nils Christe and his wife Annegien Sneep as they set the ballet *Before Nightfall* on Martin Schläpfer's BallettMainz. The piece was made to Bohuslav Martinů's Double Concerto for Two String Orchestras, Piano, and Timpani, which is certainly one of the most difficult scores in the contemporary ballet repertoire. Watching the piece is like seeing the music; one would think that a musician had become a choreographer overnight. I have rarely seen such phenomenal musical awareness in a choreographer. Mr. Christe said many wonderful things during his time here, but two really stand out. After clarifying a particularly challenging musical section, he mused, "No wonder choreographers don't bother choreographing musically; it's too hard." And after insisting on drill-team perfection in one of the sections for six people, he said, "Hide the counts"—one of the smartest descriptions I've ever heard of how to respect the music and choreography without looking like robots.

Before playing my first class for the late Bobby Blankshine in New York City, he told me he could count only in three. Since I had known him as a very musical dancer with the Joffrey Ballet, I said, "Impossible!"—but it was true. Knowing this before class prevented me from playing the entire class in three (logic and boredom would have prevented me from doing so eventually), but it's a bit hard thinking in 2/4 when a teacher is counting in 3/4—and it doesn't do the students' understanding of music any good, either. We talked about it afterward, and he came to realize that he could count in two, but changing a bad habit is much more difficult than establishing a good habit from the beginning.

Counting means, obviously, speaking in numbers. The numbers themselves are less important than *how* they are spoken: in a regular pulse, as the music will be played, and with the dynamic peaks and valleys of the movement phrases. If you don't count clearly, don't expect your students to dance clearly.

If you are embarrassed by your seeming inability to count, ask your accompanist to help you outside of class. He will probably be eager to help improve that aspect of communication between you.

My reason for relating the following incident is not to belabor the point that clear counting is vital, but to emphasize that, without a logical approach to counting, a teacher cannot really teach. It is the most extreme case of ineptitude that I have experienced, and it contains many dance-world problems which I feel should be brought out in the open, primarily the unquestioned power of the teacher (in this case, mostly ignorance as opposed to conscious abuse of power), and the powerlessness of students who are often too young and inexperienced to control their destinies and physical well-being.

A few years ago, I played for a three-day workshop in Zurich. On the list of distinguished teachers was a woman from a well-known ballet institute in a former Eastern-bloc country. (She will remain anonymous here.) She began the class by counting the pliés in duple meter. "Not unusual," I mused to myself; the "Russian systems" tend to be overburdened with duple-meter rhythms, and often use them for pliés. However, when she slowly counted four sets of four counts for one grand plié, I knew we were in for trouble. To make a *very* long story short, she counted every combination not only in duple meter but also in this same slow tempo, no matter whether she was demonstrating tendus, fondus, ronds de jambe, or petits battements. And no matter what I played (and I tried to play as well as I could—this kind of challenge doesn't come along very often, thankfully), she could not fit one of her combinations to my music. Nor was I once able to adjust a selection to her combination, because she always changed the timing ("and" tendus became non-"and" tendus, for example), and she usually changed the steps as she did the combinations with the students. The students were floundering all over the place, and I couldn't "take a poll" and follow their general drift, since they were too inexperienced to know how to make illogical combinations work—something advanced students and professionals learn to do quite well.

Oddly enough, this teacher never once stopped to try to connect the movement to the music. This lack of connection didn't seem to bother her at all, and she just kept bestowing gracious smiles on me. The crowning glory was her admonition to the class: "In between listening to the music, you have to count. You must always count," at which point she looked to me for corroboration. It was all I could do to nod and smile wanly back at her, instead of laughing—or politely excusing myself and leaving.

"Is that really such a big deal?" you may ask. *Yes.*

- A roomful of students was being taught that it doesn't matter if one's movements even vaguely correspond to the music.
- The same roomful of students was unable to derive any technical benefit from the class because they were too busy trying to figure out the combinations, and wondering whether they should follow the music or the teacher.
- It was the first time in fifteen years that I wasn't able to salvage a class taught by an inept teacher. It didn't hurt my ego, but what did bother me was knowing that one class with this teacher would either set back the progress of and confuse a less experienced accompanist, or make him quit.
- There were several local teachers watching who came up to this teacher afterward and told her what a wonderful class it had been. Excuse my bluntness: They were either stupid or sycophants.
- The teacher probably went home thinking that, because no one said anything to the contrary, everything went just fine and her class was a big success.
- How many other dance teachers graduate from teacher-training courses without a thorough—or even the most basic—grounding in music as it applies to dance?
- Yes, the teacher was probably nervous. But she should not have been sent out to teach with such a lack of experience; and if I had seen just the slightest hint that she knew she was not as brilliant a teacher as she projected, I would probably have been less agitato.
- This person will never even begin to develop her potential as a teacher until she learns to demonstrate correctly. And how many students will she confuse—and possibly even harm—in the meantime?

I was tempted to say something along these lines to her, but I have learned through experience to help only when I am asked. Most teachers—for that matter, most of us human beings—get very insecure and defensive when confronted with our shortcomings. The more experienced one is as a teacher—in such a position of authority—the less comfortable one is in the position of being taught, especially by a pianist, whose role in the dance classroom is usually seen to be totally subservient to the teacher.

So this is another reason why I wanted to write this book: to present helpful information in a nonconfrontational way. After decades of observing dancers and teachers, I have learned to identify certain problem areas as they relate to my effectiveness as an accompanist. During this process, I have also become aware of mistakes that many teachers constantly make which sabotage the teacher-accompanist and the teacher-student relationships. It is my hope that teachers will benefit not only from quietly reading and slowly digesting the information in this book, but also from recognizing the problem areas that may be relevant to each teacher's experience. I don't want to prove that you're wrong and I'm right; I simply want to improve the communication between all participants in each dance experience so that the quality of training that dance students receive will improve.

The importance of counting clearly cannot be overstressed. And counting does *not* have to remove passion from either movement or music.

~

You do not need an extensive musical background to communicate with your accompanist. For as long as you have been involved in dance, you have been learning about music subconsciously, and you know much more about it than you think. Just because you can't verbally define the difference between a mazurka and a polonaise doesn't mean that you can't recognize the difference. Your body understands it, and you can communicate as effectively with your body as you can with words—sometimes more effectively.

Mention must be made of wrong notes. Throughout this book, I encourage accompanists to branch out and augment their existing technique in order to provide a richer, more supportive musical base for dancers. This can only be accomplished by breaking through their self-imposed barriers. Just as your students fall down occasionally or mess up a step in the process of mastering it, so, too, will your accompanist hit many wrong notes. It is a necessary stage, and difficult for you, your students, *and* the accompanist. If it gets really unbearable, speak to him after class, telling him that you appreciate his hard work, but that he probably needs to practice more by himself. If he doesn't have a piano of his own, offer him the use of yours during the studio's off-hours.

A teacher's personal expression of dance extends to many areas. It is up to you to establish guidelines within which you operate your class. For instance, do you foster the benevolent autocracy of classical ballet, or do you run a looser ship? Do you start and end your classes on time? Do you throw tantrums if anyone—student or accompanist—talks in class? How do you wish to be addressed by your students and accompanists? While these questions may not seem to be within the realm of this book, you need to remember that a musician seeing a dance class for the first time sees a whole new world. It will be helpful to explain as much as possible of what you expect, since the problems he will have with the music alone will be overwhelming. Ideally, every accompanist who plays for your classes should become flexible enough to be your alter ego, and how you relate to him will provide him with a base upon which he relates to you.

At this stage in your career, you may or may not have dealt with the insecurities inherent in being a dance teacher. While I am not suggesting that you coddle your beginning accompanist, do remember how insecure he may be. He may not understand most of what you are saying to him at first, and he probably understands nothing of what you are saying to your students, especially if he doesn't speak French. (Even something as basic as the fact that barre combinations are done on both sides to the same music is often a revelation to a novice. It certainly was to me when I began.) So yelling at him for one reason or another will probably make him retreat into himself.

The relationship between teacher and accompanist is very special. It is much more intimate than a normal employer-employee relationship, and it cannot grow and thrive without mutual respect. It is important for your students to see this respect between the two driving forces of a dance class.

It is becoming an increasingly rare luxury to play for teachers who treat accompanists as collaborators and contributors, rather than beat-keepers and slaves. I am aware of at least one dance institution with a large staff of accompanists, almost all of whom are very unhappy in their work. It's bad enough that some of the teachers speak to the accompanists rudely; it is *inexcusable* that some of the dancers/students speak to them in the same way—but of course they have learned this behavior from their teachers. The accompanists are often treated with condescension and disdain, and they are made to feel that they are a hindrance rather than a help. As a result, they are not motivated to increase their repertoire, maintain their technique, or do any extra work beyond their normal workload.

If you feel your accompanist is not doing his job as well as you would like, you must help him, not humiliate him. Work with him outside of class; give him a tape of your favorite ballet class to listen to; suggest that he watch more classes and/or take some; and make sure that you are not giving him confusing information. Remember that the way in which you speak—to your accompanists as well as your students—is just as important as what you say. We accompanists are only human, and the hardest lesson for us to learn is not to take corrections personally—as an assault on our characters. Imagine how you would feel if someone corrected you constantly during a class you were teaching. For the safety of your students, this constant correction is often what must occur between you and your accompanist in the beginning stages, so an objective and sympathetic tone of voice will make corrections more palatable to him.

All experienced accompanists become extremely adept at troubleshooting, that is, covering up teachers' mistakes for the sake of continuity of the class and preserving the teacher's authority. Over the years I have become less willing to do this (except in situations like auditions or the first few times I play for a new teacher—or when I sense that a teacher is too fragile to be corrected). I think teachers need to know when they make mistakes just as much as accompanists and students do; since a teacher's authority is so rarely questioned in the classroom (and rightly so), she has no way of knowing that not only the accompanist but also many of the students are aware of her mistakes. I'm not saying that she must be perfect, but I do recommend that she not blame her students or accompanist (or both) for her own mistakes. Sooner or later, this leads everyone to question a teacher's authority and commitment to discipline.

A case in point:

Teacher: "Children! Why didn't you do the combination on the counts I set?"

Students (to the back wall): "Because you set it three different ways."

I would never embarrass a teacher by saying that to her during the class. Even when I notice a discrepancy in counting or some other problem, I don't point it out to her in class because (a) she probably wouldn't believe me;[1] (b) it would waste even more class time trying to sort everything out; and (c) I don't believe in humiliating teachers in front of their students. (I expect teachers to extend the same courtesy to their accompanists and students, but unfortunately many of them have learned neither good manners nor productive psychology.) But these days I will ask questions, even when I know the answers, just to try to get teachers to accept more responsibility for their classes.

And I try to play exactly what she sets. A case in point:

A teacher sets a combination very precisely with a balance in arabesque for seven counts at the end that finishes in fifth position on "8." I play exactly that, lifting my foot off the pedal on "8 and," so there is no more sound, and the students' legs and the teacher's arms are still in arabesque. And she goes on to the next combination, having forgotten what she requested.

These are not isolated instances. If they happened once a week, I might not even mention them, but, with a depressingly large number of teachers, each of them happens at least once a class.

Sometimes I feel like an old crab when I force new teachers to correct their mistakes. It would be so easy—and a lot more fun—to just give in and play what I know they want, not what they showed. But I am convinced that this is why there are so many musically inarticulate teachers: They are rarely shown the correct way to express their musical needs, so they perpetuate the sad reputation of dancers being unmusical, and they unconsciously teach their students that music isn't really important.

Some of us have had the good fortune to have been trained by—or to have played for—teachers who respect music, who are aware of its power to motivate and inspire, and who realize that good accompanists help teachers teach better. These teachers work in close collaboration with the accompanist in every class, demanding impeccable musicality from their students and impeccable sensitivity from their accompanists. This collaboration manifests itself not necessarily in protracted discussions of musical selections during class, but by a meeting of the minds that has been established usually outside of class by working on problem areas and defining common goals.

The best teachers for whom I have played (and I mean the best teachers for everyone in the classroom, not just for the accompanist) don't always count using numbers and "ands." They almost never know the difference between a bolero and a mazurka (and they are happy to learn it). They tell me what they want with their voices, not always by speaking directly to me, but by demonstrating every combination clearly and with vocal inflections that match the quality of movement. They look me in the eye occasionally to let me know they think I'm a person, not a jukebox. (A depressingly large percentage of teachers seem to demonstrate every combination solely for the edification of the students, absolutely ignoring the accompanist's presence.) If they haven't done so during the demonstration, they let me know when to stop. If I have chosen an inappropriate selection, they let me know diplomatically; they never berate me in front of the class. And they say thank you after class and mean it, sometimes adding, "Let's work out that problem we had in (whatever combination)." They make me feel I'm really a part of the class, not a piece of furniture. So of course I prefer to play for them—and of course I try even harder to please them.

~

You must have something to offer your accompanist besides a paycheck, especially if it's a small paycheck. The surest way to keep a good accompanist is by appreciating him and by challenging him, and there are many ways to go about that. Here are a few suggestions:

- Use a wide variety of music. Don't, for instance, always use a waltz for ronds de jambe à terre; try a tango or a moderato two occasionally.
- For a more advanced accompanist, challenge him technically. Set up your class so that there is very little time for his (and your students'!) mind(s) to wander. If practical and useful, speed up the tempo as your students repeat a combination.
- Encourage him to bring in new music. When he does, react to it, even if unfavorably; it is helpful for him to know why a piece of music is unsuitable.

- Have your accompanist give a music lesson once a month for fifteen or thirty minutes in a technique class. In the remaining time, give a barre incorporating into the students' movements everything he has discussed. Reinforce these concepts in subsequent classes. If he doesn't know how to begin, discuss with him any musical problems you have observed in your students. Or have him teach them to count, clap, sing, or walk (or any combination thereof) to basic musical forms such as waltzes, marches, and polkas.

All of the above bring tremendous benefits to your students, too.

It might be helpful to list the most common problems accompanists have with teachers. They are:

- Teachers who don't react, either by saying thank you after class (and meaning it); or by a grin at a new piece—or an old one played particularly well; or by *some* acknowledgment that we have helped a little.
- Counting and the specifications of tempo and combination length that are vague, inaudible, or nonexistent.
- Teachers who finish demonstrating a combination in one meter—let's say a two, then say, "Oh, I think I'd rather have a three. AND—."
- Constantly not being able to finish phrases, which is somewhat like a lecturer being interrupted as she is making her final point.
- Teachers who bring their personal problems into the classroom and inflict their frustrations on anyone who happens to be around.
- A hard-to-define attitude of lack of respect for music in general, and accompanists in particular.

Music and your students

So far, I have discussed your relationship with your accompanist. Now a few words about music as it relates to your students.

It seems highly desirable, if not imperative, for the teacher to demand that her students dance with the music. It is regrettable that there are many schools (and even some professional companies) whose staffs do not insist on this most basic component of dance. The results are appalling. Besides contributing to the students' general lack of discipline, this oversight not only prevents the students from understanding what dance is really all about, but also decreases their chances for a professional career. Very few directors of dance companies will hire dancers who have trouble with music, and dancers with a problem in this area stick out like sore thumbs in an audition.

Ninety-five percent of any given dance audience will notice whether a dancer is on the music more often than whether he is turned out. That doesn't mean that music is more important than turn-out, but it certainly does mean that it must be given equal emphasis. Musicality is as much a part of technique as turn-out. Once habits are learned, they are very difficult to break. This goes for good habits as well as bad ones, and if a teacher insists on musical awareness from the beginning stages of dance training, she won't have to mention it at the more advanced levels. It won't even occur to her students to be off the music.

It should be one of your priorities to insist that your students' movements correspond to the music. For instance, if a grand plié takes two counts to go down and two counts to come up, insist that their leg muscles use the entire four counts—including all the good stuff between the numbers—not two counts down, one count up, and a port de bras, as so often happens. This may be such a common mistake because I often hear teachers count a plié combination like this: "ONE and uh two - - THREE - and four - - . . . ." To get a never-ending plié, every syllable and every 8th note need to be verbalized, like this: "WUH-UN a-and uh-uh two-oo a-and uh-uh THREE-EE a-and uh-uh fo-our a-and uh-uh. . . ." And even (or especially?) professional dancers need to be reminded that what they often think of as the most boring combination of the class is the most important; demanding from their bodies the same amount of time in a plié as the music dictates produces logical movement, and trains both mind and body to automatically respond to music's essence. *Controlling one's plié is a vital step in developing expressive musicality.*

Ronds de jambe à terre are often sloughed through, also. Regardless of where the foot is on the "1" of every bar (in first position, tendu front, second position, or tendu back), equal time must be given to each location. A majority of students, whose teachers don't realize the need of giving specific guidance, make random kidney bean shapes, arriving at different geographical points at random musical times. This shows that all positions—and the difficulties inherent in getting to them—are not being given full consideration. Forcing the body to move at a tempo other than its own sluggish wishes is a big key to technical advancement, and music is the logical motivator to this end.

Many movements, such as an arabesque, are often executed in more than one or two counts of music. You must make your students aware that it is rarely logical, comfortable, aesthetic, productive, or musical to hike their legs up to an arabesque in one count and park there for three more counts. Point out to your students that they have four counts in which to accomplish this movement (arabesque is a position, yes, but it is a moving one), so they must learn to gauge the musical tempo in relation to their bodies and order their movements accordingly.

Another example is a cambré forward. If the whole movement is accomplished in four counts, it makes no sense to bend the body to the floor in one count, park there for two counts, and come up in one count. It is the moving through the movement that builds strength and muscle tone, not the parking in each position. To be beneficial, the students' torsos should be passing through a right angle at the end of count 1's measure, their chests should be as close to their knees as possible at the end of count 2's measure, back in the right angle at the end of count 3's measure, and upright (and lifting and inhaling to start a cambré back) at the end of count 4's measure. If they learn to do it right in their beginning years, they will never have to relearn it properly at a later date, they will gain technical strength more quickly, and they will start learning how to function properly in a dance ensemble.

From the foregoing discussions, it might be possible to conclude that robotlike precision is a desirable commodity. Nothing could be further from the truth.

Dancers—from intermediate to diva level—occasionally use the excuse, "I hear music differently" to account for their lack of precision. No dance ensemble can afford to have sixteen sets of ears hearing differently. The "1" can be in no other place in time than on "1." I think dancers react to music differently: sluggishly, over-anticipatingly, or productively. Or not at all; to a few dancers, music seems to be a necessary evil—something that gets in the way of their executing movements in their own personal tempos.

Dancers may also react to different orchestral lines and instrumental entrances in the music; they may prefer in certain passages, for instance, to make their movements more cellolike than trumpetlike. But "1" is still "1." An unmusical dancer is neither useful to a choreographer nor a pleasure to an audience—nor will he ever even begin to experience the fulfillment of Dance.

No matter how fantastic your accompanist is, his music alone will not ensure the development of the students' musicality. Your verbal guidance is absolutely necessary to make them aware that there are logical reasons for musicality, not just aesthetic ones. If you don't stress the importance of music, your students won't either.

Nataliya Viktorovny Zolotova once illustrated this point quite graphically. Her official title was Honoured Actress of the RSFSR [Russian Soviet Federated Socialist Republic] and Senior Teacher of Classic Dance in the Moscow Academic Choreographic School (better known as the Bolshoi Ballet School). I had the great good fortune of watching her teach for a week at the Banff Centre in Alberta. She had an interpreter assigned to her whom she didn't use the entire week (with one exception). Even when wearing what we would call a housedress and bedroom slippers, she demonstrated everything she wanted from her students through body language and the inflections of those mellifluous Russian syllables. The exception occurred the day she became absolutely incensed with her students and called the interpreter over to translate the following: "I can't describe the difference between a musical dancer and a nonmusical dancer, but there is a difference! You can't dance without the music! I won't put up with it!"

Another quote—from one of the finest teachers of all time, Vera Volkova: "You look like a typewriter person in that arabesque; if there's no dancing in your balance, it's only willpower." Now granted, there is a great deal of willpower that has to go into the mastery of dance, but the magic that dancers such as Mikhail Baryshnikov produce on stage far transcends mere willpower—and it never looks like hard work on stage either.

Technique cannot be separated from dancing. A student doesn't spend years perfecting a prodigious technique and then start learning how to dance; technique, discipline, and musicality must be learned hand in hand from the first day of dance class.

Music helps your students remember that they are engaged in an artistic endeavor, not calisthenics. Students subconsciously pick up so much from their teachers, so if you groan, "All right, we're just going to do glissades across the floor," they will groan through those glissades. But if you treat them as just another combination—and request an appropriate and especially lighthearted piece from your accompanist—you turn drudgery into productive movement. Don't forget that you probably have some years of dancing experience behind you that tell you that glissades across the floor can be a bit boring, but a child or beginner doesn't know that yet, nor does he know that facing the barre for barre work is boring, unless you imply it. A fresh, eager student will enjoy anything you give him, as long as you present it in an appealing manner.

Along the lines of how you present your material to your students must come a few words about energy. Often, the difference between a competent teacher and a great teacher is this vital element.

As you know, a dance class is made up of logical combinations utilizing physical principles. These combinations progress in an order designed to develop and strengthen different sets of muscles in isolation as well as in coordination with the entire body. Most dance teachers pattern their classes with this in mind, but the great teachers have an extra measure of being able to infuse each daily repetition with new life. The great teachers rarely teach in a monotone, and they are usually talking most of the time. They often make their corrections during the combinations, thus correcting a bad habit during its execution, instead of allowing the student to practice it wrong once again, and to rely only on thinking about it afterward to correct it—and to prevent their students' muscles from getting cold. The great teachers use their voices to transmit energy to their students and to their accompanists.

Many younger students and most beginning accompanists have never seen a grand jeté or grand battement in their final forms. A beginning accompanist will never understand how to play a piece appropriately for either of these steps—or for the preparatory movements leading up to them—if the teacher doesn't convey vocally some sense of how much physical energy is required to produce them. (This is especially pertinent when the teacher no longer demonstrates energetic steps and movements full-out.) Singing, clapping, finger snapping, and vocalizing the steps and accents of all combinations while the music is playing are all helpful means of increasing the accompanist's and students' awareness of the quality of movement, especially since the beginning accompanist understands very little of the varying qualities of movement. (I know there are some very good teachers who frown on all this extraneous noisemaking on the part of the teacher, but I really appreciate it. After more than forty years in the dance studio—and after four classes in a row—I am really grateful for a little synergistic support. And there is no question in my mind that it spurs the students on too. And, yes, there can be too much of a good thing.)

Exhorting your students, "Listen to the music!" doesn't always produce the desired effect. Students will often listen to the music when their group is not dancing; then, when they come back to the center, they seem to have tin ears. "Fill out the music" and "Use the music" (and, for more advanced students, "Fulfill the music" and "Be the music") seem to get better results, and making specific observations is even more beneficial. "The melody is telling your feet what to do" and "Your movement should match the quality of that adagio" are only two examples of ways to make your students understand that the music is there to be *used.*

Even if some of your students are taking music lessons, they don't always connect what they learn in those lessons to their dance lessons. Having them count one piece of music per class (including numbers and "ands" or "and-uhs") teaches them early on that there is a direct relationship between their movements and the music. Having them sing is highly recommended. It's hard to sing a legato line and execute a choppy movement at the same time—and it forces them to breathe.

You can develop students' awareness of music in many ways. Not everyone is born with the ability to phrase music, and some people find it hard to count too. A dancer absolutely must do one or the other extremely well. One way (and you would have to prearrange this with your accompanist) is to have your students balance in a position for eight counts after the combination is finished, then stop—even though the music continues. This forces them to count, and it is quite difficult for most dancers to stop moving while the music is still going on. (Even exquisitely musical dancers sometimes have to count—for instance, when there is a canon in the choreography.)

Another way is to ask students how many phrases of eight are in a combination. Emphasize to them that it is easier to pick up a combination in patterns and phrases than step by step by step by step by. . . .

One of the best ways to heighten the students' awareness of music, as well as to graphically demonstrate how they could improve the dynamics of their dancing, is by the accompanist playing like they dance. I never do this without asking a teacher's permission. Whenever I hear teachers talking about "soggy frappés" or "boring grands battements," I ask them if I can play like their students look. They always say yes, and I play mush: the same piece with no dynamics and the pedal held down throughout. They usually get the message—and a laugh.

Yet another way is by asking your students to identify music your accompanist plays. Even if many of your "hobby students" come to class only once a week, it can benefit them to learn to treat music as an inspiration instead of background noise. And you are also training the dance audience of the future, so it behooves them to associate specific music with specific dance works. Ask them what a particular piece is immediately after the accompanist plays it the first time, so that they can connect the name to the music. Or ask the accompanist before class if he could play a specific excerpt for a specific combination, and you can say something to your students like, "I will ask you what the name of the next piece of music is." If you ask them after the last time they hear a piece, it will be more difficult for them to remember it.

An extremely good way for your more advanced students to start becoming aware of the inextricable link between dance and music is by requiring them to teach a barre. Have each student in turn demonstrate a combination; each must decide what comes next, and must demonstrate clearly with counts and "ands" or "and-uhs" (both will hereafter be referred to simply as "ands") for the accompanist and for their colleagues. I played a class like this recently, and it was an eye-opener for all concerned. The students demonstrated exceptionally clearly in almost every area, and I'm convinced it's because their teacher always demonstrates clearly. Most of the tempos were too fast, and I felt it would help them more if I played exactly the tempos they demonstrated than if I adjusted, and I really feel that they understood how vital tempo is. My favorite reaction was from the teacher. She was amazed that all the combinations were so similar to hers, and understood clearly that students parrot their teachers. "What a responsibility!" she said. Indeed.

It might be wise to occasionally remind your students that there is a live body over there at the keyboard. Students are often too caught up in their own selves to be aware of much else. If students aren't listening to the music, there's a good chance that they also are not listening to you. If a student tunes out any single factor of dance—placement, corrections, music, his fellow dancers—he runs the risk of gradually ignoring everything but his own ego.

~

It must be stressed that any art can be learned only through doing it, not just by reading about it. This book can help teachers and accompanists become aware of problem areas and can offer suggestions, but in the end it will be up to you and him to establish a working relationship in which each of you can grow. Much of the responsibility lies with you, since you know what you want and he doesn't yet. This changes only with doing it. No one can teach himself something without appropriate resources, so much of an accompanist's growth depends on your increasing his awareness.

May I repeat what I said at the beginning: Your job—making dancers—is most difficult and fraught with responsibilities! Teaching requires the very rare gift of clear, incisive communication, and I only hope that you will enlist the aid of good music to help you achieve your goals.

How a new dance teacher deals with an accompanist

Before beginning, I want to stress to experienced dance teachers reading this that you may find some of my suggestions hopelessly picky and/or unnecessary. I must admit, I am going for Utopia here, teaching a rank beginner, who has no experience in verbalizing her musical needs, how to get the most out of her accompanist—and students—in the musical area. You experienced teachers may have learned—or subconsciously known—many of these points and, if you didn't have a solid musical grounding before you began teaching, you may also have picked up some unproductive habits along the way. Those last ones are what we experienced accompanists have learned to sort out, muttering under our breath things like, "You don't really want a 4-bar preparation for that 6/8 march" (you want a 4-count preparation) or "You said, 'last group' five minutes ago; why am I still playing?" And they are the habits that totally confuse new accompanists, sometimes to the point of making them decide this is not the job for them.

If you and your accompanist are both happy with your relationship, then don't worry about being as musically exact as I am suggesting. A couple of teachers have said to me, after reading this book, that they feel they are hopelessly inaccurate in their demonstrations. I tell them that instinctive musicality can sometimes override the necessity for accurate counting, and I can almost always translate any unclear demonstration into musically logical accompaniment. But there are, unfortunately, many dance teachers out there without instinctive musicality, and they absolutely must learn to count. And a beginning accompanist will not always be able to understand sublime musicality; they are really at the nuts-and-bolts, "one-and-two-and" phase, and you must be very clear for them.

Simply stated, most of a dance teacher's work comprises giving class—demonstrating combinations of movement—and teaching—ensuring that the students execute the combinations correctly. A thorough understanding of classical technique, the possibilities and limitations of the human body, a discerning eye for faulty placement, insistence on musicality, and psychological insight into the uniqueness of each student are necessary to the teaching aspect. In comparison, giving class is fairly easy.

In my experience, most new dance teachers begin by giving class instead of teaching. They spend hours before each class writing down each combination—sometimes with music in mind, sometimes not. Then in the classroom they often demonstrate each combination (usually reading from their notes) in a tone of voice somewhere between apology and sheer terror. If they are lucky enough to have an experienced accompanist, they just let him go about his business. If they must also deal with an inexperienced accompanist, the result is often chaos. Musical teachers are endlessly grateful if the music matches their preconceived movements. Unmusical teachers often blame the accompanist if their combinations don't work, and an inexperienced accompanist will, indeed, assume it was his fault, since he cannot prove otherwise.

After a while, teachers start to teach. They eventually realize that thinking up combinations is the easiest part of teaching, and they no longer have to rely on such lengthy, detailed notes. (That is not to say that experienced teachers don't plan their classes beforehand; many fine teachers pre-choreograph every class.) They give corrections—surely the most vital part of teaching. And they start to be more creative musically, either by delving back into their own experiences in music and movement, or by availing themselves of the accompanist's experience and willingness to contribute—or both.

What steps do you as a new teacher take when you have never worked with a pianist?

The first step is to find an experienced dance accompanist and pick his brain. Pay him for private study, if necessary. It is imperative to start off correctly—to establish good musical habits from the beginning. Otherwise, you could end up like the teacher in New York who thought he could only count in three.

If there isn't an experienced accompanist around, here is a guide to follow. It is written with the assumption that you will be working with an accompanist as inexperienced as yourself.

The following information may seem extremely detailed and picky, but it cannot be stressed enough that *it is important to start correctly.* It may take a little longer for the information to sink in, but you will have established good habits for productive communication with accompanists *and* students. And your counting will have become not only correct but also organic and natural. It is not just natural talent or pure chance that makes a teacher's class run smoothly; it is the result of much thought, an awareness of her responsibility to the students in her care, and an appreciation of and respect for the divine logic of music.

Most good teachers agree that there is never enough time in one class to do everything they want to do. Therefore, every time-saving device that doesn't hinder the class itself must be utilized. One of the most important of these devices is clear, incisive communication between teacher and accompanist.

Learning to count correctly

Your counting tells your students what and when to dance, and tells your accompanist what to play.

Counting

- defines the meter;
- should define the tempo you will want for your combination; and
- should define the quality of movement (you will probably speak a grand battement combination differently than a rond de jambe combination).

Your counting represents the music you want to hear.

Ten or twenty years from now you may no longer be using counts when you demonstrate your combinations; numbers and "ands" will possibly be replaced by names of steps and movements. And experienced accompanists rely more on the rhythm in which teachers speak, as well as on their vocal inflections, than on counts for making their musical choices. But ten or twenty years from now, you may run across another inexperienced accompanist, so you must be able to count when necessary. And tomorrow a student may ask you, "On which count do I do the arabesque piquée?"

I would much prefer to teach teachers to demonstrate more with words, impeccable rhythm, and inflections instead of numbers, but that works only with musical teachers. There are unmusical teachers out there who absolutely must learn to count. If an unmusical teacher doesn't learn to count, her students will probably never be able to use music as a help in learning how to dance, instead of thinking of it as a necessary evil. If a musical teacher is forced to count, she will not lose her inherent musicality.

Sometimes sublime musicality is not enough. I recently played for a very musical teacher who is a beginning counter: hesitant, unsure of his ability to say "one two" instead of "tendu plié." One of his recent rond de jambe combinations included eight counts of "normal" rond de jambe ingredients and eight counts of very unusual—and very smart—movements. He sloughed through the second eight because—he told me later—he didn't think he could verbalize it correctly. I didn't question him about it in class because I knew his innate musicality would never allow him to produce a weird phrase. (I wish I could say that about every teacher I play for!) But watching the dancers execute this vague phrase sixteen different ways taught him that unspecific counting produces sloppy, misdirected dancing. Away from the pressure of the classroom, I helped him realize that he could count it clearly if he just practiced a little bit—and trusted himself a little bit.

Ideally, you should be able to count correctly every piece in chapter 3, "Musical Forms for Dance." But to begin, you absolutely must be able to count—and know the qualitative differences between—a waltz, a polka, a march, a mazurka, a 6/8 for chassés or skips, and a 3/4 adagio. Most ballet classes can be taught using only these musical forms. And they comprise the majority of most accompanists' repertoires. But students learn better if their ears are challenged as well as their minds and bodies; accompanists have more variety of expression; and you won't get so bored with the "same old steps" if you eventually start to branch out into other musical forms.

You may not even realize that you *are* able to count the above-mentioned forms. If you can correctly count a "typical" rond de jambe à terre combination, you know how to count a waltz. If you can correctly count a "typical" grand battement combination, you know how to count a 4/4 or a 6/8 march. If you can correctly count a chassé combination two different ways, you know how to count both a 6/8 (a three) and a polka (a two).

It is worth repeating for emphasis: If, during a classroom demonstration, you are counting a piece you are hearing in your head, you are most likely counting the melody. If, however, you have no specific piece in mind, you will be counting the rhythm.

The terms *a two, a three,* and *a six* are included both in chapter 3 and in the musical examples. They represent the most basic terms a dance teacher uses when she speaks to her accompanist about her musical needs. The terms *a two* and *a three* refer solely to the meter of a piece, and are always in phrases of eight. The term *a six* refers to the phrasing of a piece; it will always be in phrases of six, which can be broken down into either duple meter (a bolero, example 16) or triple meter (an allegro 9/8, example 49)—and it is *never* a 6/8.

There are four steps to proper counting: getting the numbers in the right places, getting the "ands" in the right places, turning them all into organic phrases of music/movement, and verbalizing those phrases in a regular rhythm and the correct median tempos.

Numbers are counts. They are fairly easy for most beginning teachers.

"Ands" seem to pose a problem for some people. "Ands" come between the numbers/counts, and are musically less stressed than the numbers/counts (from here on, simply "counts"). For instance, a polka is counted, "ONE and two and THREE and four and . . . ," as in line A1 in the following excerpt.

You could count this polka, "ONE - two - THREE - four . . . ," making no sound where the "and" would fall, as in line A2. But an accompanist would have no idea of the meter you want if you don't say the "ands." If you put the "ands" in different places, the piece becomes a waltz, as in line B.

Polkas and marches are counted with the same words: "ONE and TWO and THREE and FOUR and. . . ." Waltzes and 3/4 adagios can be counted with the same words, but in distinctly different tempos and inflections. The words are: "ONE and uh two - and THREE and uh four - and. . . ." A 6/8 for chassés/skips is counted: "ONE - and TWO - and THREE - and FOUR - and. . . ." As mentioned in the introduction, the symbol " - " takes up the same amount of time as each word, but is silent.

To ensure accurate communication between teacher and accompanist, the word count *should always be used instead of* bar *or* measure. *Four counts of a waltz equal four bars/measures, but four counts of a 4/4 equal two bars/measures.*

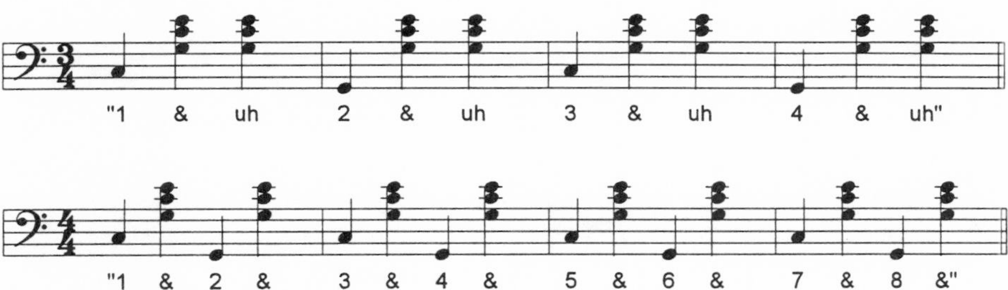

Remember that, as you start speaking a combination, neither the students nor the accompanist have any idea of what you want. (Experienced accompanists often seem to be able to read teachers' minds, but that ability needs many years to develop.) The way you count must let them all know instantly: the accompanist, so he can quickly identify the meter, median tempo, and quality, and proceed to choosing an appropriate piece; and the students, so that they know where each step will occur in the music. It is vital that at least the first 8-count phrase of each demonstration includes the counts in a regular rhythm and the median tempo. If you are clear in your counting at the beginning, your accompanist will have more time to find a suitable piece, which obviously benefits your class by wasting less time on musical problems.

It is important to start speaking the combinations in phrases, just as you speak sentences. Dancing is ultimately phrases of movement, not isolated steps; and music is phrases of sound, not disconnected notes. By counting in phrases, the students are unconsciously learning the right way to approach both music and dancing. And the beginning accompanist will be hearing the phrasing, even though at first he may be able only to play the right notes at the tempo you need.

I once worked with an extremely musical teacher who was an extremely poor counter. She counted most of her combinations, "and ONE and ONE and ONE and ONE and ONE. . . ." Only a very experienced accompanist will be able to decipher that. How was I able to figure out her counting? Musical teachers speak combinations with vocal inflections exactly as if they were speaking sentences. She was no exception, so I could hear where the ends of the phrases were. But a beginning accompanist rarely understands the French words the teacher is saying, and is even less able to pick up the inflections and what they mean.

Start getting into the habit of counting in maxi-phrases of eight counts (as 99 percent of classroom music is used). (Even sixes are in phrases of eight: Eight mini-phrases of six counts form a huge maxi-phrase of eight.) From a practical point of view, counting in phrases of eight makes it easier for students to grasp a whole combination mentally. And you will be helping the accompanist to start learning that the easiest way to know when to stop playing is by keeping track of the number of 8-count phrases in each combination.

Keeping a running count of the 8-count phrases as you demonstrate will prevent you from producing 11- or 14-count phrases, which—I hasten to add—are perfectly valid as long as you *know* they are eleven or fourteen counts, and as long as you let your accompanist and students know. Otherwise, the general rule is eight counts.

In less technically advanced classes, in which many different steps are not combined in movement phrases, you might want to go to a novice accompanist and say, "I would like a rhythm like this, please" and verbalize it (a beginning accompanist is not always able to see rhythm in movement). Then you can work slowly (if necessary) with the students while the accompanist looks for a piece with the correct ingredients.

In more advanced classes, it's always a good idea to demonstrate the first eight counts of a combination without changing tempo. (Whenever I hear a teacher change tempo during a demonstration, I'm pretty sure there's trouble ahead.) This will

- tell you whether your phrasing makes sense to both the students and the accompanist (and to you);
- reinforce to the students that they are learning to dance, not just executing steps; and
- help the accompanist choose an appropriate selection.

Demonstrating at least the first 8-count phrase in a regular rhythm and the correct median tempo is very important for all concerned: for the students, to get an idea of what the general feeling of the combination is; and for the accompanist, to assist him in the musical decision-making process. If you slow down his choice of music, it will probably become very heavy. If you speed it up, he may be technically unable to play it. And in both cases, the inherent quality of the piece will be adversely affected, which—consciously or unconsciously—affects your students' movement.

~

You can practice all four of the above steps (getting the numbers right, getting the "ands" right, and counting 8-count phrases in a regular rhythm and the correct median tempos) at home by counting along with a favorite ballet class tape. For your first classes, you might even want to make up your combinations to this tape. If you have the luxury of enough time to plan your classes without rushing, it would be a good project to figure out exactly how many 8-count phrases are in each combination—which will be important information for an inexperienced accompanist. You could also give the accompanist a copy of the tape, explaining that—in terms of sequence, musical/movement quality, and number of phrases—your class will be musically identical. Of course, he will have the option to play different music, as long as the meter, quality, tempo, and number of phrases are the same. Analysis of this tape may be a time-consuming process for your accompanist, and really not part of his job, so be sure to show your appreciation in some way.

Your counting capabilities will improve with practice (as everything does), and will eventually become not only correct but also natural and organic. You will probably have neither the time nor the desire to change bad counting habits later on down the line; that's why it is so important to start correctly. Remember that the demonstration of combinations lays the basis for the entire class.

I cannot stress enough that your counting is a major part of your inexperienced accompanist's training. If how you count bears no relationship to any of his past musical experience and understanding, he will be totally bewildered. I am convinced that, if just this one aspect of communication were improved, there would be many more good musicians who might look upon dance accompaniment as the true profession it is, instead of the last stop of a failed concert career, or just something better than being a dishwasher.

Face to face with your accompanist in the studio

Begin by greeting your accompanist, if you haven't already done so outside of the classroom. A simple hello is just fine. You will soon realize that your accompanist is a vital part of your success as a teacher, and it is depressing to say that there are many teachers who do not acknowledge the presence of their accompanists before they start class.

Where to demonstrate

Unless you have a specific reason against it, demonstrate the barre combinations next to the piano. Make sure your accompanist can see your entire body, and make sure your head is not turned 180° away from him; he must be able to both see and hear what you want. I have played for a surprisingly large number of teachers who change locations for demonstrating barre combinations; they often manage to choose the point in the room farthest from the piano, so I can neither see them nor hear them. This implies a subconscious disrespect for the music and the musician. If they really think music is important, they would certainly make every effort to ensure that the accompanist knows what they want. And the students appreciate not having to hunt around the classroom for the teacher; they know exactly where she will be.

If you are like many beginning teachers, you will not have a lot to say during the first few classes, so you might as well stand near the piano during the barre—at least for the beginning of each combination—for moral support as well as for helping your accompanist, should the need arise. Establishing the correct tempo in the first four counts is crucial. If you set a combination that could be done at different speeds (and there are many), it is wise to verbalize and—at the same time—mark the first eight counts—either with your hands or your body—in the tempo you set, in a place where the students can see you, making absolutely sure that the accompanist knows exactly the tempo you want. Adagios are usually the culprits in this area; a very simple example is your inclusion of an eight-count développé in a combination when you usually give a four-count one.

If your accompanist doesn't react when you say something to him, it can be because he simply can't hear you. The acoustics of a classroom and the quality of the piano have a great effect on your accompanist's hearing, so if you are standing next to the piano, the communication lines are better. (I used to play on a piano that had a very muffled quality, so the board in front of my legs was removed. Consequently, it was very difficult to hear what a teacher said to me if she was not within three feet of the piano.)

Once a combination gets going, an accompanist is usually concentrating more on his music than on what you are saying, because he gets used to the fact that you are speaking to the students. If you are clear in your demonstration, you shouldn't have to say anything to him (except, possibly, to make a slight tempo adjustment), and he will become accustomed to this. So when you do say something to him, he needs to know that you are speaking to him, and not to the students. Direct your voice toward him, not into the far corner of the classroom, as many of your colleagues seem to do.

Most teachers demonstrate the center combinations between the front mirror and the students. Again, make sure that your accompanist can see all of you and hear you. A good rule to remember: If you can see him, he can see you; if you can't see him, he can't see you.

What to say during a demonstration

There are basically two ways in which teachers demonstrate combinations in class. The most widely used method is for the teacher to demonstrate a combination to her own counts, leaving the choice of the music to the accompanist. If the accompanist is just beginning, his selection may be inappropriate, in which case time gets wasted while he and the teacher readjust. The second method can counteract that problem: The accompanist plays a piece according to the teacher's directions ("a slow waltz for ronds de jambe à terre" or "a huge 6/8 march for grands battements"), and she can either set a combination after hearing just four counts, knowing that the music will be appropriate; or she can ask for a different feeling, meter, quality, tempo, or whatever. This second method is better as far as wasting less class time is concerned, but its disadvantage is that it prevents the accompanist from "reading" the necessary information in your demonstrations and learning to choose appropriate selections himself. It also limits an experienced accompanist's flexibility in using a variety of suitable meters.

A combination of the two methods is a wise choice: Until he is more advanced, ask the accompanist to play a piece according to your description only for combinations that you sense are his weak spots. Don't forget to encourage him to overcome those weak spots, or else they will be forever problematic for him. Discuss them with him from a dancer's point of view. (My weak spots as a beginner were dégagé-with-demi-plié combinations [which example 29 solved], grand battement combinations, all adagios, and big waltzes.)

Adagios are a problem area for virtually all beginning accompanists, and often continue to be so for more experienced ones. You will very often demonstrate adagios in a faster tempo than you will want your students to execute them. Most teachers are no longer in prime dancing shape, which means they can no longer sustain slow leg movements off the floor, nor hold the positions as correctly as they want their students to. So they usually mark an adagio at one tempo, and then slow it down when the students execute it. More than any other type of music for dance, adagios suffer the most when they are played more slowly than their inherent median tempos demand. They become heavy and very unsatisfying musically, which is bound to affect the students' movements. So I strongly recommend that you use the second method mentioned above while demonstrating adagios: Ask your accompanist to play an adagio, and then choreograph your combination to the tempo that you know he will play. This is also recommended for more experienced accompanists, as they have probably found a wide variety of wonderful adagios that are not written in 3/4. (Are you aware that 98 percent of all dance teachers demonstrate all adagios in 3/4—even the teachers who say, "I'd like a 4/4, please"?) In case you do demonstrate an adagio without knowing what the music will be beforehand, let your accompanist know that you have finished demonstrating the first side before you go on to the second; we experienced accompanists often choose an adagio by the length required by the teacher. For instance, I have a couple of lovely 16-count adagios which I play only for 16-count adagio combinations; if I played one of them for a 32-count adagio, the dancers would have to listen to the same sixteen counts four times in a row (assuming they would do it immediately to the second side), which I find too stultifying.

When you use the first method described above to demonstrate, there is a definite order in which all combinations (and especially those at the barre) can be most efficiently announced. The first two pieces of information should be the name of the combination and the meter or form, as in the following: "Ronds de jambe à terre, a three" or "Pirouettes, triple meter" or "Frappés, coda." This is especially true when you deviate from your usual format—that is, wanting a tango instead of a waltz for ronds de jambe, or a waltz instead of a march for grands battements, for instance. Inexperienced accompanists need all the time they can get to find appropriate music for each combination, which they can do while you are demonstrating the combination for the students. By saying the name of each combination, the accompanist will be able to find a suitable piece more quickly.

I am assuming that your accompanist is reading a copy of this book also, and is becoming more familiar with the qualities of each step and movement. Therefore, when you say, "Ronds de jambe à terre," his mental computer will eventually allow him to eliminate mazurkas, codas, polonaises, marches, polkas, and a host of other unsuitable forms from his choice. Unless you have a specific meter or form in mind, naming each combination and the form or meter you want is less important for a more experienced accompanist, as he already has a good idea of "what goes with what."

Musical teachers often make up combinations in their heads with specific pieces of music in mind. If this is the case with you, sing as you demonstrate, or request by name the piece that you are hearing in your head. As a dance teacher, you are not expected to also be an Elisabeth Schwarzkopf or a Dietrich Fischer-Dieskau; it doesn't matter that your voice is not perfect. You probably sing a lot better than you think you do. Verbalizing or stressing a step's accents (or both), during both your demonstration and the students' execution, is helpful for accompanists who cannot yet visually analyze exactly where an unusual accent falls. You should use every means available to get the correct quality of music for each combination.

You must use numbers and "ands" during the first eight counts of each demonstration. This will tell the accompanist what meter you want, in case he doesn't already know. Tempo plays a big part in an accompanist's decision-making process, so he needs to know the median tempo of every combination immediately. It is really a waste of time to demonstrate many combinations (especially pliés, ronds de jambe, and adagios) all the way through in the proper tempo. (And doing so makes it harder for students to pick up the combinations mentally.) But when you speed up your demonstration to save time, remember that an inexperienced accompanist could lose the thread and become totally lost. So it's a good idea to know exactly how many phrases these particular combinations have, so your accompanist can be prepared for the phrasing while you go about a sped-up demonstration.

It is not necessary to use numbers and "ands" the whole way through each of your combinations, but it is *vital* to maintain the meter throughout each demonstration, even when you speed up. Never sacrifice clarity and exactness of which step falls on which count, just to save time; you will probably waste more time by having to go back and clear things up for your students. Also remember: If you start describing how you want a certain step done before you have finished demonstrating the combination (a common occurrence), the accompanist will not know how long to play, and the students will not have a grasp of the complete combination. Dancers need to know *what* the steps are before they can apply *how* to do them correctly.

Be specific about the number of sets in any given combination. For example, a common rond de jambe combination consists of four 8-count phrases: The first phrase is done en dehors, the second en dedans, the third again en dehors, and the fourth again en dedans. Does each of these phrases constitute a set (four sets in the combination), or does once en dehors and once en dedans together constitute a set (two sets in the combination)? Neither advanced nor beginner accompanists can be expected to know how each individual teacher calculates her sets. If you can fill in the blanks of the following sentence and say it to your accompanist, he will be most grateful: "Each set takes ___ counts, and I'd like it ___ times." An advanced accompanist very often needs only a visual grasp of the combination once through, and then you can say, "We'll do that right left right left" (or whatever).

Along the same lines, teachers should demand that their students do the number of phrases that she has set. All too often I see teachers give in to the students who use their own timing during combinations. Sometimes a teacher will even forget what she set and will blame the one dancer in the room who had the nerve to stay within the correct counts, for being unmusical. Once in a while I can understand it, but insecure teachers allow it to happen fairly frequently because they are uneasy about confronting mistakes. In these situations, experienced accompanists wonder whether to play what the teacher set or what the class is doing. Many of us choose music to fit the phrases of what teachers set, and it is neither satisfying for us nor productive for the students to have our musical choices ignored. It breeds frustration on our part and self-indulgence on the part of the dancers. (To be honest, this kind of situation was the catalyst that drove me to start analyzing combinations so that I can say exactly what the phrasing of each is. I got tired of always being blamed for playing too much or too little music.) Speaking on behalf of many advanced accompanists, I like to know how many sets in a combination beforehand because it affects my choice of music. My coda category, for instance, has pieces in phrases of 4 × 8, 6 × 8, 8 × 8, and 10 × 8. Of course I can play only the first few phrases of the 10 × 8s, for example, for a shorter combination, but I prefer to save them for combinations that are exactly that length, so that the dancers can reap the benefits of the rousing musical momentum that builds until the end.

Many teachers seem to demonstrate only for the students. They never make eye contact with me; at the barre they often stand where I cannot see them; and their comments seem to have no connection to the music, except for the counts. (There is more to music than counts!) It is especially irksome when they finish demonstrating a combination and then, as an afterthought and usually inaudibly, they mumble, "And let's go to the other side right away" or, "Let's have a balance at the end" (with, of course, no mention of how long it should be—or even whether they want music for it). They seem to forget that it is just as important for me to know this information as it is for the students.

How to get a combination started

You need to decide how you are actually going to start each combination: How will the accompanist know it is time to play? You will have been speaking for quite a while before you begin each combination, and an inexperienced accompanist cannot yet pick up a teacher's vocal inflections that signal that it is time to begin. An experienced accompanist learns to sort out the idiosyncrasies of many different teachers, and will be able to adjust to almost anything you do, as long as you are fairly consistent about it.

I do not recommend leaving these beginnings to even an experienced accompanist. He may be feeling a bit out of sorts on a particular day, and will think he needs more time to prepare himself for some of the combinations. I believe that no one but the teacher should set the pace of the class, and it's up to us to maintain it. You should start each combination when *you* want to start it. If you notice that your accompanist is daydreaming or taking an unduly long time to find a piece, just go ahead with your magic word/phrase. He must learn that *you* set the pace of the class, no one else. (All of this, of course, within reason: A new accompanist might need a bit more time to find a piece, but daydreaming does not belong in the classroom.)

To begin a combination, you can look at the accompanist and say the omnipresent "and" or his name or "please," or any number of other words, but it is helpful to yourself and to him to be consistent. I recently heard of a teacher-training program that encourages its members to vary the words they use to set things in motion. I observed some teachers trying to deal with this, and it broke their concentration trying to search for different ways to get things started. And if I happen to be rummaging around in my music, trying to find a particular piece, I am subconsciously listening for that particular teacher's magic word, and may not react if she has come up with a new one. (I became especially unfond of "Let's go!")

Even if you say your magic word, dancers will rarely start moving until they hear the music, so direct your voice toward the accompanist.

What you say between your demonstration and the students' execution is, of course, up to you. Don't forget, though: The more time there is between demonstration and execution, the greater the chance of students' forgetting the combination.

Preparations (introductions, "four-for-nothings," lead-ins, etc.)

What happens after you say the magic word can be problematic if you have an inexperienced accompanist. Most teachers prefer to have a 4- or 6-count preparation before every combination, whether at the barre or in the center. This concept is often extremely difficult for new accompanists, probably because music for preparations, as well as for transitions, balances, and finishes are rarely part of the music that accompanists play from.

Here are the words to use if you need to describe what you want: "I would like four (or six) counts (*not* bars or measures) in the meter, tempo, and quality of the piece you are going to play." If he cannot produce what you want the first time, you will just have to make do with whatever he can manage for an introduction. You will have to work with him outside of class, as you will waste a great deal of time during the class trying to get him to understand what you want. (Looking at—or using—the musical examples at the end of this book should give him a good idea of what to play for an introduction. And it will help him a great deal if you give him a copy of a ballet class tape that includes these introductions, so he can hear what seamless ones sound like.)

Some teachers request 2-count preparations, saying that four or six counts waste too much time. With the exception of a few forms which will be mentioned later, I strongly recommend a 4- or 6-count preparation for every combination. Dancers often don't get to hear each piece of music before they start moving, and two counts of music don't really establish a mood or a rhythm or a tempo. Four or six counts of music sound more like a phrase of music than two counts do. And the most time you can save by using two counts is about three seconds, which is hardly worth the sacrifice of musical integrity.

The exceptional forms are all sixes, as well as all 4/4 and 12/8 adagios. The phrase lines of these forms are so naturally long that two counts can properly establish mood, rhythm, and tempo. (If your students look blank or bored during what they think is a too-long preparation, you might remind them to think about the corrections they should apply to the upcoming movements.)

Count a 4-count preparation, "FIVE . . six . . SEVEN . . eight." (In this paragraph, the . . represents whatever will be verbalized between the numbers according to the musical form, such as, "FIVE and uh six - and" or "FIVE and six and.") If you count a 4-count preparation, "ONE . . two . . THREE . . four," an inexperienced accompanist may think it is part of the main body of the combination. And I have often seen inexperienced dance teachers continue with "FIVE . . six . . SEVEN . . eight" after they have used "ONE . . two . . THREE . . four" for the preparation. Another reason to say, "FIVE . . six . . SEVEN . . eight" is that, during diagonals, dancers will prepare for their "entrance" by thinking "FIVE . . six . . SEVEN . . eight," not "ONE . . two . . THREE

. . four." Count a 6-count preparation, "ONE . . two . . three . . FOUR . . five . . six."

How to correct faulty tempos

Reestablish the tempo you need just before you want each combination to begin and—because your new accompanist is not yet adept at translating a spoken tempo into his music—stand next to the piano for at least the first four counts of every combination, so you can adjust his tempo, if necessary. Hearing the introduction can give you a good idea of whether the tempo will be correct, but not until you actually see the dancers moving with the music can you be really sure that it is what you want.

With advanced accompanists, you can often dispense with tempo clarification if you stand in full view of him as the combination begins, and verbalize and do or mark the first four or so counts with him. An advanced accompanist knows the median tempos of most combinations (and, if he has been playing for you for a while, knows your tempo habits), and he will follow both your movements and the sound of your voice.

Saying "faster" or "slower" to an inexperienced accompanist is risky at best. Changing tempo "on demand" is something he is very unfamiliar with, and he will probably omit beats or play much faster or slower than you want—or both. Yelling "faster" or "slower" from across the room to an experienced accompanist is rude—and risky. "Faster" sounds like "last group"; and, if I'm playing an energetic piece, the "s" is usually the only sound I can identify over the din.

Many teachers who try to correct a faulty tempo through clapping are unsuccessful; they say "faster" or "slower," but continue to clap the faulty tempo. Music is such a powerful force in the dance classroom that it often requires a herculean effort to change a tempo. Without a doubt, the best way to correct a tempo that is only slightly awry is by counting very audibly, using all the "ands," in the correct tempo. A lot of "stuff" happens between the numbers; this stuff is the "ands," and your vocalization of them in the proper tempo will help your accompanist adjust to what you want.

If the tempo is radically wrong, you may have to stop an inexperienced accompanist, make yourself clear to him, and start again. It is always better to do this than to be worried about the accompanist's reaction to having to stop. It is unproductive and often dangerous for students to do a combination at an inappropriate tempo. When you are verbally demonstrating a new tempo for the accompanist, four counts will suffice. (Most of the time, experienced accompanists never play radically wrong tempos; your adjustments will be minimal, and will rarely necessitate stopping and starting over.) If you are serious enough—and committed enough—to insist on the right tempo for each combination, you won't want to wait until the second time around to change a faulty tempo.

Some accompanists have difficulty maintaining a consistent tempo throughout one piece, especially if it is a difficult one, or if they are playing a piece in a tempo that is quite different from what they are used to. You may have to, again, count very audibly within his hearing range. Some accompanists resent this, but until they can be rock-solid about tempo, it is necessary.

A few teachers seem to enjoy scaring their students occasionally with an unexpected tempo change, but, as a general rule, students will benefit from hearing the request to your accompanist to speed up or slow down; they can prepare their heads and their bodies for the new tempo without additional stress. (I discussed this once with Martin Schläpfer, a teacher whom I trust implicitly. He said he doesn't like to scare his students, but he does like to get their adrenaline going by sometimes speeding up a combination unannounced. I completely agree with him, but I also feel an unannounced tempo change during jump combinations can be potentially dangerous.)

The second side of barre combinations

Some teachers like to have a break between sides to give corrections, or to allow the students to think for themselves how they can improve upon the first side. Other teachers like to go straight to the second side without a break. You may choose to be consistent and either always stop between sides or never stop. If you choose to incorporate both ways into your class, you must be very specific to your accompanist during the demonstration of each combination. (Relying on telling him four counts before the end of each combination whether you will stop or go on is risky at best; you may be correcting a student at that time, you may be thinking of your next combination—or you might just forget.) It is part of his job to maintain the energy and momentum of your class, so he has to know exactly what you want.

If you choose to have the students go straight to the second side without a break, a 4- or 6-count preparation is recommended, seamlessly tacked on to the first side, rather than a ritard. This kind of ritard gives dancers false expectations of how music naturally flows, and they often start to expect that music and musicians will cater to their every whim. As much as possible, music in the classroom should reflect music on stage, which will never slow down for a couple of bars when a dancer gets to a tricky section or has to change directions.

How to continue a combination

If you do not specify the number of phrases in a combination, do not expect an inexperienced accompanist to know when to stop or to continue. One of the first things he should learn is calculating the number of phrases in a combination, but this process is fraught with difficulties, some of which are:

- the teacher speaking too softly;
- the teacher speeding up her demonstration (so the accompanist loses the thread);
- the accompanist not understanding that "en croix" often means, for him, "multiply by four";
- the accompanist's being not yet able to see the patterns and repetitions of steps in combinations.

So if you sense that your accompanist is coming to the end of his piece, either catch his eye and give him the standard sign to continue (a hand-rolling movement, as if you were cranking a hand organ—or any mutually agreed-upon gesture), or go to the piano and tell him to keep playing.

Many of these problems with new (actually, with all) accompanists can be dealt with by speaking loudly from the other side of the room, but he may not always be able to hear you, especially if you don't direct your voice toward him. For instance, from across the room, "It's a bit fast" sounds like, "A bit faster," and vice versa. Since you speak a great deal during the class to the students, make a conscious effort from the beginning to direct your voice toward your accompanist whenever you speak to him. After all, you never turn your head away from a friend when you are speaking to him or her.

How to stop a combination

Stopping a musician in the middle of a phrase is like interrupting someone in the middle of a sentence. Not finishing a phrase is frustrating for the musician and not beneficial to a dancer's musical education. There are, of course, instances during a class when you must stop the action immediately, but most of the time you know a few seconds before the end that you want to stop. Let your accompanist know at that time, so he can prepare to "phrase out," rather than chopping him off as he has begun the next phrase. He needs to be told at least four counts before the end, in order to have enough time to prepare a musically satisfying finish.

Teachers and accompanists should find a mutually agreeable signal for finishing. Agnes de Mille tapped her ring on the mirror (very audible); Iracity Cardoso and Riccardo Duse make a kissing sound (surprisingly audible); Marjorie Mussman puts her hands in a praying position; and some teachers make a karate chop in the air as the accompanists look in their direction (which only experienced accompanists are able to do, so the last two are not 100 percent reliable). Clapping to signal a stop is not advised. It is difficult for us to differentiate between clapping to stop, to correct an erratic tempo or rhythm, to generate energy, or just because you feel like it.

One way to stop diagonal combinations in the center is for you to go to the corner and stand there, preventing students from starting across again. Your accompanist is gradually learning to follow you with his eyes as much as he can, and he will know the end of the phrase is coming up when he sees you in the corner. It may also be a revelation for you to see your students from a different angle.

If you are a beginning teacher and wondering what the best way to stop is, there are two. Go close to the piano and say (at the appropriate time), "We will stop after this phrase of eight." Or hold one hand up, in a position reminiscent of a traffic policeman, for the last eight counts of a combination. Even the most experienced accompanist can't have his eyes glued on you every moment, but all accompanists gradually learn to look at the teacher whenever possible, especially during a phrase that could be the end.

Even if you are one of those rare teachers who tells the accompanist how many phrases of eight there will be in each combination, he may continue to play after your combination is finished. He may be playing a piece that is not written in convenient phrases of eight, and an inexperienced accompanist is not yet familiar with the "normal" length of combinations. It is especially important to help him out by using one of the two ways of stopping just mentioned.

Even experienced accompanists don't always know when to stop and continue. Dancers will almost always stop moving when the music stops, so if you have to make a choice, it's more important to let the accompanist, rather than the students, know that he should stop or continue.

It is also very important for a dancer to sense that the end is coming by hearing it musically, which he cannot learn if the accompanist continually wanders off into another phrase after the dancer has finished moving.

How to finish a combination

If a barre combination includes a balance tacked on at the end, the accompanist needs to know this also. It is surprising that so many teachers mumble as an afterthought, "Balance." A balance is not a random movement; it should be treated as part of the combination, and deserves to have especially supportive music, since it often comes on the heels, so to speak, of some fairly exhausting movement phrases. Let your accompanist know whether you want him to play something other than a continuation of what he's already playing before the balance, and be sure to let him and your students know how many counts there will be for the balance. And I think it is important for students to realize that a combination is not finished until they have returned cleanly to a finishing position (as they will do onstage), so let your accompanist know that he will play an "amen" after each balance. An amen sounds exactly like it does in church, and musically complements most finishing movements (usually the arms). Be sure you stand where your accompanist can see you during these amens; he needs to watch the quality of your arm movements, as well as to see exactly when you want the finish to take place. An example of an amen is given on page 152.

How to organize groups of students in the center

While this subject may seem to be outside the province of how you deal with an accompanist, it has a direct bearing on the continuity and momentum of the class, which your accompanist will help you maintain.

One of your objectives is packing as much actual teaching into the allotted class time as possible. The more time-wasting procedures you can eliminate from your class, the more time you will have to teach. One of the biggest wastes of time is organizing students into groups before each combination in the center. I have seen many new teachers be completely baffled by how to solve this problem, and I would like to offer what I have seen in the classes of many fine teachers. This format also makes it very clear to the accompanist how he will maintain the flow of the class.

Organize your students into groups before the center begins, and stick to it. Make your students responsible for keeping their positions in the lines, as in a corps de ballet. (We know that most of your students will never be in a professional corps de ballet, but many of you give recitals and local performances. Budding ballerinas learn to stay in line in the classroom, not in rehearsal or performance.) If you make it clear from the beginning that you will not have a separate group at the end for the ones who forget, or for the prima donnas, they will catch on quickly. (In case you haven't noticed yet, teaching dance is often similar to being a parent; consistency of discipline is of paramount importance. And it makes your job easier in the long run.)

Once a combination gets going, you can use the following format to keep the flow:

- Musical preparation (usually four or six counts);
- group A executes the combination;
- musical preparation, during which group A leaves the floor, moving to the front and sides, as group B comes in from the back;
- group B executes the combination;
- musical preparation, and so forth. The musical preparation before and after each group is played seamlessly and in rhythm, with no break at all.

Encourage your students at any level to look as if they are going to dance—even before the preparation; this will tell the accompanist that he should keep playing either until you tell him to stop or until he sees that there are no more people waiting to dance. So often I see dancers slouching around in the back of the studio during my final four counts, so I prepare to stop and then they charge into formation. Looking like dancers instead of slugs is also a good habit for them to get into.

As the students come forward in waves, you can make general or individual corrections constantly, without having to get the action going again after every group. This can also be of great benefit to the students in learning both how to dance together and how to make entrances, as they will be required to do onstage. (It should not be forgotten that all elements of a daily technique class—discipline, strength, stamina, cleanliness of execution, awareness of other dancers, and musicality—are all preparations for the stage.)

A law of physics states that it is much easier to keep an object moving than it is to stop it and start it up again. Therefore, if the teacher and accompanist establish and maintain the musical momentum of class, it won't be so difficult and time-wasteful to stop a whole group of bodies and start them moving again. This momentum also prevents the students from letting their energy drop between combinations, thus having to rev themselves up for each new onslaught. As with moving bodies, energy is more easily maintained if it stays at a consistent level than if it is allowed to stop and start and stop and start.

How to mark clearly

Only teachers who do a daily class themselves will be able to stay in good enough dancing shape to demonstrate their combinations in the tempos which they will demand from their students. Therefore, a teacher should be quick to explain to a novice accompanist that the tempo in which she demonstrates and the students mark a combination may be very different from the tempo in which they actually execute it. This is especially true in the realm of adagios, when it is often helpful to play a piece quite quickly to save time, but—at the same time—with emphasis on the musical peaks and valleys in the movements.

Frequently I notice that when a teacher speaks a combination, then marks it with her hands, then marks it with her body, there will be three different versions of where the accents fall. This is especially true with assemblé combinations in less advanced classes. And I see teachers verbalize and mark chassé combinations in two, then dance them full-out in three. (If you listen to the rhythm your feet make in a series of well-done chassés, you will hear a three.)

Musically astute students and experienced accompanists are used to this; other people aren't.

In less technically advanced classes, it is advisable for the students to mark each center combination with the music, as the students at this level are usually inexperienced in using music. At least once through, to at least one side, the rhythm and tempo should remain constant and unbroken. Some teachers get so caught up in the corrections they want to make that they interject these as the class is trying to mark or learn the combination, and the students and accompanist become quite confused. (Students—from beginners to professionals—will have a very hard time registering a correction for later application while they are still trying to figure out the combination.) Marking each center combination in all levels of classes, especially with an inexperienced accompanist, will save you time in the long run.

It is helpful for teachers to remember that marking with the hands is rarely an accurate gauge of the tempo desired. Going one step further, teachers will occasionally sit during a class and verbalize the combinations to the students, thereby making certain that the students really know the steps and terminology in their minds as well as in their bodies, and are not just dependent on following the teacher. In this instance, there must be an even closer connection than usual between you and your accompanist. You will not have done the combination physically, and you may even have said, "Four tendus en croix—AND!" So an accompanist must pick a tempo out of thin air.

After you have marked a combination, it is helpful to tell the pianist something like, "We will do it that much and then that much again, then four counts to change groups and repeat." Most accompanists gradually develop a sixth sense to subconsciously keep track of maxi-phrases as the teacher is counting, even though they may be hunting for a piece of music. This sentence—or a sentence that uses the number of counts in the marking as a basis for calculating—tells the accompanist very clearly how much he should play and when he should stop.

Dos and don'ts for dance teachers

Dos

Insist that your accompanist be treated with the same respect that you expect for yourself. I personally detest being called Mrs. Cavalli, but in the classroom I feel it is inappropriate for the teacher to be called Mrs. So-and-So and for the accompanist to be called by his first name, unless he is very young. Outside of the classroom is another matter.

Learn the difference between a slow waltz and a slow 3/4—and also between a waltz and a 6/8—and also between rhythm and tempo.

If you are looking for a piano for your studio, find one that your accompanist can see over, not a tall upright. The most obvious reason is so that your accompanist can have an unobstructed view of the entire classroom. Additionally, the accompanist's neck and shoulders take a great deal of strain, and having to keep his head turned at the same angle to see you and the students can lead to muscular problems.

If you change a tempo during a combination, be clear as to whether you want the new tempo all the way through when the combination is repeated, or whether you want the two different tempos. And if you stop during a combination, tell your accompanist whether he should start from where he stopped or from the beginning.

Put the male dancers at the end of the line in across-the-floor combinations. They very often require a change of tempo in jumping steps, and the accompanist can adjust the tempo more easily for one group of dancers than he can if the males are interspersed with the females. Also, the accompanist can prepare a satisfying musical ending when he sees the last male start across the floor.

Be sure that you count what you show (and vice versa). I have seen many teachers demonstrate frappés like this:

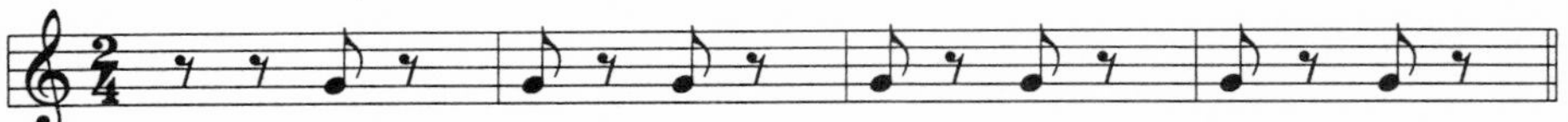

while they are counting this:

Videotape one of your classes and find a quiet time outside the classroom for you and your accompanist to watch it. Both of you will learn a great deal from an objective viewing of the class. It is an exceptionally good tool for your students' progress also.

Always let your accompanist know when something is not right with his music. If you feel that it will take up too much time during the class, defer it until later, but remember that he cannot improve unless he knows why something went wrong. Say something like, "That's nice, but it doesn't work for this combination" or, "Could you use different pedaling to make that a little lighter?" or even, "I can't describe what's wrong with that." And finish all such comments with, "Let's talk about it after class, OK?"

Tell your accompanist when a center combination is going to last longer than usual. Sometimes a teacher choreographs a combination with enough forward movement that it can be executed moving down the floor with no break between groups. If the accompanist is forewarned in this instance, he can select a longer piece of music and not be stuck playing the same sixteen or thirty-two measures over and over again.

If you are watching your students do a combination and thinking up your next combination at the same time, resist the temptation to use the rhythm and tempo of the first combination.

If you have an experienced accompanist, you could tell him he can play whatever he wants, and in any meter, as long as it fits the combination you demonstrate. This gives him more freedom—in his musical choices as well as in trouble-shooting, if necessary. Or you can tell him you would like him to play exactly what you demonstrate or request.

During the center, keep the sight line between you and your accompanist open; ask the students not to stand around the piano. A beginning accompanist may be too shy to say anything. A more advanced accompanist may have the same problem that I have: I cannot speak while I am playing. I can understand and absorb anything that is said to me without my playing being affected, but I cannot speak without both making a mess of what I am playing, and speaking unnaturally in response.

Read the section "The first class for a new teacher," in chapter 5, in order to recognize the consistently problematic areas for accompanists.

If you know that you usually demonstrate combinations faster than the students will do them, tell each accompanist before class so he can take that into account when he chooses music.

If you have something to say to your students after class that doesn't involve music, please excuse your accompanist before you begin speaking.

Mention music at least once during every class. It should not be treated like a disposable commodity.

Remember Vera Volkova's comment: "It takes at least ten years to become a competent teacher—and some people never learn."

Don'ts

Don't assume that your accompanist will stay overtime. If your class starts late for whatever reason, you might think to yourself, "We can go overtime a bit, we started late." If the pianist was there on time, it is not his fault that the class started late. Ask him in private if he is willing to stay overtime; if you ask him in front of the students, he may feel like a heel if he says no, even if he has a very good reason for doing so.

Don't make corrections while you are demonstrating steps. You will rarely speak corrections in the same rhythm and cadence that you speak combinations, so your accompanist may lose the thread and continuity of the combination. And your students need to know the steps before they can apply corrections.

If you change the speed in which you speak your demonstration, do not expect a beginning accompanist to remember the first speed you spoke. Sometimes even an advanced accompanist has a hard time keeping one tempo in his head while listening to other tempos.

Don't say:

- "steady," "easy," or "calm" when you mean slower; these adjectives do not mean slower. "Slower" means slower, and "faster" means faster.
- "not too fast/slow." Neither beginning nor advanced accompanists ever want to play anything too fast or too slow. Remember that *you* are responsible for all the tempos in your class.
- "faster/slower than usual." These terms have no relevance to beginning accompanists; they have no "tempo memory" in their mental computers yet.
- "last group" unless you mean it. When accompanists hear "last group," they will start formulating a logical musical ending. Announcing "One (or two) more group(s)" lets everyone in the classroom know when to finish. Say it after a group has done a few counts of the combination, so the accompanist is sure exactly when the last group starts. And if he keeps playing after you think he should have stopped, he may not know how many sets of the combination each group does.
- "Play me a six" when you want a 6/8. A six is never a 6/8, and vice versa.
- "One more time." It sounds like "Other side," and an accompanist would not know whether you want one more time for all the groups or for each group.

Don't discuss students in the presence of accompanists or anybody else. And don't take your frustrations out on your accompanist. I hesitate to say this, but I have seen far too many teachers blame an accompanist for something that was not his fault. In most of these instances, it wasn't the teacher's fault, either; it was an inability to communicate her needs clearly.

Don't allow your students—not even the tiniest tots—to start across the floor in a diagonal whenever they want. Show them the correct time to start in relation to the phrases of eight, until they can do it for themselves. (I am always surprised that more teachers don't make a younger student start counting to eight when the child in front of him starts across. It teaches him phrasing, it enhances his math skills, and it allows the teacher to help and to make corrections instead of just counting.)

Never yell at your accompanist, no matter how upset or frustrated you may be with him. It is rude, disrespectful, totally counterproductive, and a terrible example for your students. (This subject comes up rarely in the teachers' courses that I teach, but when it does, everyone expresses such surprise at the mention of yelling at accompanists. I hope things have changed, but in my early years I was screamed at by some very well-known teachers.)

If your accompanist plays a piece that you absolutely loathe, don't suffer in silence; tell him politely that you would rather he didn't play it again. Most accompanists like to keep track of teachers' likes and dislikes; they provide another block in the building of rapport and respect with each teacher.

Don't apologize to your accompanist for having to play a piece so long (within reason, of course) without a break, or that he has to play the same variation thirty-seven times in a row. It is a part of his job. I personally find it better not to even think about—or be reminded of—fatigue; it, too, is counterproductive.

Don't assume that an accompanist—no matter how advanced he is—will set the correct tempo if you haven't been specific in this area. If you have given an inexperienced accompanist garbled or inconsistent tempo information, he will be even more unsure of what he is about to play. If you give an advanced accompanist garbled or inconsistent tempo information, he will rely on his previous experience to decide what to play and how to play it. A hairsbreadth of difference in tempo can mean the difference between a student just doing a combination and making shapes with the body, and really doing it properly and feeling muscularly what each movement is all about. Your students' well-being and safety is your first concern.

Don't assume that your accompanist will remember a combination and its music from one day to the next if you don't ask him to remember it.

Never allow anyone—not even a prima ballerina—to dictate a tempo to your accompanist in the classroom. You must take the responsibility of tempo decisions, as well as everything else that transpires in your class; otherwise the students will be running the class instead of you. (Rehearsals for a performance are another matter.)

If you haven't asked for a particular piece or meter before you start demonstrating, don't ask for one just before the dancers start dancing. We accompanists have spent the whole duration of your demonstration looking for a piece in the tempo and rhythm that you have spoken.

Don't forget that your voice is a powerful motivation for your students *and* your accompanist.

Checklist

- Learn to count correctly: with numbers, with "ands" and "and-uhs," in phrases of six or eight, and in the tempo you will eventually want during at least the first eight counts of every demonstration.
- Demonstrate barre combinations next to the piano and stay there until the tempo of each combination is firmly established.
- If you can see your accompanist, he can see you.
- Announce the name of each barre combination and the meter or musical form (if you know it) *before* you begin your demonstration, not after you have finished it.
- Verbalize, clap, or finger-snap a combination's accents, both during your demonstration and while the accompanist is playing.
- Sing, hum, whistle, or request an appropriate piece by name.
- If there is to be a balance at the end of a combination, let everyone know how long it will be.
- Let your accompanist know if you want amens at the end of combinations. If so, do them yourself at the appropriate time, standing in a place where he can see and follow you.
- If you don't want a standard 4- or 6-count introduction, be clear about what you do want.
- Clarify the tempo of each combination just before you begin, if necessary.
- Change an erroneous tempo by counting firmly with "ands"; or stop, adjust, and start over again.
- Be clear about whether you want to stop between the two sides of barre combinations, or whether you want to go directly to the second side.
- Your accompanist should be the first to know if you want to continue or stop any combination.
- Before the end of every combination, if necessary, give your accompanist enough time to prepare a musically logical ending.
- If you are not within about three feet of the piano, direct your voice to your accompanist whenever you speak to him. If he doesn't react to your directions, he probably can't hear you.
- Twos and threes are in maxi-phrases of eight; sixes are in mini-phrases of six.
- Never forget that there is more to teaching than giving a class.

5 ~ *For Accompanists*

To be an accompanist for a dancer, singer, or instrumentalist requires that you become an organic part of something larger than yourself. As a musical majority of one in the dance classroom, you and your music exert a tremendous influence over what transpires. You will feel like a soloist playing a nonstop recital for the duration of the class, but you must behave like a partner. The fact of the matter is, you have been hired to provide a service—first to the teacher, then to the students. The service to other people enhances the enjoyment you will find for yourself in this work.

I hope that the information in this section reflects the essence of what a dancer reacts to in music, as well as how an accompanist goes about eliciting that reaction.

There are a few facts about dance and dance training that you should keep in mind. Simplistically, dance is mind over matter: A dancer's intelligence and willpower demand response from almost every muscle in the body. (Because of the nature of this book, the spiritual motivation that spurs a dancer's desire into action will be touched upon only occasionally.) A pre-professional dancer takes at least one daily class (usually three or four) and must invest nonstop mental application—a fact that is not always apparent to nondancers.

Dancers' daily classes are just like your daily practicing. However, here are a few ways in which the two learning processes differ greatly.

- Someone may teach himself to play the piano, yet dance is an art form that cannot be self-taught. Permanent, debilitating damage can be done to many parts of the body if it is not learned correctly from the very beginning. Body placement is of the utmost importance in all phases of a dancer's life. A dancer cannot see his back—a great source of strength—without putting his body completely out of alignment, so he must rely on a teacher's knowledgeable eye from the very first lesson.

- If a pianist hits a C-sharp instead of a C, he knows instantly that it is wrong. It takes years, often decades, for a dancer to learn correct technique. (I once heard Dame Margot Fonteyn say that she finally learned how to do a proper tendu at age forty-two.)

- If a pianist comes to a tricky section of music, he can almost always repeat it until it is a part of his muscle memory—for fifteen minutes, if necessary—and he can play it correctly without thinking. Because of the sheer strenuousness of classical dancing, a tricky section for a professional dancer usually cannot be repeated more than four or five times; otherwise, his muscles may cramp, and he will run out of breath.
- Classical dance is rarely practiced at home, except for certain isolation or strengthening regimes; dance must always be executed in a warm space, on a floor especially constructed for dance. (A floor that is too hard destroys a dancer's body.)

You have a tremendous responsibility to provide good music for dance students. In most cases, what you play will be the only musical education they will receive. Generally speaking, artistic consciousness in the United States is not yet at a level where it is deemed necessary (or important or financially profitable) to train artists properly; in the musical area, proper training for dancers means a thorough education in how to use and love music. In many of the state schools in Europe and the former Soviet Union, dance students are given music history and music theory, but these subjects are abstract compared to the embodiment of music that one sees in a truly musical dancer. At certain periods in their training, many dancers' ears have to be propped open to take the music in and use it as the sole reason to move. It is up to you and the teacher to provide a broad base of motivating music.

You must believe in everything you play. You must play every piece with conviction and substance, no matter how slow and/or soft it may be. Dance music is not piddly, dinky, or tinkly. Ballet music especially has gained this loathsome reputation, probably because good classical dancing is performed with a deceptive look of ease, which leads anyone who has never tried it to believe that the music should match the movement. (Classical dancing is like being a mother: if you've never done it, you can't imagine how hard it is.) This undeserved reputation also may have come about because accompanists are rarely made aware of the orchestral scope that lies beneath their fingertips. The full range of the keyboard should not be reserved only for the dancers in the rehearsal studio who are preparing for a performance to orchestral music; breadth of movement encouraged by an orchestral sound must become part of a dancer as soon as he is able to assimilate it. When hearing you play, a layman or a musician uninitiated in the demands of dance accompaniment should be able to comment, "That's music," not, "That's dance music."

There are certain guidelines you can follow to be able to translate movement into music. A good accompanist must train his eyes as meticulously as he trains his hands. This is an easy rule to forget because, unless you improvise, your eyes will be glued to the music most of the time when you begin. You must train yourself to look at—and really *see*—what is happening. Watch the teacher as she demonstrates. See and, if possible, hear in her voice the flow, accents, and quality of the steps in a combination; don't stop at merely ascertaining the meter. Since movement in the classroom is taught in patterns and phrases, a helpful approach is seeing what comes between the instructor's counts "one" and "two": how much time there is, where any accents may fall, and so on. That may sound terribly simplistic, but it works for me. By the fourth count of a demonstration, I almost always have a concrete idea of what I will play; then I observe further, to see if something else would work better.

We tend to forget the basics in our fast-paced life, and a basic of dance accompaniment is that our music should match the quality of movement. One thing that helps obscure this basic idea is that any given step, when combined with other steps, can sometimes take on a whole new feeling. You can't always pigeonhole dance accompaniment by linking particular steps to particular meters. When you hear "rond de jambe à terre" or "fondu" included in a center combination, you can't always assume that it's going to require the same music—or even the same mood—as the barre combination of the same name. *You must learn to react to phrases of movement, not individual steps.* On the best of days, each piece we play in class sounds as if it had been written expressly for its corresponding combination.

The vital area of communication between teacher and accompanist is stressed throughout this book. To establish the necessary rapport with the teacher, you must become aware of certain generalities. At its best, the teacher-accompanist relationship is like a healthy marriage: Each partner respects the other's talents and feelings; both work toward a common goal; and neither feels superior to the other. However, in this relationship, the teacher has the final say. After all, the purpose of a dance class is to teach students how to dance, and you do not know how to do that. If you feel that the teacher is mistreating the music (as opposed to being unable to communicate her needs to you—or your being too inexperienced to understand her), speak to her after class to solve the problem together. Or find work elsewhere. There is nothing more destructive to egos or to the training of students than a class in which the teacher and accompanist do battle with each other.

Teachers' patience levels vary from person to person, but most teachers are very patient with beginning accompanists. Experience has taught them that they often train accompanists as well as students. During your initial training process, teachers will very often gear their classes to your abilities. As you become more skilled and inventive technically and conceptually, they will be able to teach their students more creatively. Teachers will always respond favorably if you evince the desire to improve.

Ideally, you should work toward becoming the teacher's alter ego, and I hasten to add that this is not a secondary, submissive position unless you choose to see it that way. It seems that there are certain facets of a good accompanist's personality that give him the ability to enjoy and to make contributions to his work without receiving constant praise. (You will have to learn to accept the fact that one of the best "compliments" you can receive is the teacher's not saying anything to you during class, because you are doing your job so well that you have given her the freedom to do hers.) If a teacher could accompany and teach at the same time, she most certainly would, since there would be a perfect unity of purposes. But this is almost impossible.

During the process of finding out what dance accompaniment is all about, your ego may become terribly bruised, as it will seem that you will never understand the complexities of dance. Gradually, patterns will begin to emerge. You will play just the right piece of music for a combination (and not just by accident), and the whole room will come alive with renewed energy. You will catch a glimpse of the light at the end of the tunnel. (I remember very clearly, at the beginning of my years in New York City, feeling that I was just a necessary evil in the dance classroom. No one ever said it to me; it was just pure frustration at not being able to be consistent in producing what the teachers were requesting. A lot of the problem was that they were unable to express themselves in a manner that I could understand. [I would have given anything to have had a book like this!] This started to improve as soon as I began taking dance classes.)

Your ego will probably be your biggest problem. Possibly never before will you have felt so inept, but I must stress that your understanding will increase so that you will be in full control of what you are doing. A starving ego is not a helpful attribute anywhere, and especially not in a dance classroom—for the accompanist, teacher, or student. But pride in your accomplishments is very healthy, and the elation you will experience playing for dancers cannot be equaled.

At first, your personal musical expression may feel very restricted. It may seem that you are always required to play what the teacher wants, and are rarely given a chance to take the initiative. But as your understanding and perception increase, you will be able to take over the reins and initiate the impetus for movement. Dance accompaniment is surely one of the most creative musical outlets; it lets you play a broad range of musical styles for others' enjoyment—and you get paid for it too. (There have been times in my career when I felt I should have paid a teacher, dancer, or choreographer for the privilege of being part of such an incredible experience.)

The piano is one of the most physical of instruments. The length of the keyboard demands "controlled freedom" in the torso. Arms, feet, and hands must be in perfect coordination. The unique qualities of the instrument lend themselves to the production of full, orchestral-sounding rhythms in the left hand and rich sonorities in the right. I try to re-create the breadth of an orchestra so the dancers will feel a substantial support for their movement, and also so they will get used to the orchestral sound that they will dance with most often onstage. (This does not mean that you play loudly all the time, or that you never use quiet music.) This concept of orchestral fullness may seem somewhat elusive at first, and will be dealt with more extensively beginning on page 154.

On the subject of physicality, there is a special energy and momentum in a dance class that will come directly from you. Because of the muscularity of dance, rhythm is the first musical element that a beginning student becomes aware of. When you provide a rich, consistent propulsion for him to use, he cannot help but respond to it, and you will find yourself answering his response. It's very catalytic and wonderfully contagious. Your music will help him ignore the difficulty and exhaustion, while a classroom full of happy, moving bodies will help you ignore your fatigue. (It is not wise to complain about how tired you are or how much your arms, shoulders, or back may hurt; an aspiring or practicing professional dancer always aches more intensely and in more places than any pianist on earth.)

Watching class is invaluable for increasing your powers of observation. If you are a beginner, you can practice your ability to decipher how many phrases of eight counts there will be in each combination, and whether the quality and meter you perceive in any given combination match what the accompanist actually plays—or what the teacher actually demonstrated. As an experienced accompanist, you can experiment mentally by imagining how many different meters you could play for any given combination. I think we pick up a lot subconsciously by watching; freed from the demands of coming up with music to match each combination, we can see the class better as a whole. Regardless of your level of experience, you may want to write down questions to discuss with the teacher or accompanist after class.

Watching class is invaluable; taking class is even more so. There are many fine accompanists who have never taken a dance class, but I feel that their enjoyment, perception, and capabilities could be greatly enhanced by getting in there and physically producing what they are trying to motivate musically. My years of intensive dance training have helped me immeasurably with the art of accompanying for dance, as well as with other life-essential areas such as discipline and concentration (to say nothing of how good my body and soul feel when the endorphins are flowing from such a strenuous endeavor!). After dance has seeped into your muscles for a certain length of time, you will feel kinesthetically each movement as it progresses, even though you are relatively stationary at the piano; this cannot help but beneficially affect what you are playing.

If you take class, you may find, as I did, that it is one of the few activities in life in which you can completely lose your self. The more you learn about dance, the more challenging the physical execution becomes, and nothing else exists but the teacher's voice, the music, and your mental, physical, and emotional responses to those elements. The classes I was lucky enough to take were so draining that they acted like truth serum on me. If anyone asked me a question within about twenty minutes after class, I had to tell the truth; I had been pushed past so many mental and physical barriers in the class, and I had no resources left to be tactful, polite, or evasive. This condition was produced by Mr. Brunson's nonstop corrections and verbal support during class (as well, of course, as the musical support he demanded from every accompanist), which increased everyone's energy output. While some people may say that students can become overly dependent on a teacher like that, I feel very strongly that it is practically the only way to get students to break through their own barriers of resistance and self-doubt.

I never would have learned to accompany dance as I do now without having been exposed to—and without myself having physically produced—that kind of energy. Playing for a demanding class has the same effect on me.

~

I would like to see musicians choose dance accompaniment for a career because it is a viable profession and an enjoyable occupation. This, of course, is possible only if musicians are made aware that it *is* a career choice. When I attended a well-known music conservatory in the United States in the late fifties, we pianists were neither made aware of nor prepared for any options other than heading for Carnegie Hall or teaching music education in a local high school. (And I don't think the system has changed much.) I started to accompany for dance not because it interested me, but because my husband and I were broke, he was in school, I was pregnant, and it was the only job on the employment board that I could do.

Dance accompanists have the totally undeserved reputation of being the low (wo)men on the totem pole of musicians. This is a vicious circle which must be broken. A pianist may consider himself (or be made to feel like) a failure because he can't (or maybe doesn't want to) compete with the technical whiz kids in his class in music school. Because he doesn't respect himself, he is bitter, falls into the syndrome of believing that playing for dance is only one step above washing dishes for a living, and doesn't allow himself to see the challenge, personal expression, and just plain fun of being such an important part of an artistic whole. He may feel, as I did, that playing the piano is something he's done since childhood; it may be an important part of his life, but he has neither the technique nor the desire to devote many hours a day to practicing in order to maintain a grueling concert schedule playing a limited number of pieces. He may have a dormant sense of response to movement; he may enjoy working with others more than being a soloist; he may have any number of personality traits that make him a good candidate for a dance accompanist but, because the job is often characterized by a lack of respect from his peers, he ignores its possibilities—if he is even aware of them.

You may wonder if you can make a living at dance accompaniment. As with anything else, it depends on your level of expertise. (I have supported either myself alone, or my two daughters and myself, solely on playing for dance since 1972.) One great advantage of being a dance accompanist is that one can almost always find a job, since there are so few of us. It is usually much easier to find a competent substitute teacher for a dance class than a competent substitute dance accompanist. If you are looking for work, an often fruitful way of finding it is by calling every dance studio in the Yellow Pages and leaving your name on file. You might even offer to play an audition class for no pay.

I am sad to say that the discrepancy between teachers' and accompanists' salaries is much too large. One well-known college dance program (in 1999) pays its teachers $45 per class and its accompanists $13. This is shameful; if the powers-that-be want to improve the quality of their accompanists (which will improve the quality of their students), they will have to address this issue. Very often accompanists are treated as part-time employees or—disgusting term—casual labor, and are not eligible for any benefits. This is why I went to Europe; I was tired of having to put in at least three times as many hours as teachers in order to earn the same amount of money.

If you are at the beginning of your career, do not resist any opportunities that might come along to play for modern technique classes. I greatly regret that I was neither pushed into improvising nor encouraged to branch out into modern accompaniment when I started. Consequently, I have probably missed out on some wonderful accompaniment experiences. And versatility in this profession is a big asset; an accompanist who is proficient in both modern and ballet will never lack for work.

There is a great need for experienced accompanists in Europe too. If you are considering looking for work there, you might get an inexpensive charter flight to any of the European capitals, plus a month-long Eurailpass, and try your luck. *Stern's Performing Arts Directory* (published annually by *Dance Magazine*) includes a list of European companies (which are usually connected to opera houses or state theaters). Since many companies have unusual days or weeks off, it is advisable to write in advance, either telling them approximately when you are coming and hoping to audition, or setting up a specific audition date. Be sure to include your résumé. English is spoken in many dance companies in Europe, so communication is usually not a problem.

~

You will gradually become aware of what a vitally important service you provide. It is not at all unusual to hear the following comments: "What?! You want me to teach the six o'clock class? That will be the fifth class I've taught today. . . . Oh, so-and-so is playing? Okay, no problem. He's great!" Or: "I just *can't* take another class today. My muscles feel like cement blocks. . . . Oh, so-and-so is playing? Wow, I want to be there. He lifts you to the ceiling!" And you will gradually get to the point where you can enjoy watching the students progress; when this happens, remember that you have made a significant contribution to that progress.

I had originally considered separating this chapter into two sections: one for beginners and one for more advanced accompanists. I have decided to write it differently for two reasons: The most inexperienced accompanist must have some idea of what he is aiming for; and more advanced accompanists are usually interested in reading anything that pertains to their profession, since there is almost no literature available on the subject.

Depending on your technical level and experience, certain concepts may seem vague or irrelevant at first until you have mastered certain more basic approaches. Some of you will be able to put into practice the pedaling theories sooner than others. Others will understand the basic mathematics of 8-, 16-, and 32-count phrases. Still others will instinctively feel the inherent stylistic differences between a Schubert waltz and one by Waldteufel. People develop at different rates in different areas, so most of the problem spots will be discussed at all levels. Set aside what you don't yet understand, and refer to it as you discover the need. And don't let frustration get the best of you; use it to achieve a positive result.

Every art form has points of reference for its students. Dancers can see performances on stage or on television and thereby observe established artists. Musicians can listen to tapes and attend concerts, while visual artists and actors can go to museums and theatres. And all of the above groups can read countless books about their respective art forms. But only rarely can an aspiring dance accompanist find an example to follow. I am not a musical pedagogue, nor do I consider myself the definitive source on dance accompaniment. But I feel that a comprehensive resource should be available to anyone wishing to explore the various careers in music. And I am hopeful that all accompanists, at whatever level they may be, will find enough concrete information in this book to enable them to enjoy dance accompaniment as much as I have and do.

Background information for beginning accompanists

This section is directed specifically to novice accompanists who are as yet unfamiliar with both the technical vocabulary of dance and the way dance is taught.

Classroom etiquette

We will begin this section by examining some rules of classroom etiquette and professional behavior that you are liable to find in a dance studio.

Just as most rules of etiquette are based on common courtesy, so too are the ones found in a dance class. Eating during class, conversations with anyone other than the teacher while the class is in progress, and leaving before the class is over (unless there is a real emergency or you have prearranged it with the teacher) are generally frowned upon; normally you stay until the teacher excuses you. Smoking is usually not allowed in the classroom or—often—the entire building. Yawning without an attempt to disguise it is not very polite (this is mentioned because the air in a dance classroom loses oxygen very rapidly, so yawning is not uncommon). You may have the urge to open a window because of the lack of oxygen, but the teacher should have the final say on this; a draft—even of the hottest, most humid air—can be potentially very damaging to perspiring bodies and warm muscles, and to your back. Making faces should be avoided at all costs. If you are one of those people who makes faces or shakes his head at his own mistakes, try to program it out of your repertoire; dancers and teachers may misread it and think you're making faces or shaking your head at them. Reading or doing crossword puzzles is downright rude; if you are that bored, spare everyone concerned—including yourself—and find another job. Arguing with the teacher is inexcusable, as is being habitually late (more than once every six months is too often). It is discourteous and distracting to practice "that tricky little section," even though the teacher seems thoroughly involved in corrections. Bathing every day is an absolute must, as is a daily change of clothing. (If you "re-perspire" on a shirt already perspired on, your nose may become accustomed to it, but nobody else's will.) And *never* correct a student in class—not even about the music.

Your attitude in class has a decided influence—if not on the students, then most certainly on the teacher. A bad day every once in a while is a normal occurrence. If you are one of those people who are prone to bad days, try to keep it to yourself. Bringing your personal problems to class is counterproductive and unprofessional. You cannot really get involved in your work if you let your negative emotions get the best of you. And, while total involvement in your work certainly won't solve your problems, you'll at least get a temporary respite from them by throwing yourself completely into class.

Some self-indulgent accompanists who play quite competently one day may go in the next day and refuse even to try to help the teacher or students. Occasionally, they forget how much teachers and students rely on them to motivate and lift the class. But usually, their egos are bruised, either personally or professionally, and they need to have their presence validated. Whatever the reason, there is no excuse for deliberately undermining a class. You are being paid for providing a service, not an emotional display. If you find yourself in one of these moods, go ask someone for a hug before class; it works wonders.

Although your prime responsibility in the classroom is to be the teacher's alter ego and to support her efforts, she will be the first to agree that the reason you are there is to help the students learn how to dance. If you are having a temporary personality clash with the teacher, don't take it out on the students. Don't let your grumpiness affect their progress.

There is more to accompanying than just playing music.

The structure of a dance class

The technique of classical ballet is very logical, though hardly simple. However, people tend to complicate it. Idealistically, it is a system by which the body is trained to meet the demands of the artist's mind. There should be an unbroken line of approach, understanding, and commitment from the beginning of the barre, through the center work into rehearsal and on to the ultimate testing ground: performance. Students tend to lose track of this because they must often spend many years in the classroom before they are technically equipped to set foot on the stage. Students who form good habits, and understand the reasons behind the demands that are made on them, will automatically carry those habits into their professional work, as well as into their daily lives.

The reverse, of course, is also true. If a teacher doesn't demand that her students develop good working habits—among other things, doing the combinations as she sets them and on the music—the students more than likely will be unable to remember a choreographer's steps, and will have no understanding about how to work both with other dancers and within the framework of the music. There is more to dancing than pointing one's foot and turning out.

Teachers usually repeat movement phrases without stopping because the brain has to transmit an essentially new pattern throughout the body. The first (and sometimes the second) execution of the movement phrase often are taken up with memorizing and assimilating the shapes of the patterns; once these are mentally anchored, the brain can command the muscles to get down to the profitable business of full muscular, mental, and motivational response. Robert Joffrey once said, "Dance is muscular memory." (So is playing the piano. Before I discovered engrams—see note 14—I used to look at my fingers during a fast passage and think, "If I had to consciously think about every one of those notes, I could never play that passage." Now I know the process that enables me to play a fast passage.)

It is important for accompanists to remember the process behind the execution of any given combination. Because a dancer's output of energy is considerably greater than a pianist's (rarely do we gasp for air after playing a 32-count grand battement combination, whereas after performing one dancers usually do), the accompanist must continue to maintain the energy and build toward the end of a combination, and to never slacken in intensity.

A teacher owes it to her students to demand from them certain qualities—technical execution, discipline, musicality, and professional behavior—in the classroom that will stand them in good stead in the professional situation toward which some of them may be striving. You are working hand in hand with her in this endeavor. Although you may not be aware of the techniques she is using, know that there is usually a method to her madness.

Beginning accompanists cannot be expected to have the faintest notion of the structure of a dance class unless they have taken one. There is a logical development to each class, and it might help to explain some of the basic rudiments here.

The barre (sometimes called side practice)

The barre is a series of combinations of steps and movements done holding onto a barre (usually a thick wooden rail), which helps a dancer find his balance. These combinations are given in an order designed to improve technique, as well as to warm up, strengthen, and elasticize muscles, tendons, and ligaments.

A teacher rarely varies her own particular order of barre, but it often differs from teacher to teacher. It is advisable for a beginning accompanist to write down the order of the barre combinations and the corresponding musical possibilities of teachers for whom they regularly play. Most teachers like to vary the way steps are combined within each combination, in order to train the brain to be as responsive as the body. (There are some valid teaching systems that believe in doing the same single class all week in order to perfect it; the music should change, however, or the class will become stultified.)

Just as you would not begin your first practice session of the day with a Liszt concerto, neither would a dancer start his first class with movements requiring great strength or sustaining power. Therefore, the barre starts slowly, either with the traditional pliés or—as more and more teachers seem to be doing these days—with a floor barre or a warming-up foot combination.

We will not go into the whys and wherefores of every barre movement here; only the qualities of steps and movements will be discussed in the next section. If you are the curious sort, ask a teacher to explain the physical structure of and reasoning behind a barre—and then go take one.

All barre combinations are executed on both sides. You will be asked to accompany these combinations in one of three ways:

- stopping after one side and repeating exactly the same thing on the other side, including any given preparation and balance;
- at the end of the combination, continuing seamlessly—with no break in the rhythm—with another preparation and repeating the entire combination again to the other side; or
- if the teacher has included a turning movement at the end of the first side, repeating the same piece without preparation (with ritard at the transition, if requested) as the dancers continue on the other side. (Information on preparations and balances begins on page 144.)

The center (sometimes called centre practice)

The center defines the combinations done in the center of the room without the support of the barre.

The same rule applies to the center as it does to the barre: logic. After a concentrated period of warming and strengthening muscles and improving technique, it doesn't make sense to go into the center and do the most strenuous movements until one's balance is regained without the barre. The ways teachers approach this are as varied as the teachers themselves.

The act of jumping—probably the most potentially injurious movement in all of dance—should never be attempted until all muscles are thoroughly warm. Therefore, jumping almost always comprises the final part of class, preceded by any number of terre-à-terre (non-jumping; literally, floor-to-floor) combinations including adagios, pirouette and port de bras combinations, coordination exercises, and so on.

Whether or not you are able to recognize and label each step is less important than being able to read movement phrases and remembering that the momentum of each combination and each class continues to build. Just as each selection you play builds in energy until the students are back in a finishing position, so too does the support for the entire class—from pliés to révérence—depend on you. Some pianists think that a pianissimo on "1" in a grand allegro is a welcome change of pace for dancers. It *is* ear-catching, but startlingly so; they need support all the way through a combination, especially at a place where the most interesting—and possibly difficult—movement happens. Remember that a step may be easy, but the physical exertion that has come before sometimes makes just standing still an exercise in stamina.

Center combinations are repeated too, but not in the same way as those at the barre. The following is one way in which many teachers organize their center combinations:

- Musical preparation; group A executes a 16- or 32-count combination that may or may not include both right and left sides;
- (no musical stop) musical preparation for group A to move forward and to the sides of the room as group B moves onto the floor;
- group B executes the combination;
- (no musical stop) musical preparation for group B to clear and group A to move onto the floor;
- and so forth.

This allows the pace of the class to continue while the teacher makes corrections during execution of the combination.

If a teacher says four groups, I stop after four groups, even if I see another group wanting to go. Some dancers think I'm being lazy, stubborn, or mean when I stop like that, but I do it because (a) the teacher makes the rules in class, not the students or the accompanist; and (b) it wastes time to have more groups than necessary.

Eventually, the structural patterns of the dance class will become clear, and it won't seem quite so mysterious.

How teachers demonstrate

There are two ways that teachers demonstrate their classroom combinations. The method most often used is for the teacher to demonstrate combinations to her own counts, leaving the choice of music up to the accompanist. The other method is for the accompanist to play a piece according to the request of the teacher ("a slow waltz for ronds de jambe à terre, please" or "a rousing 6/8 march for grands battements, please"); then she will either set a combination after hearing only four counts because she will know that the piece will suit her needs, or she will ask for a different meter, tempo, quality, or whatever. How the teacher speaks is often just as helpful as what she says. For instance, it is difficult to describe legato movement in staccato phrasing, and vice versa. That's why it is a good idea to really listen to what the teacher is saying all the time; you will have a better idea of what she wants musically. The voice of the teacher is a strong motivating force for you, as well as for the students.

The demonstration of combinations lays the basis for the entire class.

In case you become aware that you constantly misunderstand some request of the teacher, take the initiative and discuss the problem with her either before or after the class. One mistake I made for a long time was, after asking the teacher to clear up something, to say, "I understand," even though I didn't. I didn't want to look like an idiot. But it is absolutely not stupid to be confused if you (still) don't understand something. Being honest about still not understanding helps the teacher know that she must be clearer in her explanation. Additionally, if you say, "I understand," she will assume that the problem is solved, and will wonder why you still make the same mistake.

The confusion generated by faulty communication from the teacher is extremely frustrating to the beginning accompanist, but you will gradually learn to sort out what teachers really mean. One of my editors, a conductor, wrote over and over in the first version, "Teachers *must* understand something about music if they are going to teach dance." I couldn't agree more. However, it is counterproductive to make a teacher so paranoid about her musical abilities that she doesn't dare to open her mouth. Until every teacher-training course insists that its graduates are properly schooled in the musical needs of the dance classroom, accompanists need to have as much practical information as possible concerning the way teachers currently conduct their classes.

Qualities of steps and movements

The following is a very general discussion of the basic qualities of steps and movements in classical ballet. Its purpose is to assist the beginning accompanist in choosing appropriate music for each step and movement. I have emphasized that an accompanist should choose his music from the observation of movement phrases and not from the names of the steps. But there are numerous instances whereby you can eliminate many musical choices simply by hearing the name of the combination, which can save a lot of time. For example, when a teacher says, "pliés," an accompanist knows a coda is never suitable; when a teacher says, "frappés," an accompanist knows a smooth waltz or adagio is never suitable.

Knowing the quality of a particular step will expedite your choice of music. For instance, it is possible to count many combinations of tendus, dégagés, fondus, grands battements, pirouettes, and jumps in a medium-tempo duple meter. However, you would probably not choose the same piece for tendus as you would for grands battements, not only because the movement quality is different but also because a rousing march is usually not appropriate for one of the first barre combinations. An important aspect of effective dance accompaniment is the ability to maintain the pace of the class that the teacher establishes. Therefore, the accompanist has to learn to find perfect musical choices as quickly as possible.

In some cases, the direction of a step or movement will affect your choice of music. While it is impossible to suggest sideways or across-the-floor movement other than by rhythmic drive and melodic movement, the verticality (the up-and-down motion) of some movement can and should be reflected in what you play, as well as how you play it. This verticality will be mentioned in the appropriate places.

Some steps and movements begin with leg motion before the "1" (the first count of the combination), and will be so noted. This will help the novice accompanist to know that there can be movement before he plays the "1."

When a particular meter or musical form is generally used for a certain step or movement, it will be duly noted. Otherwise, a step or movement can be given to practically any meter or form, as long as the musical quality matches the movement quality—unless, of course, the teacher requests something else.

The *standing leg* or *supporting leg* is the one that remains on the floor while the *working leg* is usually off the floor. (In reality, both legs are working legs.)

There are instances when a step or movement can be duplicated musically in a specific way. These instances will be dealt with as they arise.

A description of classical ballet's steps and movements would, in many cases, be too confusing for beginning accompanists to understand, so they have been described instead by personality. (In the glossary you will find brief descriptions of all the terminology used in this book.) No one told me at the beginning that there could be many different musical forms in varying characters for one combination, or that different teachers could ascribe varying qualities to the same movement or step. Accompanists should keep this in mind when they play for many different teachers.

I hope some readers won't get caught up in what they think is incorrect terminology. It may be different from what you use, but it is not wrong. I have tried to be as clear as possible; for example, my term *dégagé family* denotes dégagés, jetés, and glissés. You may call a step sissonne simple, I call it temps levé; your retiré is my passé; your sur le cou-de-pied is sometimes my coupé, and so on. In America, the word *battement* is often omitted from many steps; hence, *battement tendu* becomes simply *tendu.*

Not every step/movement category will appear in every class you play. For example, grand allegro (big jumping steps) is almost never done in classes below the intermediate level. And it should be noted that all of the qualities described herein reflect the ultimate personalities of each step and movement. In other words, a pas de bourrée, for example, is done as a three-or four-count step for beginners in a medium-to-slow tempo, but is often a crisp one-count step for more advanced dancers.

At the barre

The barre combinations listed in this section are arranged in the way most teachers structure their barres. Teachers of less advanced students may omit some of them.

Barre combinations are rarely marked—that is, practiced with music before dancing them full-out.

Some teachers give a "pre-barre" or a floor barre, consisting of movements to help the body warm up and to improve alignment. These movements can be given to such an endless variety of meters, tempos, and musical qualities that I have chosen not to enumerate them here. It is safe to say, though, that the mood is usually calm and gentle.

Pliés

Pliés are always smooth, flowing, never-ending, and legato.

To an untrained eye, pliés go down and up, but in reality they are a study in contrary motion. If a dancer allows his full body weight to sink into his legs during a plié, his thigh muscles will become bulky from pushing all that weight up again. If, however, he breathes correctly and thinks of lifting his torso up and away from his legs as they bend, it is much more beneficial—and easier.

It is very difficult to re-create contrary motion musically in a dance-related fashion, but the first thirty-two counts of example 65 illustrate the concept fairly well. This is a very advanced concept of dance accompaniment, and certainly not something for a novice accompanist to lie awake nights over. However, an awareness of the reasons behind it will help to keep all elements of plodding and heaviness out of plié music.

It is safe to say that pliés must be reasonably slow. They are the first, most important, and most basic movement in a dance class, and must be executed diligently. The vast majority of teachers use slow 3/4s for their plié combinations. Slow waltzes are sometimes requested, but their "OOM pah pah" structure at a slow tempo does not lend itself to the flowing quality that a plié must have. Younger students, however, need a slow waltz for pliés, since the counts are more easily heard in a waltz than in a slow 3/4. Many of the 3/4 and 9/8 adagios in this book are in the correct tempo for pliés, but their high emotional intensity makes them unsuitable. Example 74, for instance, is so overwhelmingly powerful that it is not qualitatively conducive to the first combination of a class. The purpose of pliés is to begin the process of warming up and building technique and strength, not, at that point, to express emotion. By the time a dancer gets to the adagio in the center, his body should be thoroughly warmed up, making him prepared to express the motivation behind his movement.

In this book I have tried to steer clear of stating my own personal preferences as much as possible. The preferences of teachers and the needs of dancers have provided the basis for the observations and suggestions contained herein. But I would like to state my musical preference for pliés. This preference has also grown out of observing teachers and dancers in their response to music.

I vote for the medium-tempo flowing waltz as the form most conducive to pliés. It gives me more leeway in being able to express motion than other forms because the music is moving at a faster pace. And I find it easier to make dynamic changes which evoke the soaring, uplifting quality so appropriate to any movement of the cambré/port de bras family, which are almost always included in plié combinations. A demi-plié uses two counts of the waltz to go down and two counts to come up, and a grand plié uses four counts down and four counts up; the movements remain slow, but the music is alive and energetic. There is more substance in the rhythmic structure, which helps to generate fuller execution of the plié throughout the whole leg, rather than just bending the knees. (I don't mean to brag, but just today I played one of the group waltzes from *Swan Lake* for pliés for the Bern, Switzerland, company class, and they all applauded. That is not a normal occurrence from a group of professional dancers. I'm sure they were grateful for something to really lift their spirits on a Saturday morning after a hard week of work. The applause surprised me, and made me feel great—and the music probably made them feel even better.)

Example 65 is one of everybody's favorite pieces for pliés. The choreography included with it is the plié combination that Mr. Brunson's students did in every class he taught. The choreography never changed (which was never the case in all other combinations), and we were *never* bored.

To be fair, I will state the three complaints I have heard concerning the use of this form.

- "It's so heavy on the legs." *All* musical forms are heavy on the legs if a dancer "sits" at the bottom of the grand plié. I know teachers who have used this form for many years in their classes, and their students have well-developed—*not* bulky—thighs. If a dancer uses the music logically, he will never get heavy legs. The key to the logic here is for the dancer to start down in the plié more slowly than he is used to, so he won't have to sit and wait at the bottom for the right time to come up. It is the static parking that produces tree-trunk thighs.
- "It's too grand for anything but professional-level classes." I agree with that, for the most part. But I've watched what happens when I play this kind of waltz for a class of students who come "once a week to dancing school"; their eyes pop, the adrenaline starts flowing, there are actually one

or two beads of perspiration on their bodies, and they think maybe there's something to this dancing business, after all. As a steady diet, maybe not, but as an occasional taste of what pliés can really be like, I feel it's a great idea. And adult classes love it.

- "It's too loud!" This was from a dancer in a professional company who said she wasn't awake enough for that much energy. I politely refrained from saying, "That's the whole point. Pliés deserve as much, if not more, energy than any other combination."

Tendus

Tendus defy qualitative categorization. When the quality of a particular step cannot be succinctly described, the tempo in which it is executed often defines the quality. Hence, slow tendus with demi-pliés suggest an "andante con moto"—a moderato two with a smooth 8th-note figure or Alberti bass in the left hand, or a slow and flowing waltz. Don't forget dynamics; just because the movement is slow, that doesn't mean that the music is "sleepy" or lacking in energy and contrasting dynamic levels.[1]

Medium-tempo and fast tendus suggest a host of different meters, depending on whether the leg goes out on the count or on the "and." (A detailed discussion of "ands" begins on page 196.)

The dégagé family

Dégagés, jetés, and glissés are, from the accompanist's point of view, the same step, and are usually referred to throughout this book as the dégagé family. The term a teacher uses depends on which system of dance she studied.

These steps are a bit easier to define qualitatively than tendus. The action of the leg going away from the body is always brisk and crisp; the return of the leg is either equally brisk or, if the leg's return ends in a demi-plié, legato and melting.

Some teachers emphasize geographical locations—the outs and ins—of this step, in which case a duple meter works best, since it reflects those locations. Other teachers emphasize different facets of the step—for example, they want might more of a rebound, in which case a triple meter works best, since it doesn't have an accent on the "out" movement.

I am including a dégagé combination (example 66) that is typical of some that used to be a problem for me for many years. Many teachers like to give dégagé combinations in a medium-tempo two that allows for clean, turned-out closings in fifth position, immediately followed by sixteen counts tacked on at the end for dégagés in first position to emphasize speed. A change of music for these last sixteen counts not only perks up the dancers' feet *and* ears; it also is helpful for the accompanist, who may already be playing the first section as fast as he can.

Dégagé-family combinations also can start either on the count or on "and," and can be done to as large a variety of meters as can tendus.

Ronds de jambe à terre

Ronds de jambe à terre are usually called simply ronds de jambe. Another movement of the same family, ronds de jambe en l'air, always includes the words en l'air.

There are definite geographical locations for the leg and foot in a rond de jambe à terre (a perfect one is in the shape of a D), and the musical accent may be requested in different locations. There are two different kinds of rond de jambe à terre combinations, and the meter of the music is different for each.

In two

One kind of rond de jambe combination includes the following pattern: two slow ronds de jambe and three fast ones. (Sometimes when I dissect this movement phrase, I come up with three slow ones and two fast.) Example 9, a moderato two, shows this pattern written, between the staves, where it can occur. Neither a rhythmic nor a melodic figure complementary to this particular combination of movements can be found easily in a waltz. Carefully chosen legato tangos will also work for this type of combination.

In three

The other kind of rond de jambe combination usually contains no quick ronds de jambe, so the inherent roundness of the movement is best enhanced by a smooth and flowing waltz or gentle ländler. I like to fill in the melodic holes with eighth notes in the left hand, which is demonstrated in the A section of example 75.

Ronds de jambe à terre normally start in one of two different ways:

- from first or fifth position, so the first actual leg movement occurs on "1"; or
- from second position, which is usually preceded by the teacher saying, "Preparation." This can be confusing to the new accompanist because, theoretically, there is a preparation before every combination. But this rond de jambe preparation is unique. During the 4-count introduction, one complete rond de jambe is accomplished in the following way: The student fondus on one leg while the other leg tendus to the front ("5" and "6"); the fondu leg straightens as the tendu leg goes to second position ("7"); on "8," the tendu leg completes the preparatory rond de jambe.

Fondus

Fondus are always melting, smooth, legato, and extra-controlled.

Fondus may not look as vertical as, for instance, grands battements or grand allegro, but they definitely are, and are also one of the most demanding steps in the dance vocabulary. Ideally, they should be executed smoothly from the lowest depths of the demi-plié to the highest point of the demi-pointe. The standing leg has to press the entire weight of the body up with no help from the rebounding action of jumping, so you can imagine how important it is to have the torso correctly placed and as lifted and buoyant as possible, as described in the plié section. Therefore it is helpful to reflect this motion in melodic lines and in your pedaling. I maintain a legato melodic line throughout, and use the pedal as the dancers use their bodies: Depress the pedal when they are down, lift it when they are up.

Some teachers will begin fondu combinations by having the students' working legs tendu to second position before the "1."[2]

Fondus may be done to waltzes, barcarolles, the lassú section of czardases, and—in more advanced classes—to carefully chosen tangos.

Frappés

Frappés are always bright, crisp, and staccato. Vera Volkova once said, "Frappés are never sad."

Frappés and the dégagé family share the same energetic footwork, but their rhythmic structure is often quite different.

Dégagés, when given in a duple meter, are usually executed rhythmically evenly, as in the following example:

Teachers are often very specific about the rhythmic execution of a frappé, calling upon their students to do four single frappés either in the rhythm of the above dégagé example, or in the following rhythm:

Four double frappés look like this rhythmically:

Single and double frappés are the usual form of this step; triple frappés occur occasionally.

Since most melodies are not written to the rhythmic specifications of frappés, an accompanist can either invent some, or use pieces whose melodies contain notes where the frappés' accents fall, and stress them with contrasting dynamics and pedaling, as in examples 67 and 68. Both examples contain the correct accents for single and double frappés.

Many teachers devise their own preparations for frappés, getting the working leg out to the side in tendu so that the inward movement to the ankle can be executed on the "and" before the "1."

Adagios/développés

The quality of these movements is sustained, controlled, deceivingly powerful, smooth, elongated, reaching, and extending beyond the body.

These movements can often be grueling to a dancer at the barre because of the stamina required. In the center, the class is divided almost always into at least two groups of dancers, allowing one group to rest while another group works. This is not the case at the barre; all the dancers do every combination with no rest in between. Therefore, strong, substantial, helpful, supportive—but always legato—music is called for here.

(Although the following information may not seem relevant to this book, I want to mention an important "discovery" that is just starting to take hold in the dance world. This revelation is something I have retained and cherished from my first years of dance study with Mr. Brunson, and it seems to have fallen out of favor these days: strength and stamina developed through aerobic execution of dance classes. Sweat seems to have become a dirty word; it boggles my mind to see how few dancers—even professionals—come away from the barre with barely a sheen on them. We used to be dripping after pliés. Sweating doesn't necessarily prove that one has good working habits, and I have known a very few dancers who just don't sweat, but an entire roomful of barely damp bodies suggests that something is missing from the execution of such a physical endeavor. Dr. Eileen M. Wanke has done extensive research and tests on a number of dancers, and the results of executing aerobic ballet class on a regular basis show that the dancers are not only stronger and happier, but also less injury prone. I will not go further into this subject, as it will comprise a large chapter in my next book but, for those of you whose interest is piqued, you can get more information from Dr. Wanke at the following address: Bereich Tanzmedizin, Sulingerstrasse 20, D-27211 Bassum, Germany. (This information is available in both English and German.)

Adagios are comprised of a number of different steps and movements, some of which are développé, relevé lent, grand rond de jambe en l'air (whose shape and texture is decidedly different from a "normal" rond de jambe en l'air), attitude, and arabesque.

Passés/retirés are often included, too, as they are the first movement of a développé. The personality of a passé depends on the mini-phrase of movement in which it appears; in the case of adagios and développés, it will require the same quality as the rest of the combination. It has a distinctly different personality in pirouette combinations, as we shall see.

Accompanists must learn immediately that the longer a leg is held in the air, the harder it is for a dancer.

Adagios in all the meters I have discussed are suitable for this family of movement. A more detailed discussion on your choice of music will appear in the section on adagio center combinations.

Petits battements serrés and battus

These movements are always brisk, crisp, repetitive, "busy," and staccato.

An accompanist's ability to musically reflect the quality of this movement family will increase as his technique expands. As a beginning accompanist, you will probably start out by playing a medium-tempo two, preferably with a lacy, filigreed melodic figure in the right hand to reflect the shape, speed, and texture of the movement. As your confidence, understanding, and technique increase, you will graduate to a fast waltz, such as Chopin's "Minute" Waltz (op. 64, no. 1), or a coda. Both a fast waltz and a coda have more notes in the rhythm—and often in the melody—than the medium-tempo two; these notes reflect the dancers' movements more accurately.

Battements serrés are often given in the same rhythm as single frappés, and teachers may improvise the same sorts of preparations.

Ronds de jambe en l'air

This step is a chameleon, like a tendu. Ronds de jambe en l'air can be executed to a variety of musical forms, depending on which particular quality the teacher is stressing.

Their oval or teardrop shape suggests that they are always smooth. But when they are done at a brisk tempo with the foot just slightly off the floor, there is a definite, almost staccato, finishing accent as the foot and leg stretch to complete each one (see example 12). When the teacher demonstrates ronds de jambe en l'air in a fast tempo, a brisk waltz, 3/8, or non-coda two is usually suitable. When she demonstrates them in a slow tempo or smooth quality, the same rules apply to "en l'airs" as to "à terres": a legato waltz if they are all done at the same speed (see example 69), or a slow two if there are three slow and two quick ones (see example 70).

Teachers occasionally start en l'air combinations in almost the same manner as à terres. The main difference is that, on the accompanist's last count of the 4-count introduction, the working leg will often dégagé to second position and do one rond de jambe en l'air, arriving in second position en l'air again by the "1."

A grand rond de jambe en l'air bears slightly more resemblance to an à terre than to an en l'air. It has the same shape as an à terre (the letter D), but it is executed with the foot and leg off the floor at varying heights, and is almost always executed as part of an adagio combination.

Grands battements and battements en cloche and en balançoire

These movements are perhaps the most spectacular of the steps executed at the barre, often earning a respectful "Wow!" from an audience during a lecture-demonstration. Verticality is very much in evidence in grands battements; the height of the movement, as well as the power necessary to get the leg to that height, must be reflected in both the musical structure and the dynamics. Melodic lines as well as leading tones in octaves in the bass, leading to the peaks of the movements, are most helpful to the dancer.

Most teachers, and probably many pianists, think that all marches are written in 4/4, so accompanists often end up playing only 4/4 marches for grands battements. More experienced accompanists like to vary the musical forms they use for each step/movement group at the barre, and the grand battement group includes 4/4 and 6/8 marches, grandiose waltzes, and—occasionally—polonaises.

Grands battements with the leg going up on the count

Duple meter marches and grandiose peaks-and-valleys waltzes are recommended for this kind of combination.

A polonaise, not a mazurka—as is so often requested—is called for when teachers give grands battements in three counts: The leg goes up on the first beat of a bar, descends to tendu on the second beat, and closes in fifth position on the third beat. (Polaccas and boleros have the right tempo and rhythmic structure for this kind of combination, but their quality doesn't match the power necessary to support it.)

Grands battements with the leg going up on "and"

Almost all 6/8 marches work for this kind of combination. A few duple-meter marches, such as example 80, work also, depending on the melodic accents.

The quality of this and the previous grand battement combination is always broad, loud, energetic, and uplifting.

Grands battements en cloche and en balançoire

These are very swinging movements, and require a triple meter with stress on every count, as in 3/8s. Mazurkas have stress on every count, too, but they are generally too slow and too heavy for this movement.

The quality of this combination of movement is more relaxed and free than the two previous ones (see example 71).

Battements en cloche may also be done very quickly with the toes barely off the ground to the front and back. They have a radically different quality from the "grand" variety.

Stretching

Stretching is the only end-of-barre combination we will deal with here, as the others are as personal as each individual teacher.

The quality of stretching is self-explanatory. Other applicable adjectives are *smooth* and *elongating.* For dancers who are not loose in the hip joints and/or hamstrings, another applicable adjective is *grueling,* but this should not be reflected in the music.

I often "audition" new adagios during stretching combinations to see if teachers like them. If a teacher rejects one for use as a barre or center adagio, she will usually be amenable to your playing it for stretching. Since I prefer to save my "inspirational music" (as a dancer once called it) for adagio combinations, and since no rhythmical impetus is necessary to help a body or a leg get off the ground, I use adagios with flowing rhythmic structures and relatively quiet dynamics. Even dancers with loose hip sockets can often be in pain from stretching, so a serene, peaceful atmosphere generated by the music is always appreciated.

The cambré family

Cambré, port de bras, port de bras en rond, port de corps, circular port de bras—these are some names of movements that are designed to warm up, stretch, and strengthen the entire body from the ankles up. They often directly follow a period of intensive leg activity, providing not only a rest for the legs but also the opportunity to work on the vital stomach and back muscles. For the sake of brevity, cambré will be used as a generic name throughout the text, unless otherwise specified.

A closer look at any movement of this family can illustrate the difference between just making shapes with the body, and doing the movement so it is both pleasurable and beneficial. The cambré can be done correctly only if the tempo of the music accommodates it. If the tempo is too fast, which is usually the case, a dancer usually sits back in his hips and sloughs through the movement. It takes concentration and the right amount of time to use the stomach muscles, activate the back, and maintain perfect verticality from the hips down to get the stretch in the backs of the legs.

A lot of dancers execute cambrés in a hum-drum fashion—as just another exercise. Mr. Brunson, bless him, exhorted us to experience them as soaring, liberating movements at the same time that they were doing great things for our muscles. (I am convinced that that liberating feeling contributed to the benefits our muscles received; without the emotional motor behind the movement, it would indeed feel like an exercise and produce less technical improvement.)

There is a distinct change in dynamics whenever any movement of this family is done, and this change starts before the movement begins: A leading line, a crescendo, and a breath with the pedal all help the dancer to inhale and renew his energy—and to change the position of his arms, if necessary.

We will discuss two of the most common movements of this family here. To facilitate reading, they will be referred to as cambré and circular port de bras.

- A cambré exhibits obvious verticality. It is executed in four sections: The torso bends straight down from the hips, comes up, bends back, and returns to an upright position. (For the purposes of this discussion, I will use the cambré in which the back remains straight during the second section, not the one that rolls through each vertebra.) It really feels good to a dancer to bend his body down so that his chest touches his legs; the back enjoys not having to support so much body weight for a few seconds, and the blood gets a chance to refresh the brain. You can reflect breaths in your pedaling at the two vital points where a dancer should inhale: just before he starts down and just before he starts back.
- A circular port de bras is not at all vertical; it is two huge, sweeping circles of the body from the waist up. There is one inhalation before the dancer starts diagonally out, down, and around; and another before he reverses the entire movement. Each movement and musical phrase is accomplished in a seamless, roundly flowing fashion which builds dynamically to each finish.

The tempo is not the same for the cambré and the circular port de bras. That may explain why the circular port de bras is given less often than the cambré; many teachers and most accompanists don't realize that the two movements need different musical tempos to be effective. Some teachers seem indifferent to tempo in general, while most are very specific about it, but sometimes they forget that a cambré or circular port de bras section needs a different tempo than what preceded it. (For years I have watched dancers attempt to do circular ports de bras in a plié combination in four counts—their usual allotment—and it is sad to see them producing movement that only warms up instead of also strengthening and lengthening. Especially if a dancer has been taught properly during his pre-professional training, he will just give up trying to do it correctly if he hasn't enough time.) Establishing the tempo for every combination is always the teacher's responsibility. It is up to her to watch her students' movements in order to discern whether a tempo is so unsuitable as to prevent the beneficial execution of a step or movement.

The following illustrations will show the accompanist how to translate these movements into music.

Cambrés and circular ports de bras within plié combinations

Medium-tempo waltz. Example 65 is a plié combination. In bars 21–28 there is a cambré forward. In measures 89–104 there are two circular ports de bras. Notice that this latter section is slightly slower.

Slow waltz, slow 3/4, or 9/8. Example 52 is part of a plié combination, and contains a cambré forward.

A circular port de bras in these three forms is not recommended. Four counts in this tempo is too little time to execute well the circular port de bras, and slowing down the already slow tempo would produce a heavy, plodding quality with none of the uplifting brea(d)th necessary for the movement. Speeding it up, in order to accomplish the movement in eight counts, would be not only difficult technically but jarring musically. Changing to a waltz, which will be covered in the following rond de jambe section, is too much of a musical jolt for the first combination of the class. I think this is why I have observed that most good teachers include circular ports de bras in later combinations at the barre.

Cambrés and circular ports de bras added onto rond de jambe à terre combinations

The majority of rond de jambe combinations consists of thirty-two counts of ronds de jambe and related steps, followed usually by eight, sixteen, twenty-four, or thirty-two counts of the cambré family and a balance.

Slow waltz. If you are playing a slow waltz—one rond de jambe per measure—most teachers keep a cambré at the same tempo, so each of the four sections is executed in two counts. However, I prefer to speed up or change the waltz (or both) so that each section is accomplished in four counts. I do this to emphasize the dynamic changes and soaring quality of the movement. I never do this without explaining my reasons to the teacher before class and asking her permission.

The tempo during a circular port de bras must be sped up so that each "sweep" is accomplished in eight counts. Otherwise, the same problem as in pliés occurs: The same tempo means not enough time to do it correctly, and a slower tempo means music that does not evoke the liberating feeling of the movement.

Moderato two or tango. After the 32-count (usually) rond de jambe section, I prefer to change to a waltz for the cambré or circular port de bras section. The change in dynamics and meter is especially effective and uplifting after thirty-two counts of duple meter. Because radical transitions are often problematic for beginning accompanists, it is advisable to stay with the duple meter for the cambré section. But it is not a satisfying evocation of the movement quality, and it is especially unsuitable for the sweep of a circular port de bras.

Medium-tempo waltz. If you are playing a medium-tempo waltz—one rond de jambe in four bars—you are probably playing for a children's or beginners' class, in which circular ports de bras are rarely given.

The medium-tempo waltz is already the approximate tempo of a cambré, as we have seen in the foregoing plié section.

Movements of the cambré family included in combinations of a non-legato quality

Rarely will a teacher tell an accompanist during her demonstration that there must be a change in the musical quality to accommodate a movement of this family. Often, she will just say something like, "Cambré at the end."[3]

The teacher must decide how many counts a tacked-on cambré needs, and communicate this to her accompanist. For instance, she could say to her accompanist, "Thirty-two counts of dégagés, followed by a 16-count cambré, plus an amen." Translated into musical terms, this becomes, "Thirty-two counts of a staccato two, followed by sixteen counts of legato music, plus an authentic cadence." The teacher would, of course, demonstrate the tempos to both her accompanist and students.

Cambrés can be included in any combination (unfortunately, most teachers restrict their usage to plié and rond de jambe combinations), and teachers should decide how they want them treated musically: whether the accompanist should continue with the same piece, changing the dynamics, quality, and tempo as necessary; or whether he should change over to a waltz.

In the center

The first combinations in the center

The first few combinations in the center—usually until the adagio—are mainly comprised of various steps that have been executed at the barre. None of these first combinations will be dealt with here, as they are almost identical to some of the barre combinations already described, and are as varied as the teachers themselves. But a fairly standard one will be covered in the pirouette section.

The tempos of these first combinations are usually fairly slow, and the moods are fairly low-key, in order for the dancers to get fully "on their legs"—to establish correct body placement without the support of the barre.

Discussion of the vocabulary used during the remaining part of the class will be primarily in terms of families of steps, rather than individual steps and movements.

Adagios

Adagio combinations in the center can be basic academic practice of typical adagio movements (which were listed earlier in the barre section), and they can also include expressive movements of the arms, head, and torso that are not found in a dictionary of classical ballet. These "atypical" movements are just as important as the classical steps, since choreography on the stage these days rarely is limited to pure classical technique. And a student doesn't suddenly learn how to move expressively on the day he signs his first company contract.

I have heard that the young girls in Alicia Alonso's school in Cuba are taught to blow a kiss as they move their arms from first to second position. While this may seem a bit flowery and overblown to us, it teaches them from a very early age that movement is *not* empty; it expresses something to an audience, if only the sheer joy of moving. After all, the classroom is the first preparation for the stage. Even in a school for amateurs, expressive movement should be encouraged. Classical ballet technique is not just about stretched legs and pointed feet; it is also a language of expression, just like English or music or Russian or painting. If the students come (or the parents want the students to come) only for physical exercise, they are probably better off in a gymnastics class.

To novice accompanists, adagios may sometimes look like a series of static poses, but in reality they are moving positions that require a great deal of strength to both maintain and—often—elongate. While some teachers feel it may be beneficial and strength building for a student to park in an arabesque and hold it there through sheer brute strength for eight counts, it is also beneficial and aesthetic for him to be aware of the length of a musical phrase and to make his movement grow proportionately within and to the end of that phrase. Parking in a position is beneficial only when the proper muscles are being used, which requires a great deal of strength in the torso. (It is sad to see a male student trying to hold his leg up in second position for eight counts in preparation for à la seconde turns when the strain on his face, the misplacement of his body, and the bulge of his thigh are obvious signals that he is using and developing the wrong muscles.)

The turn/pirouette family

The adagio turn or pirouette

This is an exquisite, controlled, slow, single turn that can finish in a melting lunge to the floor, and is usually found in adagio combinations. The quality of this movement needs no further elaboration.

"Normal" pirouette combinations

"Normal" pirouettes are revolutions of the body on the ball of one foot or on the tip of one point shoe, with the other leg usually in the passé position. Remember that the quality of passés in adagio combinations is always smooth, matching the quality of the rest of the movement. In pirouettes, the quality is decidedly different: The passé must zip up the leg to the knee as quickly as possible, and pirouette music needs to reflect that.

While the various qualities of pirouettes cannot be defined in a manner helpful to a beginning accompanist, dancers who are natural turners almost always say that coordination, a fluid demi-plié before the sharp takeoff, and rhythm are absolute musts in the accomplishment of good pirouettes. Except in the case of adagio pirouettes, every pirouette combination should be supported by a very firm rhythmic structure which the dancer will use for his "spotting" and for the pistonlike action of his legs during turns in succession. No matter what you play, the rhythm must be especially firm in the turn section, and uncluttered by arpeggios, which detract from the steady rhythmic pulse. A crescendo on the demi-plié preparation before pirouettes not only reflects the verticality of the turning position but also reminds dancers that sneaking gently up to demi-pointe will never provide enough impetus to go around more than once. The height of the crescendo should be maintained throughout the duration of the turn(s).

Sometimes beginning "pirouetters" need to just lurch around at their own tempos, either to overcome their fear of turning or to just get used to this strange new sensation. But the rhythm in the music, combined with the teacher's comments, will eventually sink into their consciousness, and they will gradually learn to use that rhythm.

Some teachers request that the pirouette section of a combination (often in the first tendu combination in the center) be slowed down, presumably to allow for more pirouettes. I feel that this practice leads dancers to unconsciously expect slower tempos for pirouettes, which will never occur in choreography for the stage. And it will adversely affect a natural turner's turning tempo, which he has already established in his body through the foregoing music. It makes more sense to have two separate sections within one combination, with music suitable for each section, as in example 72.[4]

Pirouettes can be combined with virtually every combination in the center, but when a teacher demonstrates a "normal pirouette combination," the forms most commonly used are waltzes in a variety of dynamic levels (especially if the combination includes balancés), mazurkas, and medium-tempo 3/8s. When they are danced to pieces in duple meter, the head spot rhythm is usually faster.

Turns in attitude and arabesque

Turns in attitude and arabesque are rarely called pirouettes, but they are a part of that family. They can be done as parts of so many different combinations of movement that it is impossible to suggest a particular meter or musical form.

Turns in succession

Turns in succession will be discussed after the grand allegro section, since that is where they usually occur.

Chaînés/déboulés

Chaînés/déboulés should eventually be executed at lightning speed, but they need many years of sometimes excruciatingly slow tempos for the body to get used to doing them correctly before speed is attained. I have been asked for so many different kinds of music for chaînés for beginners that I can't remember them all. Suffice it to say that, whatever you play, it should not sound as heavy as the students will look during their first attempts at chaînés; light-footed music should remind them what they are striving toward.

Because of the difficulty of the step, some teachers turn a blind eye to their students' lack of rhythmicality as they start learning to do chaînés. I agree with this, having myself plodded around at one point, trying to do chaînés; I could stay within my own tempo, but it was decidedly different from that of my neighbors in front and in back of me. (This is definitely an unusual exception to the necessity of ordering one's movements to the music's demands; rhythmicality is the first step toward—and an innate part of—not only musicality but also technical improvement. Anything less is self-indulgence.)

Soutenu turn

A soutenu turn (they are almost always singles) is done on the toes or the balls of both feet, can be either legato or staccato, and is often used at the barre to change from one side to the other.

Tour en l'air

Tour en l'air (usually double in choreography) is a turn that is part of the basic vocabulary of male classical dancers; it is often included in the variations and codas of traditional pas de deux. Music similar to these variations and codas (if not they themselves) are recommended, as well as robust waltzes and marchlike twos (very rarely tarantellas).

Balancés

Balancés deserve their own category, simply because they are probably the most dancy (for lack of a better word) movement in the dance vocabulary. How a dancer does balancés shows clearly how he feels about dancing in general. They are danced to threes 98 percent of the time. One exception is a fast friszka—usually the finale of a rousing character dance.

Sautés/jumps

There is a very specific order in which jumping steps are given. The logic of it may not be visibly apparent to the accompanist, but it is certainly there.

The first jumps in every class are almost always executed from two feet to two feet. In the next category, referred to here as petit allegro, the jumping becomes progressively more difficult as the jumps are executed from two feet to one foot, from one foot to two feet, and from one foot to one foot. Then come medium allegro (slower and higher) and grand allegro (even slower and, when applicable, as high as possible). Many of these steps can be beaten.

Changements

Changements often comprise the majority of steps given in the first jumping combination of the class. Most teachers are very specific about the tempo, since this combination is about warming up the feet and preparing the body for jumping, not about how high one can jump. There are often other steps included in this combination, and it is usually done to a two in the median tempo of a polka. Certain 6/8s (similar to example 45) are also possible and highly recommended.

Many teachers give combinations that include three changements and a demi-plié. There are two different ways of doing this, with decidedly different tempos. The first version is faster than the second, and needs a polka or a rag:

A dotted melodic rhythm is suitable for the second version:

Unless the teacher has a specific reason for changing the accent, changements begin before the "1." The dancer pliés on the last count of the introduction, jumps into the air on "and," and lands on the "1." (I greatly regret not asking Mme. Volkova why she occasionally asked her students to reverse this process and be up in the air on "1" after they had just executed it the "normal" way. What a can of worms! The students had a very difficult time changing the accent. It was another instance that proved that the dance vocabulary was set up according to organic, sometimes indefinable, laws that often relate to music.)

Petit allegro

Most petit allegro steps exhibit verticality, but the height of this family of steps is seldom as important as the cleanliness of execution.

Many of these steps (glissade and pas de bourrée are but two) can be combined with adagio movement, giving them a completely different personality. Many petit allegro combinations can be done in either duple or triple meter. And some of them can be done "grandly," such as assemblé and jeté.

Many petit allegro steps start before the count. It seems to make more sense to advise beginning accompanists to watch for the accents than to analyze them all.

Because they are so prevalent in so many different kinds of combinations, four steps deserve mention here.

Glissades are usually not jumping steps, but they are components of a large number of petit allegro combinations, so they are included here. They are normally executed as they are pronounced, with the accent falling on the second syllable/movement: "glis-SADE"—"and ONE." There is also a noteworthy mini-version of a glissade, called a précipitée (sometimes glissade piquée), that usually has the personality of a hiccup. These are also found occasionally in adagio combinations, at which time their hiccup quality is slightly mellowed.

Pas de bourrées are also not jumping steps, but they are very often combined with petit allegro movement. They look like three-part steps, but are often taught to beginners in four counts, a plié on the supporting leg being the fourth part. And advanced dancers often execute them in one count.

Pas de bourrées can be done to almost every conceivable musical form, and can begin on every conceivable beat in a bar. It would require a separate volume to demonstrate all the possibilities. Suffice it to say that, if a teacher gives a combination of only pas de bourrées, watch and listen carefully: First, ascertain whether she wants a two or a three, and then observe where the more stressed parts of the step fall, so you will know where the "1" is.

Consecutive chassés are especially popular in children's classes. They can and must be done to both duple and triple meters, but the feeling of the step—and the sound that the feet make—are definitely in three. If the teacher you play for always requests a two, ask if you can play a three now and then. (And vice versa.) Teachers often speak and mark chassés in two, but they will normally dance them full-out (as opposed to marking) in three (usually a 6/8).

Assemblés can occasionally cause problems. Teachers and accompanists must work especially closely to prevent any hint of heaviness from intruding upon assemblé combinations. I have played for many "Russian system" advocates who give consecutive assemblés in duple meter every day. If dancers have to do this combination on a daily basis, I think they should occasionally do it to a three; they will not always dance assemblés to a two, and a three changes the emphasis of the step. Twos with a dotted melodic rhythm are usually reliable choices for this combination, but the same type of music every day with the same combination deadens the ears, to say nothing of its effect on the body. Assemblés for beginners are done slowly, of course; slowing down a waltz to accommodate the necessary slowness produces lighter-feeling music than slowing down a two.

I find that 6/8s rarely work for assemblés in triple meter; waltzes seem to be better, and "Take Me Out to the Ballgame" works wonderfully. (I get no reaction from it in Europe, but I wonder if I would be laughed out of an American studio for playing it.)

~

There are legions of meters and forms that effectively complement petit allegro steps: rags, polkas, some gavottes, boleros, jigs, reels, schottisches, hornpipes, medium-tempo waltzes, Spanish waltzes, fast waltzes, tarantellas, polaccas, some 3/8s and 6/8s, and allegro 9/8s and 12/8s.

Medium allegro

These combinations are slower than petit allegro and faster than grand allegro. They can often be done as comfortably in duple as in triple meter, and the teacher can jump back and forth between the two meters during her demonstration (which happens quite often with petit allegro combinations, too). When this happens, inexperienced accompanists should ask her which meter she wants; experienced accompanists can either ask or surprise her.

A two with a dotted melodic rhythm often works well for medium allegro combinations in duple meter, and some duple meter marches are also effective. Certain kinds of 6/8s (like examples 43 and 48), medium-fast waltzes, some Spanish waltzes, and some 3/8s can be used for medium allegro combinations in triple meter.

Grand allegro

Grand allegro tempos are never as fast as what a musician thinks of as allegro.

Many grand allegro combinations can, like all the allegro families, be done in both duple and triple meters. Many duple-meter marches, big waltzes in 3/4 and 6/8, as well as occasionally codas and some 3/8s are good choices for grand allegro combinations.[5]

The qualities of grand allegro steps are always big, broad, powerful, robust, extending into space, and soaring.

Turns in succession

Turns in succession is a generic term for combinations of turning movement that is repetitive. In other words, a single piqué turn, a single fouetté turn, a single chaîné turn, or a single grand pirouette à la seconde (the four most well known) will rarely occur in a phrase of movement; they are almost always done in a series. Many steps of this family can be done diagonally across the floor or en manège (in a circle)—not ménage (household).

In advanced and professional-level classes, a coda is almost always used for these steps, because they are almost always included in the codas of traditional pas de deux. In less advanced classes, a simple, uncluttered, rhythmically clear triple or duple meter may be used. Tempo is of the utmost importance.[6]

Révérence/port de bras

Révérence/port de bras varies from teacher to teacher, and sometimes is not used at all. A révérence has various purposes, depending on the teacher's taste and heritage. Some people have accused this practice of being a ridiculous holdover from the formal French court days. Most agree, however, that it is invaluable for practicing one of the most important elements of a dancer's stage performance: the final acknowledgment and thank you to the audience.

The teacher may ask for eight or sixteen counts of a slow waltz during which her students bow to her and to the accompanist. (Be sure to look at the students and acknowledge this bow; they are being taught to appreciate you and your work!)[7] Or she may ask for an adagio in which her students execute a combination of, usually, adagio movement combined with cambré/port de bras, which may or may not include bows. (Ninety-five per cent of the révérences/ports de bras I play include cambrés that are executed in two counts bending forward and two counts coming up. Since the students don't have a barre to help them with balance, I usually play a 4/4 or 12/8, to give them enough time to attempt to execute the cambré/port de bras properly.) Or she may ask for a robust piece of music to which she may improvise, expecting her students to react immediately and follow her movements. This is an invaluable aid in training the students to be instantly responsive to a choreographer.

The two most common ways a révérence is given are:

- as a separate combination (as noted above); or
- tacked onto a grand battement combination or a series of small, fast jumps; in either case, both the tempo and quality of music must change.

If you know that the teacher will use a révérence or port de bras at the end of class, be prepared for it. Before the class starts, put your chosen piece in a place apart from the music you might use during the class, so you won't have to hunt for it when the teacher says, "Révérence—AND!"[8]

~

Being familiar with the individual qualities of dance movement will gradually allow you to become quicker in your choice of appropriate music. However, because teachers want to keep their students' muscles warm and moving, class rarely moves at a pace leisurely enough for you to analyze all the material that is bombarding you at once. The teacher may begin a combination without you if she feels the class has waited long enough and the students' muscles are beginning to cool down. There will be times when you completely "bomb out" and choose something laughingly unsuitable. That's fine, as long as you learn from it. Not even Baryshnikov started doing every step perfectly at the beginning.

Start developing the ability to analyze your mistakes when you are in the middle of them; try to figure out why something was inappropriate. Did you misjudge the tempo? Was the piece too technically advanced for you at this time? Did you misread the quality? And so on. Whatever you do, *don't stop.* Don't give into yourself in this manner. Pushing ahead and making it work will do you much more good than stopping. That is just as important to remember as the fact that it is better for the students to continue too. You can often get away with an inappropriate selection, but improvement, no matter how gradual, will give you more enjoyment and fulfillment in what you are doing than just getting by.

Periodic sessions for the teacher and accompanist together, outside the pressures of the class, are vitally important. Whether it is five minutes just before class starts, two minutes at the end to clarify something, an hour a week, or a pleasant "dinner-music" session once a month, the increased exposure to each other's problem areas, needs, and abilities will reap mutually rewarding benefits.

The tools of an accompanist's trade

Repertoire

How to develop it

There are two choices for playing suitable music for dance: improvising and using written music.

Improvisation

Some of the finest dance accompanists don't use or even read music. Because their eyes are not glued to the printed page in front of them, they are free to observe the teacher as well as the class. They more easily gauge the teacher's and dancers' reactions to their music. Accompanists who consistently improvise for dance, however, run the risk of repeating themselves stylistically. Much of their music may tend to sound the same after a while, not only in style but also in key signature. And improvisers tend to "noodle" inventively with their right hands, leaving the left hands to fall where they may, thereby short-changing rich rhythmic propulsion. It is therefore important for the accompanist to remain open and free with regard to melodic inventiveness, harmony, texture, tonality, and stylistic approach.

Dance teachers very often choreograph their classroom combinations to specific musical lines or accents, which must be reflected consistently—in the same place each time in a given combination—in your improvised music.

When you *must* improvise

If you are an accompanist who relies completely on printed music, you may still be required to improvise occasionally. While the music selections in this book have been carefully chosen to give as complete a range of rhythms, tempos, and styles as possible, there is the possibility that a teacher will ask for something not included here.

This happened to me many times with allegro 9/8s before I finally got up the courage to improvise something that fit. After several embarrassing instances of having to sit silently during a combination while the teacher clapped, my pride got the better of me and I managed to play something that only I knew was pretty rotten. The first time was the hardest. After that, I knew I could cope with nearly anything thrown at me as long as my sense of inadequacy didn't immobilize me.

Some inventive teachers have asked for 10-count phrases, and one even asked for a 9-count phrase with silence during "5" and "6." As diabolical as this may sound, it *is* possible to do. Such phrasing forces students to count the music *and* the silence, and it keeps us accompanists on our toes, so to speak.

Using written music

Your repertoire will eventually become an extension of your personality. In the beginning, it may seem small, not particularly challenging, and possibly obscure with regard to why one piece works and another doesn't. You may feel that your particular personality is best reflected in a specific style of music, such as baroque or contemporary or impressionistic. The joy of movement is communicated onstage through—and enhanced by—every conceivable style of music, from that of the seventeenth-century Jean-Baptiste Lully to the contemporary Philip Glass. You can only benefit (musically as well as spiritually) by branching out into other styles of music, keeping in mind, of course, the needs and requests of the dance teacher.

You will be influenced in your choice of repertoire by the dance teachers for whom you play: One may detest baroque music and be ecstatic over anything from *Swan Lake,* while another may insist on nothing but Bach, Beethoven, and Brahms. One of a dance accompanist's prime assets is his adaptability to each teacher's classroom demands, and this certainly includes the realm of repertoire.

Two other factors influencing your choice of repertoire are:

- Dancing demands incredible physical endurance, so a classical solo variation rarely exceeds sixty-four counts. Therefore, a complete dance statement must often be accomplished in a relatively short time, compared with the length of, for instance, a symphonic movement. This factor is evidenced in a dance class as well as onstage; rarely will a dancer at any level be asked to execute a classroom combination in the center that is longer than sixty-four counts. However, because groups of dancers often repeat combinations consecutively in the center, you may often be asked to play a combination as many as eight times without stopping, so you will need some pieces that have at least 128 counts.
- Contrasts and changes of mood are factors to keep in mind while searching for new repertoire. For instance, many waltzes are quite long and have many contrasting sections. Those sections sharing the same dynamics or

quality or tempo can be used consecutively as one waltz. Often, another waltz of a different mood can be made up of the remaining sections.

If you don't improvise, the search for new repertoire never stops. What actually comes from your fingertips can be derived from a host of sources.

Syllabus music

If you are playing for syllabus classes (for example, Royal Academy of Dancing [RAD] or Cecchetti or Bournonville), your repertoire problems are already solved, since the music is included with the teaching syllabi. However, beginning accompanists must remember that playing only syllabus music prevents the development of one of the most important—and most creative—facets of dance accompaniment: choosing suitable music for each combination.

Most teachers are very thankful for free music for their syllabus classes (except, of course, when examination time approaches). But the teacher needs to let the accompanist know that. My first ballet-accompanying job was for a Cecchetti teacher who put the syllabus music in front of me wordlessly, and I played the same music for months. It was my first experience in a classical dance studio, and I had no idea that I could or should play something different. To this day it amazes me that I didn't quit. And it also amazes me that the teacher stood it for as long as she did.

As soon as possible, begin to add pieces to your repertoire on your own, especially as alternates to syllabus music (if the teacher is agreeable, of course). Bring in pieces you have studied with your music teacher, making sure either to warn the dance teacher in advance if the pieces are not in conventional 8-, 16-, or 32-count phrases; or to "square them off" (see page 136) yourself in a musically satisfying manner. You or the dance teacher can invest in some of the material mentioned in the next section (it may be tax deductible as a work-related expense). You should purposefully expand your repertoire to reflect the wide range of music that is danced to onstage.

Collections of music

If I had to choose the single most important staple of my repertoire, it would be the Scribner (Radio) Music Library ("the Red Books"). This series contains nine volumes, the most useful of which are *Light Opera and Ballet Excerpts, Standard and Modern Dance Music* (which is 95 percent waltzes), *Grand Opera Excerpts, Modern Compositions,* and *Light Compositions.* (Use the last one judiciously; it contains many examples of piddly music for dance. These pieces are technically easy and adaptable for class, but are hackneyed and insubstantial. On the other hand, it is probably better to play a variety of hackneyed but suitable pieces while you are expanding your repertoire, than to limit yourself to one or two great ones.)

The Red Books are out of print, and every effort I have made to contact Scribner's about either remainders or reissuing has met with silence. I have found partial sets at junk shops and Salvation Army stores (see the next section), so you could be lucky, too.

Another possibility is the Agda Skjerne books, published in Denmark by Wilhelm Hansen. Be sure to familiarize yourself with each piece in these books; some of them have odd numbers of phrases. Most of these pieces are labeled with the name of a common step or movement. When you become more experienced, you will realize that a piece labeled with one step (dégagés, for instance) might also work for another step (in this instance, frappés).

You may want to invest in one—or a few—volumes like those I fondly refer to as *Ninety Thousand Pieces the Whole World Knows.* Many of them are similar in quality to those in the *Light Compositions* Red Book, but you may be lucky, as I have been, and find an obscure volume that has lots of relatively unknown goodies in it.

Scott Joplin is probably America's most famous ragtime composer, and you will find him well represented in the *Golden Encyclopedia of Ragtime* (New York: Charles Hansen, 1974). Included therein are also a number of absolutely sensational rags by more obscure composers. This volume is also, unfortunately, out of print. You might have luck contacting the nearest library; I originally found it accidentally at the Seattle Public Library. I have heard that the best way to track down out-of-print books is to contact a used book or music store and ask them to initiate a search. The web site Sheet-Music.com is also a great resource for finding music.

There are a number of John Philip Sousa volumes on the market; my favorite is *Sousa's Great Marches in Piano Transcription* (Dover, 1975), probably because it contains facsimiles of the originals. These contain a large selection of 4/4 marches, 6/8 marches, codas, and pieces I call "one of those." They are well worth the investment, even though you will have to add octaves in the left hand of almost every piece.

Czerny études

Czerny études provide a wealth of workable music for class. Whenever I mention my fondness for Czerny during seminars for accompanists, a groan invariably arises from the participants. I have learned to be prepared to go straight to the piano and play a few of my special favorites to prove that a goodly amount of his voluminous output is *not* boring.

An interesting comparison can be made between Czerny études and barre combinations. Many pianists consider all such exercises a bore, executing them as a warming-up process for "real music." But so many of Czerny's études are quite enjoyable musically and very beneficial technically—exactly what barre combinations should be. It just depends on one's approach. Some dancers just slough through the barre, waiting to "really dance" in the center, while others truly enjoy the barre, realizing it is more than just a warm-up. I once asked Violette Verdy (surely one of the world's most musical and beautiful dancers) toward the end of her active dancing career whether she ever got bored with daily class. "Oh, no!" she exclaimed; "I love class! Even the barre is fun!" I'm willing to bet that, if she didn't love music so much, she wouldn't love the barre so much.

While almost every volume Mr. Czerny ever published contains suitable classroom music, three in particular have an unusually large percentage: *One Hundred and Ten Easy and Progressive Exercises* (op. 453), *Six Octave Studies in Progressive Difficulty* (op. 553), and *Perfection in Style* (op. 755). Many of the pieces in the first of these three volumes must be adapted for suitability to dance. (The subject of adaptation begins in the next section.) They are melodically engaging but sparse in texture, which is true for almost all of Czerny's easier études.

Operas and operettas

The operatic literature has also been a major source of my repertoire, and it became especially so after Mme. Volkova said, "The body sings when it dances. Play me an opera." The special quality of a singing phrase can be a great inspiration to a dancer. (Interesting that *inspire* means both to literally breathe and figuratively move.) And trying to emulate the human voice on the piano can do nothing but increase the quality of your tone production.

The *Grand Opera Excerpts* and *Light Opera and Ballet Excerpts* Red Books contain a stylistically broad range of selections, but complete opera and operetta transcriptions offer even more music. It takes a fair amount of time to go through an entire opera or operetta in piano reduction, but it will be worth your while: You will have many new usable classroom pieces, and you will have improved your sightreading. Many public libraries have opera transcription sections.

Salon music

What is sometimes disparagingly called salon music is often a very good source of class music. Some of it is technically challenging, and most of it is very adaptable for class. Some well-known salon composers are Theodor Leschetizky, Auguste Durand, Adolph von Henselt, Théodore Lack, and Benjamin Godard. Moritz Moszkowski seems to be a borderline salon composer, and has written some wonderfully adaptable music. And I am told by one esteemed musical pedagogue that Frédéric Chopin was actually a salon composer. (He and his music are discussed in more detail in the section on rubato.)

The traditional ballet repertoire

The area of traditional ballet repertoire in the classroom is a very personal one. Most dance teachers have had some stage experience, and they have developed strong feelings about certain music. Some dance teachers hold particular ballets in almost reverential esteem, and feel that music from these ballets belongs only onstage and not in the classroom. Three such ballets are *Les Sylphides* by Chopin (orchestrated by Stravinsky, Liadov, Tcherepnine, and Glazunov), *Giselle* by Adolphe Charles Adam, and *The Green Table* by Fritz Cohen. Other teachers may have danced *Nutcracker* so often that they turn green at the sound of any music from it. If you are going to be playing for any teacher for a considerable length of time, it would be wise to ask how she feels about the traditional repertoire. Develop your own repertoire accordingly.

Generally speaking, most dance teachers respond very positively to the traditional repertoire; it was, after all, written specifically for dance. However, some of it has become hackneyed over the years; it has been massacred by unaware accompanists, and so overplayed that it is sometimes laughable.

The following ballets are available in piano transcriptions, have a large number of usable excerpts, and would be a very fine foundation from which to start building the ballet-excerpt section of your repertoire.

Nutcracker *Sleeping Beauty* *Swan Lake*	by P. I. Tchaikovsky
Raymonda	by A. Glazunov
Coppélia	by L. Delibes
Giselle	by A. Adam
La Source *La Bayadère* *Don Quixote* *Le Corsaire* *Paquita*	by L. Minkus, L. Delibes, A. Adam, R. Drigo, or E. Deldevez[9]

Some selections from certain transcriptions of Tchaikovsky (in the version of Peter March/Tchaikovsky Foundation, New York) and Glazunov are technically quite difficult, but are definitely worth the trouble to learn. Their difficulty stems from an accurate rendering of the orchestral scope; the fullness of a large symphony orchestra is not always re-created in piano transcriptions. (It took me two years of intermittent work to get Peter March's version of the waltz Finale of *Nutcracker* into my fingers.)

Ballet Musik, volumes 1 and 2, decades-old compendia published by Wilhelm Hansen in Denmark, contain many usable excerpts from not only the well-known traditional ballets but also some obscure ones. Some of the excerpts are watered-down versions of the originals, though, and have no orchestral substance whatsoever.

Some beautiful ballet scores (such as Glazunov's *The Seasons*), as well as more recent music composed specifically for dance (such as Stravinsky's *Petrouchka*), have not been included in the above list because there is a smaller percentage of usable excerpts from each composition. (Contemporary works like *Petrouchka* are rarely composed according to the nineteenth-century practice of stringing many short variations [perfect for classroom use] together with a loosely binding theme.)

Show tunes

Broadway show tunes and popular old standards are played in class according to personal taste. Some dance accompanists play nothing but these tunes, possibly because they don't know where else to look for suitable repertoire. And many dance teachers accept these tunes, possibly because live music in any style is usually preferable to tape. But, just as all-baroque or all-Czerny classes are stylistically limited and ear-deadening, a steady diet of show tunes can be stultifying, uneducational, uninspiring, and insubstantial. A judicious sprinkling of them, however, can be a welcome change and pick-me-up.

Dance accompaniment, like everything else, is subject to fads. The preponderance of show tunes for ballet class in New York City is hopefully just that: a fad. Most teachers feel that classical ballet should be taught with classical music. And, again, remember that what the students hear in class forms their musical experience and taste to a great degree.

Where to find it

You will become more and more aware of the needs of the teacher(s) you play for, and will want to find music to fit those needs. Music stores, of course, are the logical places to look, especially ones with secondhand music sections. (During the years I lived in New York City, part of every day was devoted to rummaging through the used music racks at Patelson's on 56th Street, and much of what I found over forty years ago is still in my active repertoire.) Salvation Army and Goodwill stores, garage and estate sales, and junk shops are great places to find old, used, inexpensive, suitable pieces. *Etude,* the magazine published for music teachers beginning around the turn of the century, is full of obscure but very usable selections.

The radio is a good source of music, too. Keep a note pad handy in your car for jotting down the name—or the melody—of something you hear while driving. (I heard a Weber bassoon concerto—a piece a pianist would certainly not be likely to happen upon at Patelson's—one day on the radio, and it had such a catchy 24-bar theme that it has become a permanent favorite of teachers, students, and myself.)

How you go about deciding what will work for class when you are in a music store without a piano is another technique that improves with experience. At first, you may buy a lot of music that looks adaptable but turns out to be unworkable, for one reason or another, when you try it out on the piano. It would be wise not to throw any music away. Although I have often been chided for being a pack rat, this questionable trait has been beneficial regarding music. I used to look at pieces written in 9/8 and categorically dismiss them as useless; since my understanding of music for dance has increased, I treasure them, and have gone back through all my rejects (about three cartonsful) and found several that are wonderfully appropriate.

What I look for first in music are a singable melody and phrasing that either is in, or can be adapted to, eights, sixteens, and thirty-twos. (Rhythmic structures eventually become very easy to alter, so don't look at that first.) If you can't already produce music in your head from a printed page, work toward developing this sense. It is handy in a music store, and it is essential in the classroom for the purpose of deciding what to play.

As restricting as dance music may seem at the beginning, there is an endless supply of music that can be adapted to its so-called restrictions.

~

Your active repertoire should be in a constant state of flux. Your increasing understanding of the needs of dance, playing for new teachers, and the broadening of your musical taste will contribute to the evolution and expansion of the music you play.

In the beginning, one category of my mental repertoire was "utility waltzes"—waltzes that were not quite piddly but that were hardly memorable. Because of decades of music seeking, I have finally been able to eliminate that category, and each of my waltzes now has at least one distinguishing factor: a lovely melody, an especially legato flow, unusual melodic accents, or unique phrasing.

I repeat: At the beginning, you cannot be expected to understand what constitutes suitable music for dance. But ideally, throughout the intellectualizing you must do to sort out all this seemingly foreign data, you will remember to exercise your creativity and approach each class with an open mind.

How to organize it

You cannot function efficiently and rewardingly in the classroom if your music is not easily accessible. Therefore, this section is designed to help you decide the most effective way for you to organize your repertoire according to your personal needs.

In binders

One of the things you want to avoid—for a variety of obvious reasons—is lugging fifty pounds of music around with you wherever you go to play for class. The expenses involved in condensing your music into transportable, efficient packages are usually tax deductible, as long as you save the receipts: photocopying, three-ring notebook binders (heavy-duty and with round silver rings, not D-shaped, which hinder smooth page turning), mending tape (Scotch brand Magic Tape lasts longer than most others), and sheet protectors—clear pockets of plastic or Mylar or other clear material (again, heavy-duty), preferably glare-free, with or without black paper inserts. Sheet protectors can be bought more inexpensively in bulk, and you will probably be using a lot of them if you are serious about dance accompaniment.

A few words about putting music into the sheet protectors. This is something, like many other things in this book, that you can learn through trial and error, but you will save a lot of time, energy, and paper if you do it the efficient way from the beginning. If you have a piece that is two pages long, put the pages into the sheet protectors in such a way that they face each other in order, thus preventing a page turn. (In any page-turning situation, you almost have to choreograph the page turn; you have to anticipate when it is coming up and find a suitable time to do it without interrupting your musical flow. If necessary, write TURN in the measure where a page turn will cause the least distraction.)

In the process of putting your music together, you may want to square it all off, marking the eights, sixteens, and thirty-twos with a highlighter before putting it into the sheet protectors.

In order to reduce bulk and to avoid a lot of page turning, use repeat marks when possible. A great deal of suitable classroom music has an "A-A-B-A" structure; to save space, make it look like " ||: A :|| -B-A."

The extra cutting and pasting will be worth it in the long run. To really reduce bulk, use double-sided copies. This requires meticulous planning before you get to the copy machine, but is also well worth the effort.

If you have the luxury of access to free or inexpensive photocopying, the ideal method for organizing your repertoire is to photocopy every piece of suitable class music that is in a volume with other, unsuitable pieces. If this is not possible, decide which volumes you do and don't mind cutting up.

Early in my career, I decided to leave the Red Books and some Czerny volumes intact. My reasoning was that there was so much usable material in them that it wasn't worth cutting them up. It proved to be a good decision with the Red Books. Although they are dog-eared, warped, yellowed, and scribbled on (lovingly, with many Volkova combinations and maxims, notes to myself, and even autographs of Alexandra Danilova and Léonide Massine), they are still in usable shape because they are hardbound.

The decision was ill founded with the Czerny volumes. Their condition became so pitiful that I finally photocopied the pieces I use all the time and laid the originals to rest in a box with all my other originals.

I think it's a great mistake to cut up *any* ballet score. You may need the complete version some day for a performance, or you may, unknowingly, have a very valuable edition of some extinct ballet. (I fell heir to a piano score of Glazunov's obscure *Les Ruses d'Amour,* which may not be so valuable, but I am a great Glazunov fan, and wouldn't take a pair of scissors to that volume for anything.) Photocopy what you need out of it, then put it away in some safe place.

To use binders with maximum efficiency, buy some colored plastic inserts with "offset file" tabs that you can label. There are two common ways of labeling. You may choose to do so by dance step, in which case you would have a "plié" tab, a "slow tendu" tab, a "fast tendu/dégagé" tab, and so on, adjusted to how the majority of your classes are set up. Or you may choose to label by form, in which you would have tabs like "waltz," "rag," and "9/8." These approaches will become clearer in the next section.

Next, you need to decide whether you want to organize your binders by step, by complete class, by meter, or by composer.

By step

When I first began to accompany for dance, I was so overwhelmed by the amount of different kinds of music that was called for that I had to organize it somehow. The method best suited to my inexperience was by step. I organized my tabs in the order of most of the classes I was playing for, and had as many suitable pieces for each step as I could find. As your experience and understanding increase, you may find this method unrealistic and counter-creative. You will discover that much classroom music is interchangeable (one particular piece will often work for the dégagé family, frappés, and petit allegro), and it is restricting to think that you can play a certain selection only for tendus or only for ronds de jambe.

By complete class

When I worked in New York City, I played for several different studios on any given day. This necessitated reorganizing my music by complete classes. This meant that I had three or four different binders, each of which had a few selections appropriate for the combinations that teachers usually give. These binders were a true pot pourri of music, and were organized by step. Each binder had selections different from the other binders, so I could have taken "the grubby black binder" to the four different studios I played at on Mondays and played out of it all day, then "the flowered binder" Tuesday, "the new blue binder" Wednesday, and so on. (I never did use them quite like that; it would have become quite boring—and totally uncreative—to use the same music all day, so I tried—and learned—to play a lot from memory.)

If your needs indicate the "complete class" binder approach, be sure to include at least one polonaise, one bolero, an allegro 9/8, and a good sampling of "nonstandards" (meters you're usually not required to play). That way you won't get caught when a teacher suddenly asks for one from out of nowhere. (If you do get caught unprepared in this situation, improvise something!) The nonstandard section might even be the same in each binder, since its contents probably won't suffer from overexposure.

By form

When my career took a different turn and I found myself staying pretty much in one place for class, I decided to reorganize my material into binders by form. My repertoire in binders now consists of two thick waltz binders; a relatively skinny binder that has only long (128 bars and over) waltzes; a 2/4 binder; a binder of Czerny études, tarantellas, and miscellaneous non-adagio 3/4s; a binder of slow 2/4s, "ands," and marches of all meters; a binder of rags; an adagio binder; a stretching-music binder; plus two other "complete class" binders, should I ever need them (one of these is the first one I ever put together, the grubby black binder, which I can't bear to disrupt).

I also have three "touring binders." When I came to Europe and began working with companies that tour a great deal, it was hardly practical to carry around all those binders, so I photocopied only the pieces I hadn't yet memorized, put them into two spiral binders for easy page turning, and reduced the weight of my luggage considerably.

If you decide on the "by form" approach, the most efficient way is to organize the pieces by tempo within each meter: slow waltzes first, then medium, then fast, then big (also by tempo). If you want to be super-organized, you can put pieces of similar quality on adjoining pages so that, if you get caught unexpectedly with a long combination, you can change the music without frantically turning pages. Better yet: Improvise a second piece when the first one wears thin, thereby freeing your eyes to respond more readily to the dancers.

By composer

Organizing by composer seems to be the least efficient, since you will choose a piece for its meter or tempo (or both) much more often than for its style. Also, as your repertoire increases in size, it will become correspondingly more difficult to remember who wrote each piece of music. (One of my editors suggested omitting this "by composer" discussion, since it isn't a recommended method. I mention it so that novice accompanists who are just beginning to set up their repertoires in an organized fashion can be aware of its pitfalls.)

~

If you have already organized your repertoire in a fashion unrelated to any of the foregoing, you will probably have discovered that somehow, miraculously, you can adjust to any crazy system you set up for putting the material together. I was incredibly fortunate to receive copies of the repertoire Mme. Zolotova brought with her to Banff, and I immediately put them all into one binder—waltzes, marches, tarantellas, adagios, you name it. It was totally disorganized to anyone but myself (my internal computer recognized it as "the Banff binder"), and it gradually took on its own character and organization; I somehow knew where each piece was. But I do not recommend this; it is not a workable, efficient method for a beginner who has too many other new situations to cope with.

In your head

Whether you improvise or use written music—memorized or not—you will gradually develop categories in your internal computer. These categories will be organized mostly by form and by step, and will be accessed according to how you "read" the teacher's movement—how you perceive the teacher's demonstration. For instance, if I see a typical rond de jambe combination, I access my "rdjàt" category, which used to be exclusively slow, smooth waltzes, but now also includes moderato twos and some tangos. When I see a petit allegro combination, and the teacher says she is not sure whether she wants a two or a three, I access my "petit allegro" category (which includes 2/4s, 3/4s, and 6/8s),[10] and sing along in my head all the possibilities while she is demonstrating. In this instance, it is *essential* for the students to mark the combination through with music before actually beginning; a teacher's hand marking combined with an accompanist's head marking can produce chaos.

Head marking—humming the melody in your head as the teacher demonstrates—is especially helpful when choosing music for combinations whose tempos can be problematic or misread during a demonstration. For instance, I always hum in my head during fondu and adagio demonstrations.

"Reading" the teacher effectively is our most important stock in trade (this assumes, of course, that she is "speaking" effectively with her body), and will be the prime motivator for calling up the appropriate music for each combination from all the billions of musical notes floating around in our brains. When an unusual request comes along, different approaches are called for.

Two examples:

- Teacher: "I'd like a six, please." Me (to myself): That's the "pol-bo-min" category (polonaises, boleros, allegro 9/8s, and some minuets). To the teacher: "What quality: grand, light and bouncy, or delicate?"
- Teacher: "I'd like something like this: DAH - dah dah DAH - dah dah DAH. . . ." Me: "Oh, that's the rhythm of" and I play example 68 from *Carmen*—"but is that the quality you wanted?" (Advanced accompanists have a pretty good idea of the quality of each combination just by where it is given in class; inexperienced accompanists don't know this yet.)

The second example illustrates the "no-category" way of organizing music in your head. Its success depends (a) on the teacher articulating vocally what she wants in such a way that it reminds you of a piece with the identical melodic rhythm; and/or (b) on your ability to impose vocalizations on the accents of her movements and translate them into music.

An accompanist gradually becomes aware of the patterns in ballet classes, and of why certain musical forms absolutely do not fit certain steps (marches aren't used for ronds de jambe à terre, for example), and learns to mentally organize his musical needs accordingly.

And the reverse is true: One of the two most important things that experienced accompanists have developed is knowing all the different possible forms that work for teachers' demonstrations. For instance, most teachers count at least one tendu combination so that it sounds like a march. We experienced accompanists have learned that tangos work, too, as well as some American popular songs, and a host of unnameable twos, as well as—if the teacher has no objection—medium-tempo waltzes, some Spanish waltzes, 6/8s, and so on. In other words, give us experienced accompanists free rein, and not only will we prevent classes from being musically boring but we will ensure that the students get to dance the same old steps to just about every form of music possible, thereby broadening their kinesthetic understanding of movement.

Adaptation of music

Throughout this book you will find references to adhering to the composer's intent. The main reasons for this are respect for the composer, the maintenance of stylistic authenticity, and your own personal musical growth. However, rule number one in a dance class is to provide music that helps dancers. So there are instances when you must alter what the composer has written to make it suitable for the needs of dancers. I am now discussing *altering* what appears on the printed page, not *augmenting* it. As you become more experienced, you will probably find yourself augmenting many pieces with octaves (which will be discussed starting on page 163).

It is almost impossible to be a musical purist in the field of dance accompaniment. The following anecdote may be of some help in understanding the need to "add a little something here and there"—in this particular case, to emphasize the preparatory steps in a grand allegro.

When I first started working with the Royal Winnipeg Ballet, Arnold Spohr—the artistic director, who also holds a degree in music—said, "Harriet, your waltzes sound like a band in a beer parlor." To add further to my embarrassment, Neal Kayan—the conductor and a very fine pianist—came down to the studio one day and said, "Harriet, just play what the composer wrote; you don't need to add all that stuff." David Moroni—principal of the Professional Programme, not a musician, and one of the most exquisitely musical dancers I've ever seen—overheard Mr. Kayan's remark and said, "Harriet, you know, 'all that stuff' is what gets me off the ground."

How often—and *how*—you alter pieces of music is completely up to you (although you will certainly get input from the teachers you play for). Because of stylistic ignorance and lack of understanding of the importance of each piece's inherent tempo, I butchered a great deal of music for the first eight years or so of my career. I had no one to turn to who was articulate in both musical and dance terms. It gradually dawned on me that this butchering was neither beneficial to the dancers nor musically satisfying for me—nor necessary. I realized that, if I had to distort the nature of a piece to suit the dancers' needs, it would make more sense to find a piece whose inherent tempo and personality fitted what was needed. This thinking occurred when I realized that there is a vast amount of music in an almost endless variety of styles that is adaptable for dance, not just the few books that beginning accompanists seem to start out with.

A specific example might be helpful here. Mr. Brunson's fourth barre combination was always some form of dégagé with demi-plié in a triple meter at a slow tempo. Since he emphasized the sharpness going out in the dégagé, I knew I couldn't play (or mutilate) an adagio 3/4, and a polonaise—which had the correct median tempo—was too grand. I thought my only recourse was to butcher mazurkas and waltzes; I slowed them down to one mousepower, and they were ghastly to listen to if one was familiar with how the composer wrote them. Madame Volkova's penchant for boleros (I had never played one in class—or even heard of that possibility—until I met her), combined with the dissatisfaction of excruciating musical distortion led me to rethink this problem and to examine boleros more closely. While the pieces in my bolero category are bouncy and light, some of them can be adapted for this particular combination, which needs sharpness on the odd-numbered measures and a melting quality (produced by the pedal) on the even-numbered ones, such as the Gypsy Song from *Carmen.* I also went back through all my rejects and found a number of unnameable pieces written in 3/4, mostly from operas, that are eminently suitable, such as example 29.

If you find altering music a loathsome practice, you may change your mind if you get to know dance and dancers a little better, thereby gaining insight into why it is occasionally necessary.

Mechanical phrasing

Neither mechanical phrasing nor kinesthetic phrasing has anything to do with the composer's phrasing. I certainly do not encourage musicians to ignore the inherent phrasing of any piece of music; it is almost always perfectly compatible with the needs of dance. It is mentioned so seldom in this book because either it is obvious through the melodic lines of a piece, or the composer has written the phrasing bows in.

Mechanical is a word almost as odious in the dance world as *exercise,* but it is necessary to define certain constants in the elements of music, technique, and execution. For example, one of the mechanics of octave work is using the fourth finger on black notes; the mechanics of a coda rhythm are shown in example 6, among others.

Eight-, 16-, and 32-count phrases are generally the mechanics involved in the teaching of dance. Why? If someone has the definitive answer, I hope she or he will let us all in on it. One factor in particular seems to have made some contribution toward the perpetuation of this mechanic. The technique (mechanics) of any art form is acquired through repetition. In dance, phrases of movement—and eventually whole dances—become ingrained in the muscles of the body, exactly as scales and arpeggios—and eventually whole pieces—become ingrained in a pianist's fingers. Music notation has been in a state of evolution for centuries, but dance still has no universally understood system of notation, and has had to rely primarily on transmission by word of mouth down through the generations. Notation systems, such as Labanotation and the Benesh System, are being used more and more frequently, but in a random sampling of a few hundred dancers, there is probably not more than one who can use either of these systems effectively.

Music for dance has also been transmitted by word of mouth—so to speak—with the musical phrase lengths being handed down with certain movement phrases. The technique of classical ballet began with the court dances of the sixteenth century. Dances such as the minuet and gavotte had specific structural forms, and each maintained its own special set(s) of phrases. As classical technique grew in complexity, it may have been expedient to retain the familiar phrasing of the court dances, which were almost invariably in multiples of four.

Whatever the reason, 8-, 16-, and 32-count phrases are the traditional vehicles in which dance movement travels. We have inherited this structure, it is here to stay, and trying to change it will probably meet with as much success as the left-handed piano. So we shall explore the most creative and efficient ways to function within these parameters.

An important term for every beginning accompanist to learn is *en croix*. It literally means "in a cross," but for accompanists, it means "multiply by four."

When a teacher asks her students to execute one tendu en croix, they will do one tendu to the front, one to the side, one to the back, and the last one to the side again. (Obviously, the human body doesn't permit movement to be accomplished in the shape of a true cross with one leg.)

Teachers are arbitrary in their use of en croix (and some never use it at all). Sometimes a teacher will use a time-saving shortcut when demonstrating a combination. She will show leg movements in one direction (front, for example) and then say, "Do this en croix." This means that the same movements are to be repeated to the side, to the back, and to the side again. The accompanist must therefore multiply the number of counts the teacher has demonstrated by four.

Another tendu pattern that could be executed en croix is: tendu, coupé, tendu, close ("1–4"); tendu, close ("5–6"); two fast tendus ("and 7 and 8"). This would need thirty-two counts, as you would multiply the movement phrase of eight counts by four. This pattern has been included here because it is less obvious to the beginning accompanist than a pattern of consecutive tendus.

You must keep your ears open for the phrase *en croix* so that you will have some idea of how many phrases to play.

The following barre steps can generally be done en croix: tendus, the dégagé family, frappés, fondus, and grands battements. Also some adagio movements can be executed en croix, such as développés. Pliés, ronds de jambe in any form, and petits battements cannot be done en croix.

~

Now we will deal with the basic mechanics of "squaring off" music into packages of eights, sixteens, and thirty-twos, if the composer has not already done so.

The first question you have to answer for yourself is whether you think it is ethical to cut four bars, for instance, of a waltz in order to square it off into a workable 16-bar phrase. Stylistic awareness and good taste are of the utmost importance in this area. I personally find it heretical to cut the music of the great classical masters, such as Bach, Beethoven, and Brahms. Consequently, my repertoire doesn't have as large a selection of these composers as I would like. You may feel differently.

Example 73 is a beautiful waltz in maxi-phrases of twenty-four measures, and it is so lovely in its original version that I feel it's not worth cutting. Besides, adding an extra eight to a normal 16-count phrase is not a problem for most dance teachers. Advise them ahead of time, though, of its unique characteristic.

Adagios pose a special problem, as usual. Really good ones are hard to find, and if cutting music is a crime, the area of adagios is the one in which I'm the guiltiest. Example 74 is representative of a full-blown cut-and-paste job. With the exception of one transitional chord that I felt was necessary, the essence of the composer's intent is maintained. Why, asks the purist, did you cut it all? I have discussed the limits of physical endurance as it applies to dance, and the piece in its uncut state is too long for a student in the classroom to sustain his energy constructively. Then why, asks the unconvinced, didn't you leave it alone, like you leave the Goldberg Variations alone? Because, even in its abbreviated version, moving to it is such a valuable emotional, physical, and educational experience that I felt it was worth it. And I absolutely love the piece. Again, you may feel differently.

You will notice that even the cut version is not in convenient eights or sixteens; really sensational adagios rarely are. The teacher must understand its phrase construction before she choreographs a combination to it, so you must either play it for her several times, or make a tape of it so she can take it home and live with it for a while.

Example 75 is the musical format of Mr. Brunson's rond de jambe à terre combination in every class he taught.[11] (The choreography included in the rond de jambe section—the first thirty-two counts—is typical of what he would normally give; the tempo was always this slow, even in company classes; and the rest of the choreography—the last thirty-two counts—never varied.) The piece as a whole has three different tempos and three very different moods. Composers rarely write music that is instantly adaptable to classroom combinations of this kind, so cutting and pasting is the only solution.

The waltz in a minor from Khachaturian's *Masquerade* is made up of phrases of various lengths, all of which are divisible by four. Rather than cutting and pasting it into 8-count phrases, I save it for 4-count movement phrases across the floor, such as this simple one: tombé pas de bourrée, glissade pas de chat.

If squaring off doesn't come easily to you, you may want to mark or cut and paste each piece according to your needs, so you won't have any guesswork in class. The effect you want to work toward is producing phrases of whatever necessary length that have definite beginnings and endings, but that also progress smoothly, seamlessly, organically, and—above all—musically.

Kinesthetic phrasing and accents

Kinesthetic phrasing involves being able to see phrases of movement and to match them with complementary music. This process is developed through learning to read movement in much the same way that you read a book.

Movement has punctuation, just like language. (Actually, movement *is* a form of language, as is music.) There are commas at the end of short phrases (for instance), semicolons at the end of longer phrases, periods at the end of combinations, and I see new paragraphs, dashes, or exclamation points in some movement. In the words of Gretchen Ward Warren, one of my editors, "I always tell students that their combinations of movement should be conversational, not a monotone."

Movement is not limited to these punctuation marks. To make movement a vital, living, human experience, one has to take it beyond the "written word" stage and add dynamics, shading, nuances, and breath. This occurs in the same way that you would read a section of a book out loud: pausing at the commas, pausing a bit longer at the semicolons, pausing even longer and changing vocal inflection at the periods, raising your voice at the exciting parts, and so forth. The pauses we would naturally make during reading rarely translate into pauses—interruptions of the regular pulse—as we produce music for dancers; they translate into breathing with the pedal (especially during legato music) and dynamic shading.

The best ways to develop kinesthetic awareness are by watching people dance, by observing great teachers teach, and by dancing yourself. Firsthand experience, of course, is always the best, so by taking class, you will feel in your body what you are trying to re-create musically. Feel where the movement phrases start and finish, being aware of the lift and extra energy you feel if the accompanist crescendos into a phrase for a port de bras, providing new impetus. Since breathing produces not only physical benefits but also well-turned phrases, take advantage of the silences (rests) in music. Tune in to your aural, physical, and emotional responses to the music, and carry those reactions over into your own approach at the piano. Taking five classes in one week would be more beneficial to you than one class per week for five weeks; you will feel the daily muscular progress and mental adjustment after five classes in a row more than you would with a week in between classes. (Learning to dance in some ways is like learning how to play the piano. How much progress would you make at the piano if you practiced once a week?)

If you decide to continue studying ballet, and you work at it, you can probably reach an intermediate level of technique. You may never experience certain aspects of dance, such as grand allegro, multiple pirouettes, and complex batterie/petit allegro, but your observational powers and your expanded kinesthetic awareness will take over where your body leaves off.

If taking class is not for you, watch as many classes as you can. Without the pressure of having to produce music for the class, you can start to make sense of this seemingly foreign language. You will start to become familiar with the steps through their constant repetition, which is how dance is and must be taught. You will recognize that dance combinations are not monochromatic, although their subtleties are hard for an untrained observer to discern. (You already know that a 16-count phrase of music is not monochromatic; it is not just a bunch of notes played with no change of tone or dynamic level.) Even the most basic combination of four tendus en croix has inflections, and if the beginning dance student is so absorbed in the execution that he misses these inflections, it is up to you to remind him with the music.

~

The following two 8-count maxi-phrases are both very suitable selections for ronds de jambe; they have the necessary qualities of a naturally slow tempo and a legato feeling. But their phrasing is different. (To fully understand this discussion, you may have to elicit the aid of someone with a bit of basic ballet technique to demonstrate the combinations as you play.)

Example A is composed of two mini-phrases of two counts each and one mini-phrase of four counts, and the combination included with it has exactly the same phrasing:

Example B is composed of two mini-phrases of four bars each, and the combination included with it has exactly the same phrasing:

Musical example A played for combination B would certainly not be wrong; the basic qualities are there. But when the movement phrases are supported with similar musical phrases, the marriage of music and dance is definitely enhanced.

As has been said before, beginning accompanists will be doing quite well to properly judge the meter and tempo at first. An awareness of the ultimate approach, however, will remind you to include phrasing in the decision-making process as soon as you are able.

Here is another example of kinesthetic phrasing. Within a standard 8-count phrase of petit allegro, teachers will almost invariably subdivide this phrase by two, as shown in example 5. However, a creative teacher could ask for something like this: glissade jeté assemblé, glissade jeté assemblé, entrechat quatre, changement. This subdivides the eight counts into three, three, and two. You have three choices:

- play the standard "divide-by-two" phrase, which works—you and the dancers come out together on count 8—but does not reflect or enhance the movement phrase;
- improvise a piece with complementary phrasing; or
- use a perfect polka by Bartók, example 76.

Much of a fine accompanist's claim to fame are his powers of observation and his sensitivity to dance: *seeing* the little running steps that are the preparation for a huge jump and choosing (or improvising or augmenting) music that has that figure in it; *listening* to the teacher's voice for clues as to the quality of any given combination; *knowing* that, while the last step of a combination may be technically easy, the physical demands of everything that has preceded it precludes ease of execution, so your own energy must never slacken; *sensing* when the class atmosphere is in need of a boost and surprising everyone with a new piece; and *breathing* with your lungs and with the pedal at the ends of phrases.

One of the fine(st) points in phrasing is your awareness of certain steps that would be more exciting or fulfilling if held a shade longer than the already-established tempo.

In adagio combinations, dancers sometimes behave more like acrobats than dancers: "I'm going to get my leg up in arabesque today even if I'm behind the music." I tend to ritard more than usual in adagios only if I see the dancers striving toward expressing something other than an acrobatic feat—and then only if I sense that the teacher is amenable to it. (Dancers can always practice the calisthenic aspect of an arabesque—or more pirouettes than the teacher called for, or a grand allegro slower than the tempo the teacher set—in the back of the room while another group is dancing. When they are dancing to music, their movements should be measured by, respectful of, and related to what they are hearing—or we accompanists might as well go home.)

In other combinations, it is a passé (with or without a pirouette attached) or a fast développé en avant that asks for a little breath or hold, emphasizing the "up-ness" of the movement, before the leg is lowered. Musicians often call this effect suspension.

Again, these ritards, breaths, and holds are executed within the bounds of good taste, as well as with the teacher's agreement. The breaths and holds are rarely long enough to be called fermatas. They emphasize the corresponding step, and give an added and contrasting dimension to the dynamics of the movement.

Something an accompanist should always ask himself during his execution of classroom music is: Would a conductor be able to produce the same music with sixty musicians? It doesn't make sense for us to play music in the classroom that bears no resemblance to the music with which the dancers will dance onstage. Only a sensitive, experienced conductor would be able to get sixty musicians to breathe in unison for the same amount of time that these breaths require. However, in the hands of an experienced accompanist, these breaths are invaluable aids in making dancers aware of shading and dynamics in their movements.

~

As your kinesthetic awareness develops, and as the dance vocabulary becomes more visually familiar to you, you will become aware not only of the "normal" accents within each step (for instance, the "out" of a frappé is almost always more accented—*not* more important—than the "in"), but also of where accents occur in unexpected places in the course of a combination. Musicians, of course, refer to this as syncopation. As your responsiveness to these accents sharpens, you may start wanting to do something with them musically, to more fully complement the movement. You can improvise corresponding accents into a piece you are playing; you may gradually get to the point where your repertoire is large enough so that a pattern of unusual accents in the movement triggers a specific melody in your internal computer; and you can emphasize these accents with reverse pedaling (discussed beginning on page 169).

Accents occur in every type of movement, from the most sustained adagio to the most soaring grand allegro. For instance, dancers are often self-indulgent in their execution of arabesques piquées on—let's say—the ninth count of an adagio. Since "9" is the beginning of a new 8-count phrase, it is prominent, anyway, but you can help remind them that they have to be in a definite position on this "9" by making a tasteful but pointed crescendo during "8," leading so obviously to "9" that they will have to be either deaf or totally self-involved not to go with you. (Naturally, you won't want to impose a triple forte chord into a quiet adagio to emphasize a particular movement; as always, good taste should prevail.)

The same device is applicable in grand allegro. The first step after the introduction in the male variation of the pas de deux from *Le Corsaire* is often an attitude piquée. Even though most male variations are at the dynamic level of at least forte, a crescendo leading to that "1" is not only the most musical way to play it, but also the most helpful to the dancer.

The previous two examples involve accenting notes that are already within the music. The following discussion deals with movement accents that aren't written into a piece of music.

A very popular petit battement serré combination is mirrored in the melody of example 77. (Although Johann Strauss, Jr., called this a polka, it is firmly entrenched in my coda category; it just feels like a coda, probably because the left-hand structure is what I think of as a coda.) The rhythm of one foot beating against the other ankle is identical to the melodic rhythm of the first four counts. This is a perfect melodic complement to the combination, despite the fact that the melodic rhythm changes in some of the ensuing phrases. You will probably not want to play the same piece every time the combination is given (a dancer I know once remarked, "One can even get bored with perfection"), so you can accent another light coda, as in example 78.

Or—because I find my improvisations totally boring—I might play the same piece, humming it in my head so I don't lose track of the melody, but playing only those notes where movement occurs (a variation on stop time), as in example 78a.

Awareness of and response to movement accents often make the difference between an acceptable accompanist and a really good one. If you are just beginning, it will be all you can do to get the right meter and tempo for each combination. Incorporating the combination's accents—especially ones that seem to run counter to the flow of your musical selection—will probably be one of the last facets of effective accompaniment that will become a habit. As with many other concepts in this book, it helps to keep in mind what you are working toward.

~

I have learned more about phrasing music from a very few dancers and dance teachers than I ever did from any of my piano teachers. It is certainly possible that I was too young and inexperienced to understand what the piano teachers were talking about. But I think there is another reason. Those few dance teachers and dancers had or have very special ways of moving. They are not just precisely rhythmical; their personal ways of moving (literally) incorporate the music: They make it visible, producing graphically the essence of the music's message, and re-creating it so clearly that one can't help but respond to the logic and beauty of it. The voices of a few teachers also taught me how to phrase, talking the students and me through combinations—especially adagios—and making us aware of high points, of places to "rest," and of the all-important breathing. People who move and speak like this don't come along all that often. If you always keep your eyes glued to the music, you may miss one of life's special treats.

Important musical additions

These are difficult areas for beginning accompanists because they mainly involve music that is added onto or into classroom combinations, but that is not on the printed page.

Starts (preparations, introductions, "four-for-nothings," "four ins," lead-ins, vamps, and who knows what else)

In every style of dance class, the word you will hear most often is "and." When a teacher counts a waltz, she will rarely count, "ONE - - two - - THREE - - four - - . . . ." She will more than likely say a variation on this theme: "ONE - and two and uh THREE - and four and uh. . . ."

The most noteworthy use of the word "and," however, comes before each combination begins. It requires precise timing to get a whole classroom of bodies moving at the right tempo on the first beat of a combination, so the teacher usually expects the accompanist to help her out. She will usually say "and" when she wants the preparation to start, and her personal preference dictates how the accompanist matches her preparatory demands.

I strongly recommend 4- or 6-count preparations. (There are a few forms and meters for which 2-bar ("2-count") preparations are acceptable. They will be discussed also.) They are by far the most clear; they provide the students with a 4- or 6-count mini-phrase in the meter, tempo, and quality of each piece to which they will dance—and they will often not have heard these pieces before they start dancing. They tell a dancer when to begin moving much more clearly than other preparations. And they provide a bit of time for the students to think about placement and corrections.

As you have probably noticed, it is very difficult for dance teachers with a minimal understanding of music theory to grasp the difference between a measure and a count. (See the first paragraph of the four-count preparations section below for a description of this confusion.) If I could be sure that the two terms would be understood correctly, I would, of course, use them. But because of my observation of inexperienced dance teachers dealing with inexperienced accompanists, I am convinced that it makes the most sense to use the word *count* exclusively. It cannot be misinterpreted. Experienced accompanists eventually learn to translate teachers' confusing information into musically comprehensible data. The aim of this book is to try to establish a common language between teachers and accompanists, so that inexperienced accompanists will have to translate only French words, not confusing directions.

I have also included every other kind of introduction that teachers have requested over the years.

Two-bar or six-count preparations

Teachers often request 2-bar preparations before sarabandes, polonaises, polaccas, boleros, minuets, all 9/8s, and 4/4 and 12/8 adagios. They do this because the phrases of all these forms are very long, and it saves time to halve the introduction. But if a teacher does not expressly ask for a 2-bar preparation before one of these pieces, I always play a 4-bar preparation (sometimes slightly sped up, but definitely at the required tempo by the fourth bar of the introduction) because I feel it sets the mood better, and it is much clearer than a 2-bar preparation, especially if the dancers haven't heard the music before they start moving.

Six-count introductions are the same as 2-bar introductions before all of the above-named forms except, of course, for 4/4 and 12/8 adagios.

Four-count preparations

When a teacher requests a preparation before a waltz, she expects four bars. But when she wants a preparation before a 4/4 or a 6/8, she wants two bars. She could even say, "I would like a 4-bar preparation, please," but she probably knows as much about meter as you do about turn-out. *What she wants is a 4-count preparation.*

You can produce a 4-count preparation by playing the last four counts of the piece you are going to play. The only drawback to this is the fact that the piece almost always ends on the tonic, so it will sound like an ending, instead of having a preparatory, anticipatory nature. You can counteract this by converting the harmonic nature of the last bar into dominant seventh (V7), but this sometimes sounds clumsy. The last four bars of example 79 fortunately lend themselves very well to this kind of preparation; a banal 4-count introduction for this quiet, slightly mysterious piece would be totally out of character.

The most basic waltz preparation, but least suggestive of the musical quality that follows, is:

My "old reliable" waltz preparation includes a harmonic progression that is clearly leading toward the "1," as in example 65, among others.

If you subtract the second beat of each bar in the above preparations, you have suitable preparations for non-adagio, non-coda, medium-tempo 2/4s and 4/4s.

There is a funny kind of 2/4 that hasn't got a convenient name (such as coda or polka); it is labeled "one of those" in the 2/4 section of my mental computer. Its tempo is very quick, but it doesn't have what I call the "doubled-up" driving rhythm in the left hand of a coda. I find it very difficult to improvise a satisfactory 8-count preparation, and four counts of this piece go by too quickly for the dancers to be really ready. So I play a short fermata of a single note, then play the 4-count introduction in tempo. That single note is such a departure from what I normally play that the dancers always sense that something unusual is coming up. More advanced accompanists will recognize this kind of 2/4 as being suitable for quick, light jumps à la Bournonville across the floor, and for ultra-fast dégagé combinations that often include piqués/pointés.

If you are a beginning accompanist, you may find yourself playing for a teacher who—just before a combination begins—counts, "five . . . six . . . seven . . . eight" without saying anything to you. Most teachers prefer music, but they may feel you aren't quite ready yet to play the preparation. When you are more comfortable with the proceedings, you can start playing as the teacher counts, even waiting until "seven . . . eight" to come in. Or practice this together outside of class time. Be sure and let the teacher know when you feel you are ready to take over the reins completely in this area.

Some teachers want their students to do barre combinations without stopping between sides, and may ask for four (or six) counts in which to turn around. I play an "old reliable" preparation, so there is no chance of their mistaking it for the first four (or six) counts of the actual combination.

~

Examples for all the above preparations will be found with their corresponding musical examples at the end of this book. They all contain harmonic progressions that clearly lead to "1." This is especially important if the teacher is not clear that she wants either a 2-bar or a 6-count preparation. Dancers are so used to starting after four counts that they do it automatically unless they hear something that tells them to perk up their ears.

Two chords

If the 2-chord preparation is used, it is usually because teachers feel it saves time—and occasionally because teachers are not familiar with 4-count preparations. (I remember how pleased Mr. Brunson was when I introduced him to 4-count preparations which I had learned at another school; he recognized their efficiency immediately.)

Music in and for dance evokes and demands action, and chord preparations are generally coordinated with the action of the arms before the legs begin moving. So it is important to know exactly which chords you are going to play, so that you can execute them as you watch the teacher demonstrate them. The sticky part is that there is still an "and" just before the actual combination begins, and this requires even more awareness. There is absolutely no way to verbalize the timing, but know that you can learn to do it very quickly by matching the teacher's movements and vocal commands. Since this "and" is not always visible in the movement, you must listen more than you watch, in this instance, until you realize that it is mostly a matter of tempo.

If the teacher gives a combination in which the first leg movement is executed on this "and" (as in many tendu, dégagé, and grand battement combinations), you must listen *and* watch very closely. The "ands" in this case will always receive more stress than a normal "and." In this situation, a 4- or 6-count introduction is definitely recommended.

My chord preparations are always two dominant-seventh (V7) chords (which emphasize the anticipatory nature) in contrary motion and slightly arpeggiated (to help counteract any wooden arm movements). They are followed by the "and": a single note or octave (usually the dominant) in the register of the melody I am going to play.

A 2-chord preparation (actually, *every* preparation) should reflect as much as possible the quality of the combination it precedes. Two rousing, martial chords don't make sense for a développé combination, nor do two lyrical, mezzo piano chords for grands battements.

Without preparation

Preparations are often dispensed with when the students are facing the barre with both hands on it, thereby eliminating the need for music to match the preparatory arm movements. In elementary classes, students will be facing the barre much of the time. It seems to me that they should prepare with arm movements and the corresponding music to get them used to that practice, as well as to help them understand one of the basic principles behind it in the first place: Arms are just as important as legs in dance, in terms of both placement and aesthetics—a concept often ignored nowadays with the current emphasis on legs and feet.

In more advanced classes, however, it becomes appropriate to get students used to occasionally starting without the aid of a preparation, as they may be called upon to do when performing onstage. The waltz Finale of *Nutcracker,* for instance, can be a nightmare for the first-year corps dancer who has never worked with a conductor. There is no introduction; the melody starts immediately at double forte; and the dancer must read the conductor's arm movements as accurately as you will learn to read the body language of teachers and dancers.

Teachers often dispense with a preparation before a révérence, preferring instead a protracted "a-a-a-and," during which you play a single dominant note and start the piece when she begins her count "1."

Another common stage device is a simple step in silence as a cue to begin moving. Inexperienced dancers and accompanists don't realize that there is a comfortable margin of time between the initiation of the step and when the foot actually makes contact with the floor. The dancer(s) must initiate the step as a cue for the accompanist, and this takes practice. Mr. Brunson used to make his more advanced classes start many adagios in this way. The dancers in each group would walk to their places in silence, stop, then use the common stage rule of "guide right" (the last person on the right side of the line starts the action) to let the accompanist know when to begin.

Transitions (also known as bridges)

Sometimes you will want to connect two different pieces of music. These situations are normally the following:

- I don't like to deaden the ears of the dancers by playing the same sixteen measures in the same key for each position of pliés. So most of my plié music is two different pieces—for example, the Quartet (in F major) from

Rigoletto for first and second positions, and the Sextet (in D-flat major) from *Lucia di Lammermoor* for fourth and fifth positions.

- Sometimes a teacher will specifically request a change of music—for example, thirty-two counts of light, quick music for petits battements at the barre, followed by eight counts of a broad waltz to balance by.

- Many combinations in the center go diagonally across the floor—for example, chassé and polka combinations in less advanced classes; and pirouettes, some petit and medium allegro, and most grand allegro combinations in more advanced classes. All these combinations can last as long as six minutes without a break. The longest I ever play the same thirty-two measures of music is three times; after that a change of melody *and* key is a must.

- Sometimes a women's grand allegro combination will be set to a waltz and the men's to a two. This requires a 4-count introduction between the two pieces, to signal the change of meter, tempo, and—often—key.

Connecting two pieces is easy, of course, when the pieces are in the same meter and key. But if the keys are not closely related, you have a number of theoretical approaches to use in order to accomplish a seamless transition. The easiest is the use of the common tone: finding a tone in the tonic of Piece One that is common to the dominant of Piece Two and building your transition on that tone. This process is shown in bars 71–72 of example 65.

If the two keys are very distant relatives, you can use leading tones to arrive at a common tone. Leading tones are notes you insert in both the melody and the rhythm of Piece One that take the music where you want it to go in a harmonically pleasing way. An additional challenge occurs when you need to make a bridge between pieces of different meters. The key to success in this case is finishing the rhythm of Piece One completely. The first few times you do it, you may slough through and rush the last bars of Piece One because you are nervous, but work toward maintaining a steady rhythm. Practicing these transitions alone outside of the pressures of the classroom will reap rich rewards. Example 72 shows a solution to both of these occurrences.

Something requiring a kind of transition is a piece—a rousing coda, for instance—that has an exceptionally "final-sounding" end, but you want to repeat it. To prevent anyone from thinking the end of the combination is coming up, I add a full descending scale of octaves in the left hand starting on "7," adding some dominant notes in the melody at the appropriate time.

It should be stressed again that you need not be formally schooled in theory (although it is certainly helpful) in order to be able to do these things. If you have been playing the piano for a reasonable length of time, you probably have been practicing many of these principles already, and you can re-create them according to your own needs as long as you know what to look for and how to approach each situation. You probably have pieces in your own repertoire that go from one key to another. Figure out how it has been done in something you are familiar with, and apply that to other situations. Again, your ear, stylistic awareness, and taste will tell you whether you are within the bounds of good musicianship.

Balances

Music to balance by is very helpful for dancers. Balancing almost always comes at the end of a combination, when a dancer has already expended a considerable amount of energy. Music will help spur him on when he feels he has run out of steam.

A teacher may ask for a 4-count phrase to balance by at the end of a combination. I always found it difficult to tack on an extra four counts that sounded like a continuation of the piece, so I "composed" the following harmonic progression that produces a harmonically satisfying solution. It is my standard transition into a short balance.

If she asks for an 8-count balance, you can repeat the last eight bars you played, preferably with a different left hand or a different flavor.

If I am given no information as to how long the balance should be, I always continue the piece I'm playing, and inject it with an extra measure of energy and volume until the very last note. If necessary, so the balance isn't illogically long, I speed up, which contributes a sense of urgency to the balance, and counteracts the heaviness that is often produced by playing the final section of a piece more loudly and more slowly. As you become more experienced, you will sense the median proportion of time that is beneficial for a particular balance if the teacher hasn't requested a certain number of counts. You may sense that a 16-count phrase is too long, an 8-count phrase is too short, and twelve counts offends your sensibilities. So you might play eight counts with a ritard beginning on "5." Again, aim toward increasing the dynamic level—and try to make the melodic line ascend the keyboard—to the very end. This should help unmusical dancers—and forces musical dancers—to keep growing in the balance.

Beginning accompanists should not be expected to cope with deciding how long a balance should be in addition to everything else they have to deal with. So if the teacher has not been specific about how long a balance should be, by all means ask.

(See also the comments on fermatas beginning on page 191.)

Finishes

If movement occurs in any part of the body after the music finishes, it will be the teacher's preference that dictates your reaction. It is usually the arms that are not in a finishing position when the last musical phrase is completed, although a leg is occasionally left hanging in space at that time.

Teachers may not request "music to finish by" because they think either it is superfluous, or that accompanists can't do it, or even that it has never occurred to them because it is so rarely heard. But, as has been said before, music for dance reflects action, and music to finish by makes a dancer feel that these "after-the-fact" movements are as much a part of the combination as the combination itself, which indeed they are. These movements are also a necessary adjunct to discipline; a dancer should never finish a movement sloppily or with random timing, since he will seldom, if ever, do so in a classical piece onstage. Much of the audience remembers only the last movement they saw, anyway, so it has to be worth remembering.

The most frequent device used for music to finish by is the standard dominant-to-tonic cadence, which my former recording partner, Roni Mahler, and I refer to as amens, since they sound like the finish of most hymns in church. This cadence is played in a feeling of diminuendo, with the two chords matching the tempo of the teacher's movements or commands or—if she leaves the timing up to you—the tempo of the class's movements. (Dancers gradually acquire a collective sense of timing in these areas—a feeling of working together as a single unit.)

The following example is representative of standard music to finish by in the key of C. Half notes have been used because, while there is no set tempo, the amen approaches the feeling of half notes, rather than quarter notes. The 8th-note C is included to make the harmonic progression smoother.

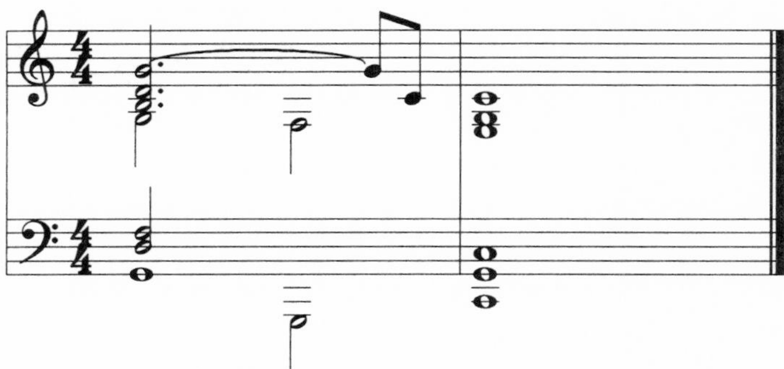

Professional dancers don't always react to amens with the same discipline as students, but I always play them in company class at the appropriate time just to remind them to finish cleanly in their own time.

There are some three-part steps in dance (balancés and pas de basque are two) that use all three beats of a three or six. This does not pose a problem unless a combination finishes with one of these steps. Waltzes almost always finish on the first beat of the last bar. They occasionally finish on the second beat, and rarely on the third. So it is advisable to improvise any missing beats in order to support the dancers' movements. This is especially helpful when a strenuous combination is being executed. It frustrates a dancer to have the musical impetus drop out from under him when he has reached one of the most difficult parts of the combination.

If you accidentally finish a piece and the dancers are still dancing, you can pick it up again. The rhythm usually goes on in your head for a few seconds, the students are still pretty much together, and the teacher is probably counting like mad, expecting you to rejoin the action, so jump in.

As I have said before, when you are finishing any piece of music in the classroom, try to remember that the physical energy and intensity build to the very end of each piece, regardless of the dynamic markings on the printed page.

Arpeggiation

The tempo of an adagio will help you decide on the most suitable rhythmic structure for maintaining smoothness. Learning to calculate the correct tempo should be cultivated as soon as possible. If you play for a teacher who always demonstrates in the proper tempo, you are fortunate indeed. Most teachers demonstrate adagios more quickly than they will want, and 98 percent of the world's dance teachers demonstrate adagios counting in three, which would theoretically prevent us from playing the abundance of wonderful adagios in 4/4, 9/8, and 12/8. This problem will be discussed starting on page 194.

Every accompanist misjudges an adagio tempo at one time or another (sometimes with depressing regularity, and often through no fault of our own), so arpeggiation can be resorted to in order to get oneself out of a musical jam.

This concept consists of filling in the holes of a sparse rhythmic figure with substance. This device is not arpeggiation in the strictest sense of the word, because you will be adding either arpeggios or chords in specific patterns of inversions. But arpeggiation seems to be an all-encompassing term that makes sense here.

To be able to use this device efficiently, analyze and learn the rhythmic structures of triple-meter adagios on page 36. If you have chosen a 3/4 adagio that needs to be slower, you can change to a rhythmic structure with more notes and time between the three beats. When you can make these standard rhythmic patterns as natural a part of your pianistic habits as waltz and coda structures, you can always turn a plodding adagio into a piece supportive for dancers, providing the correct tempo *and* the necessary flow to sustain both the music and the movement.

Because arpeggiation turns a ponderous left hand into a flowing rhythmic structure, it is extremely helpful for the adaptation of legato music that wasn't written for the piano.

The following example in its original form has a highly unsuitable bass line.

The rhythmic structure in bars 2 and 4 have almost complete silence; bars 5 through 8 have plodding repeated chords; and bars 13 through 15 bear no relationship to the flowing quality that music for pliés and adagios must have. Simple arpeggios, with octaves reinforcing the "1s" of each bar, turn it into an appropriate selection for pliés or an adage. (See example 54.)

Arpeggiation—the filling in and smoothing out of a ponderous rhythmic structure—serves two purposes: complementing full, rich substantial movement with flowing music; and turning what may be an unpianistic selection of music into one that is pianistic in approach, orchestral in scope, musically satisfying, and helpful to dancers.

Pianistic approaches to producing an orchestral sound

Throughout this book, mention has been made of full, orchestral-sounding music being helpful and supportive for dancers. Again, as your kinesthetic awareness increases, you will recognize which movements almost beg for a rich, lush musical support; and which ones need light, less full musical accompaniment.

The production of orchestral-sounding music is accomplished mainly through the use of octaves, which are covered in detail starting on page 163. What follows now is information dealing with pieces of music that, for one reason or another, are unsuitable for the dance classroom in their original form.

The music on the next page is an excerpt from the piano transcription of Boito's *Mefistofele.* At first glance (and twentieth glance—I looked at and bypassed it for years), it seems unsuitable. Pianistically, there is no flow in the rhythmic structure until bar 9/count 17. The melody includes many long tones which are impossible to sustain on a piano. It is easy to see that this excerpt is a faithful rendering of a vocal line and orchestral accompaniment, but it is useless for music in the dance classroom.

One day I accidentally noticed the bass figure in the recapitulation beginning in bar 9 and thought, "I could use that throughout the whole piece to maintain flow." (I distinctly remember that day as the one when I began to consciously put the concept of arpeggiation to work; the adagio section of my repertoire took a great leap forward.) But the melody didn't flow, so I added what I think of as reinforcing tones that help to sustain the melodic sound. (There are only two limitations of the piano that really frustrate me: its inability to sustain and intensify a single note, and the lack of four extra notes at the bass end of the keyboard.) Then I added more substance to bars 4, 8, and 12—moving lines to maintain energy and decrease the feeling of just rhythm where the melody/voice takes a rest.

f
allarg. un poco
con forza
in tempo.
ff
p
f ravvivando
ff
cres. con impeto
ff
rall.
ppp

While some might consider this distorting or tampering with the music, I justify it by saying that the composer's intent—a soul-bursting aria with full orchestral accompaniment—has been left intact, and has been re-created as faithfully as possible for the keyboard. (See example 64.)

Most piano reductions of orchestral works are written in the same registers in which the instruments play them. This poses a problem, especially in sections marked mezzo forte and louder; a single note on the piano cannot re-create the substance and breadth produced by fifteen violins playing the same tone. To more accurately render the dynamics of an orchestra, play the melody in octaves (always retaining the harmony if it is there), and double in octaves the primary beat of every bar, as well as the secondary beat, if there is one—the "OOMs" but not the "pah (pah)s." In other words: In the left hand, anything that is not a chord is an octave.

An excerpt from Prokofiev's *Romeo and Juliet* (example 80) needs this kind of treatment. It was a sore spot with me for a long time. I played at the Joffrey School in New York City for several years. Two of the studios are right next to each other, and the pianos are less than two feet apart, separated by only a thin wall. When my colleague in the next studio would launch into this piece without octaves in the right hand, I would cringe, because the tone produced was incredibly shrill and strident. I resolved never to play it—until I learned that doubling in octaves produces rich, substantial tone with no hint of banging. The additional octaves make all the difference in the world to a dancer who is executing virtuoso steps in a rehearsal (and who will eventually be dancing to the grandeur of an orchestra), or to a student who is learning how to do grands battements with the proper dynamic approach. (Why not, you might ask, use octaves in the right hand from the beginning? Two reasons: [a] Neal Kayan mused once, in passing, "It is much more musical and interesting to somehow change a repeated theme, either with octaves the second time around, or a different register, or *something* to avoid boredom!" and [b] octaves the second time through will give the students an extra lift for the next sixteen counts of an exhausting combination. How do I know it's exhausting? Because one would never play such a grandiose piece for a combination of movement that is less than robust.)

Czerny's *One Hundred and Ten Easy and Progressive Studies* (op. 453) has many adaptable selections in it. Mr. Czerny, however, wrote them with his piano students in mind, not dance accompanists, so they are often extremely basic and sparse rhythmically. The following excerpt is one of the studies, and it certainly looks boring.

By providing a rich, octave-laden left hand for support; by fleshing out the melody with reinforcing tones, if necessary; and by adding some harmony if it is not included (to provide a fuller—not necessarily louder—support for the dancers), you can easily enlarge your repertoire and improve your piano technique at the same time. (See example 16.)

Repeated notes or chords in the rhythmic structure are problematic. They are generally subordinate to the melody (especially in selections not originally written for the piano), functioning more to maintain the tempo and substance than to be consciously heard. Would it be heretical to say that rhythm fulfills a more vital function in music for the dance studio than in music for the concert hall? Anyway, these repeated notes can sound very plodding and heavy, as in the following excerpt.

The string section can play these repeated chords with the hushed quality necessary to complement a voice and sustain a mood. I have found this an extremely difficult effect to produce on the piano. Call it cheating if you will, but I reduce the ponderous effect by changing the inversions of the chords, thereby producing a sense of movement instead of static monotone. I also add impetus to the "1" of every measure in the left hand (if it is missing), and maintain the beautiful harmonic line of the rhythm. The augmentation provides more of the substance necessary to support the movements of a dancing body. (See example 53.)

Speaking of chord inversions, I change them in almost every waltz I play, if the composer hasn't already written it that way. It eliminates the plodding feeling often produced by playing the same chord for each "pah pah." Rather than the static sound produced by the same tones, you can express a feeling of movement, which is what dance is all about.

The sound of pizzicato strings is another orchestral effect that is difficult to duplicate on the piano. I confess to eliminating the pizzicato completely in all adagios through the use of arpeggiation, in favor of producing a flowing, smooth quality.

Throughout this book, I have discussed many reasons why the breadth of orchestral-sounding music is particularly suited to dance. Another reason is that, when a teacher asks for a specific excerpt from the traditional repertoire, she is hearing in her mind's ear the orchestral version (to which she may have danced), not the often skimpy piano reduction, and she may have choreographed a particular combination to that special orchestral fullness.

During my years of working with dance accompanists, I have often said that I don't improvise. Many of these accompanists have said, "Oh, but you do," referring to the ways in which I augment the printed page to produce orchestral fullness. But I don't consider that improvising. To my mind, improvising includes being able to create an original melody. I can create a melody whenever I have to, but it always sounds like someone else's. Augmentation is a technical habit I have acquired over the years that has become completely natural.

Some of these concepts may seem to be beyond you technically (they were definitely beyond me technically at one point, too), but if you understand the approach, you will be able to gradually incorporate them into your playing. The rhythmic configuration in the *Mefistofele* aria, for instance, is exactly the same rhythmic structure I use in many adagios. The chord progressions are almost identical; the only difference is the key signature. The pattern is essentially reflected in the first six 8th-note chords. Memorizing this pattern will speed the process along for you.

What you are essentially doing in much of this adaptation work is putting theory into practice. When you look at a page of music, you can find theoretical techniques and principles if you know what to look for: contrary motion, pedal points, classical structure (sonata form, A-A-B-A, etc.), proper voicing, and so forth. In your growth as an accompanist—and, after all, as a musician—don't neglect these principles. If you don't have classical theory training, a good ear is most beneficial; it should tell you when your voicings are wrong, or when your bass line is too thick or in the wrong register, or when something is stylistically inappropriate. Above all, practice the art of good taste.

Pianistic methods

The purpose of this chapter is not to discuss basic piano technique, but to offer suggestions in areas of technique that are vital to dance accompanists. The sole reason I am being presumptuous enough to mention technique at all is because I have had the luxury of having a piano teacher only once during my professional career—someone to turn to for help in technical areas I hadn't yet mastered or, in some cases, hadn't even heard of. I had neither the time nor the money to continue taking piano lessons, and would have been very grateful for some helpful hints, which I hope these prove to be. (My sole teacher was the late Neal Kayan, former music director and conductor of the Royal Winnipeg Ballet, and his assistance more than twenty-five years ago is still of inestimable value.)

It is probably safe to assume that no one goes into the field of dance accompaniment with a perfect, well-rounded technique. Therefore, if you don't currently have a piano teacher, this chapter may prove helpful.

Never forget that technique is a means to an end: a vocabulary with which an artist communicates with others. Without it, he is restricted to monosyllabic, monotonous (in the literal sense) utterances. With it, he is capable of broader expression. But a danger lies in the fact that students (of every art form) often lose track of the essence of the art during the acquisition of technique. Pianists often end up communicating consecutive octaves, brilliant arpeggios, and glittering scales in thirds and sixths—instead of music.

Freedom at the keyboard is a gradual process, and technique evolves in gradual steps. Some of these steps will be very obvious to you, as they are a result of conscious effort on your part to bring your fingers under control. You may not be aware of other steps until one day you realize that your playing has improved in scope, not just in technical feats. Your tone is fuller, your phrasing is more meaningful, your pedaling is cleaner, you use more of the keyboard, and you feel freer.

Freedom is one of the ultimate goals of every artist, but freedom is often misinterpreted. True artistic freedom is gained only through the most intelligently applied discipline. If anyone thinks discipline is restricting, he or she is not a true artist. It is a vital, never-ending fact of artistic life. Freedom without an understanding of discipline is usually self-indulgence.

One of the many beauties of dance is that its instrument is the natural purity of the human body. You should strive to make your instrument, the piano, part of yourself—to feel as if it is an extension of your own body. When you can sit at the piano and find middle C without looking, you'll be well on your way.

Playing the piano is a very physical activity. It depends on muscle memory as much as dancing does (but, of course, with fewer body parts involved). Much of the ability to re-create consistent tempos comes from this difficult-to-describe sensation. Through repetition, your hands and arms develop senses of their own, and will eventually go to the right places at the right times without a conscious message from the brain. (If you do anything often enough, it becomes a habit, just like brushing your teeth in the morning.)

The direct tactile connection between you and your instrument happens in your fingers, so you will be constantly increasing your ability to *feel* the music digitally, as well as to *hear* what you are producing, and to *see* the effects on the dancers.

All pianists have problem passages. Obviously, your eyes can't register each individual note under your hands, so you need all the help you can get to execute them properly. Sometimes it takes herculean effort to become an active participant in getting them right, instead of remaining a bystander, thinking, "I'm going to get it right this time!" and then mentally just sitting back and watching how it comes out. When I finally became aware of the fine line between these two attitudes and realized I had a choice in the matter, I no longer blamed my sloppy playing on a bad day or a bad piano; the guilty party was a sluggish brain.

A helpful hint may be what I've been told is a Zen concept. In any troublesome passage, think the name of the note(s), chord, or passage; hear the pitch or visualize the shape so convincingly that you become that pitch or shape.

Posture and stamina

Every piano teacher should teach pupils to sit correctly at the keyboard. If you have not been taught properly, you must learn now, or else find a good chiropractor. Next to being a drummer for a jazz or rock group, being a dance accompanist is the most physically strenuous musical occupation. It often requires many consecutive hours of playing at an unrelenting pace, and you must accept that as part of the job and learn to see the advantages therein. (One hears a great deal about endorphins these days, and I find them very helpful little creatures. They are hormonelike substances: natural opiates that are three times more powerful than morphine. They are released by the brain through strenuous activity, and probably explain the blockage of the sensation of pain. I have gotten a fingernail caught between piano keys a few times in my career, and have often wondered why it didn't hurt, when it is excruciatingly painful if it happens outside the dance studio. I think endorphins are the answer. And I also think they are responsible for what we term a second wind—that great feeling that sometimes happens when we are ready to drop from exhaustion. If you play for a teacher who challenges your stamina, don't complain; be thankful! You probably wouldn't push yourself that hard during your own private practice time.)

Your back is essential to endurance. Since it is such a large area, it is the logical repository of strength to produce long passages of vigorous music, as well as to sustain long hours of work. Standing up and bending over between classes is good for the back and gets extra blood to the brain.

You must sit squarely at the piano with both feet on the floor; crossing your legs produces a distortion in the upper torso that affects how you address the keyboard.

I hesitate to make any comments about the position of the arms and fingers, as there seem to be several schools of thought in these areas. But I would like to relate what has come to be the most logical and effective carriage for me.

I feel a natural slope of the arms downward from the shoulders to the keyboard. My elbows never bend toward the floor; I position myself far enough from the keyboard so there is a minimum of elbow bending. This produces a direct line of energy running from the big muscles that start in the middle of the back (the *latissimi dorsi*) straight through the arms, wrists, and fingers. (I often feel that my physical music-making apparatus is in the shape of a horseshoe: one rounded, unbroken line from one hand to the other.) My wrists never drop. (I sustained a minor hand injury in an auto accident several years ago, and whenever that hand hurts, I know I've been ignoring this concept.) Dropped wrists seem to break up the natural, linear flow of energy, and also may contribute to carpal tunnel syndrome, possibly because it seems harder to maintain flexible, breathing wrists when they are dropped. And my wrists are surprisingly flexible. An accompanist complained recently of her wrists being extremely painful; when I observed her playing, her wrists were absolutely rigid, no matter what she was playing. As I observed my own playing, I was pleased and astonished to see that the left wrist relaxed after each chord stroke. I thanked God and Mrs. Mackown, my first piano teacher, for having been taught correctly from age four.

The only area of my body that suffers from long hours at the keyboard is in my upper back, between the shoulder joints and neck. It has been a constant throughout my career; I usually ignore it, and I always have my trusty gray sweater around my shoulders, no matter what temperature it is outside.

Mobility and freedom in the torso are prerequisites for the execution of full-keyboard music making. As you gradually branch out into a wider use of the keyboard, make sure your body works in synchronization with your arms; don't keep it in a static position. (On the other hand, I feel that excessive movement in the upper body adversely affects accuracy.)

The chair you sit on is of paramount importance. Whether it is a chair, stool, or piano bench is less important than its height. If you don't sit high enough, your arms will take much of the strain that your back is better equipped to handle. The weight to produce large volumes of sound comes primarily from the strength in your back, not in your arms. If a piano bench is not adjustable, I sit on telephone books with a pillow on top, to prevent callouses on the derrière.[12]

Do not sit on your binders! If the silver rings are bent the slightest bit out of alignment, page turning will become a nightmare.

There is an astonishing number of similarities between many basic concepts of music and dance. One of these is the matter of posture, which a dancer calls placement. You will often hear the teacher correct the dancers' placement. Usually it will be in the form of a forceful vocalization to the whole class, such as, "Pull up!" or, "Lift!" or, "Stomachs in!" These exhortations are made not only because of the aesthetics of the art form, but also because the stomach muscles are connected to the back muscles; a dancer's technique benefits greatly from having these powerful muscles lift some of the weight off the legs. You would do well to respond to these directions, too; your playing will benefit from better posture, and you will be able to partially counteract "pianist's derrière"—backside spread produced by sitting for many hours.

Octaves

By now, it is probably apparent that octave work is vital to the production of full, substantial dance accompaniment. Effective octave execution can be acquired through understanding the need for it, willpower, an intelligent application of the technical principles, diligent and consistent practice habits inside and outside of the classroom, a certain degree of confidence, and occasional flashes of inspiration, adrenaline, and endorphins.

When I first got into dance accompaniment, my memorized repertoire consisted of one Bach fugue, two Beethoven sonatas, one Debussy prelude, "The Star-Spangled Banner," and a wide assortment of popular tunes, such as "Tea for Two" and "Oklahoma." (My unmemorized repertoire was larger by only about four pieces.) My technique was pitiful. I had no conception of what technique really is, and I had yet to discover the purpose of discipline. (To this day, I do *not* understand why my piano teachers thought I was talented.) My approach changed when I started to realize that dance accompaniment offered infinite opportunities of creativity and enjoyment (to say nothing of employment as a musician instead of as a bank clerk or salesperson). I didn't begin to understand the principles of technique or the art of discipline any better, but a subconscious channeling of energy must have begun. To this day, I cannot describe when conscious application of much of the technical information in this book began. In other words, I didn't go home and say, "Tonight I'm going to work on octaves." In fact, I didn't even have a piano during the first three years I worked in New York. All my "practicing" was done during classroom time, and that was the most intense growing period of my career. (Imagine what you can do with the luxury of time to yourself for quiet practice!)

The need for broad, supportive music for dance must have become apparent when I started taking dance classes regularly, and my technique grew to accommodate that need. I learned to identify and analyze the ingredients of effective dance accompaniment and the production thereof only when I started to teach it.

This is probably a good place to mention the breaking of piano strings. I lost track of how many strings I broke during those first years in New York, and my nickname was Madame Liszt. I was often exhorted to "Play fuller!" which I thought meant more loudly. As soon as I started producing more sound through more notes, rather than through more force, the breakage—and the exhortations—decreased dramatically.

The point of relating this short professional history to you is to describe the levels and stages you may also go through in your own development. Some aspects of your development, such as string breaking, will be different than mine—and hopefully nonexistent. The main reason for writing this book is to help eliminate, as much as possible, trial-and-error learning, which unknowingly stymied my progress for so long. If you understand intellectually why you need to use octaves, and how to produce them, half the battle is won.

The elusive arm muscle

My first conscious understanding of the similarities between piano technique and dancing involved muscles. There is a muscle in the inside of the thigh (the *adductor*) that is vital to—among other things—sustaining the strength necessary for holding the leg off the ground for a protracted period of time; it basically assists the *quadriceps* in this function. I was astonished to discover that there is a corresponding muscle under the back of the upper arm (the *triceps brachii*) whose function is exactly the same: sustaining the strength necessary for long octave passages. I learned this after the fact, so to speak; when I finally became aware that I was getting fairly competent in this area, I tried to analyze why, and realized that this relatively obscure muscle was mostly responsible. It seemed to brace my elbow in a position that allowed maximum flexibility in my wrists with a minimum of extraneous movement, and my forearms never cramped, once I mastered it. I didn't even know I was mastering it.

"Wow," you are saying, "now she's going to tell me how to find it, and octaves will be so easy." How I wish I could. I have never completely regained the use of this muscle after taking a year off from the piano some years back. At that time, I was still unaware of the basic muscularity in technique; it didn't occur to me that, during that year, my muscles would lose all their tone as well as their ability to produce what I hear in my head. My octave work is still competent enough, but I never experience that incredible high I used to when I could play allegro, crystal-clear octaves for seven minutes without a stop.

However, there are three factors that seem vital to the activation of the triceps. One is your posture. Just as the inside thigh muscle is incapable of being activated if the body placement is wrong, so is the triceps muscle in the arm difficult to activate if you slouch, play with your arms too close to or too far from your sides, or keep your weight too far away from or too close to the keyboard.

The second factor is taking dance classes. Along with all the other benefits you enjoy when you take class, the accomplishment of a perfectly executed second position of the arms will awaken the triceps.

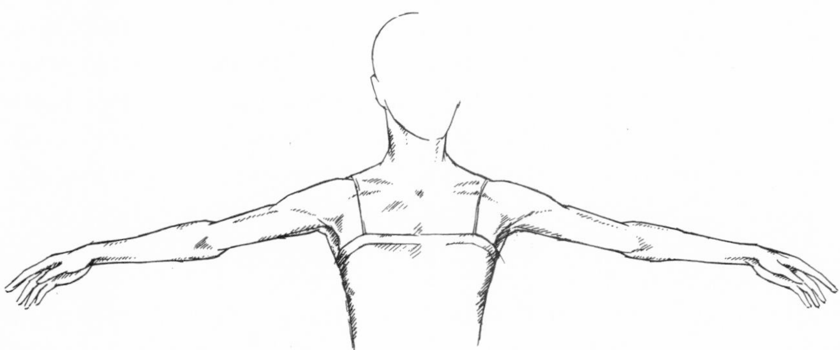

In a proper second position, the arms feel like they start in the back, and are supported with that very same muscle; elbows should never be visible. When it hurts under your upper arm, you will know you have found it. (Once the triceps gets used to being used, it won't hurt any more.) I do think that one reason I haven't regained its full use is because I have not had the luxury of regularly attending dance class in several years.

The third factor involves how much is physically demanded of you in class at the keyboard. If a muscle isn't needed or used, either it remains dormant or its strength dissipates.

There was a summer at the Joffrey School in New York when I played my first class at 9 A.M., and my last finished at 7 P.M. I had one thirty-minute break during those ten hours, and I learned more subconsciously that summer than at any other time in my career. (My greatest conscious learning period was the six weeks I played for Mme. Volkova in Banff.) I developed physical strength, too, to sustain that marathon schedule. Without knowing the triceps muscles existed, they came into play because the physical demands made upon me activated them. I don't think it was the quantity of hours I played that activated them (I still occasionally play eight hours in one day, and these muscles are not in gear as much as they used to be), as much as it was the quality of the classes I played. Mr. Brunson taught three of the seven daily classes I played, and he demanded as much of his students and me in the last class of the day (in 95° heat and 100 percent humidity) as he did in the first. I could have played the same number of hours for a less-demanding teacher and probably not have benefited as much.

Throughout the entire class, there was never more than a two-second pause between barre combinations, as he preferred the music to be played while he was demonstrating. Since there were between fifty and seventy students in class, each center combination would last at least five minutes. It never occurred to him that I might need a break, and it never occurred to me, either, because—even though my forearms occasionally cramped—I would have been too embarrassed to stop, admit defeat, and waste valuable class time. There *may* have been a point—when my forearms felt like knots—that my brain said, "Find a way to minimize the strain on your forearms," but I certainly don't remember it. The triceps muscle took over so gradually that I was unaware of it until another pianist complimented me on my technique, which I had always thought was nothing more than merely competent. Once I became aware of the function and strength of that muscle, I was able to maintain and improve upon it.

The use of the fourth finger on black keys

Another facet of effective octave work is the use of the fourth finger on black notes. This will allow you to play faster, cleaner octaves. Force yourself to use the fourth finger instead of the fifth on every black key, even in slow passages. It will eventually become a habit you won't have to think about any more. (One of the most incisive maxims I have ever heard is scribbled in one of my Red Books: "June 24, 1973: 'Technique is a series of habits'—Benjamin Harkarvy.") Habits are easy to form and very hard to break. However, if you consciously understand the benefits to be gained from breaking a bad habit, the change is more easily accomplished.

When I stopped formal piano study, I wasn't far enough along technically to need this concept of fourth-fingering in octaves. I discovered it accidentally one day when I cut my fifth finger quite badly with a knife, and had no choice but to use the fourth. My octave work improved astonishingly rapidly.

Example 81 is yet another Czerny étude. It is also one of the most exciting and brilliant sections of Harald Lander's ballet *Etudes,* which has been mentioned before. It is also a great vehicle for developing freedom in octave work. It is also a favorite with almost every dance teacher (it has the structure of a coda). And it is *also* not as pianistically frightening as you think if you look at it objectively. Many of its patterns are quite obvious immediately, and they are often repeated. The time it takes to learn it would more than repay you with its benefits to you, the teacher, and the students. Start slowly with it, and be sure, of course, to use the fourth finger on every black note. It may take you months or years before you feel confident enough to play it in class, and I assure you that teachers will be just as pleased with your accomplishment as you will be.

~

In the area of technical improvement, octave work seems to be the aspect that pianists shy away from the most. I have heard a variety of excuses and apologies for this. One pianist said he had a "harpsichord technique," and could never play music that was orchestral in scope. Another said his hands were too small to develop an effective octave technique. (A former colleague in the Royal Winnipeg Ballet, Linda Lee Thomas, had the smallest hands I've ever seen, and she played every single note, every single day, of the Galop from *Raymonda*/"Pas de Dix," which is in C major, mostly in octaves, and one of the most fiendishly difficult pieces in the dance repertoire. Another colleague once asked her, with a touch of jealousy in his voice, "Why do you bother playing all those notes?" "Because they're there," she replied.) If you set limitations on yourself, you restrict your ability to both make and enjoy music.

The most understandable reason for shying away from octave work is because so many wrong notes are hit that it can become very depressing. It is imperative for you to remember that the dancers are seldom bothered by the wrong notes unless they are truly colossal. While your mistakes may not go unnoticed, no one but you will know how monumental they are as long as you maintain a steady tempo and rhythm. Get used to the fact that you won't have as high a degree of accuracy for a while until your muscles get used to producing octaves as naturally as anything else.

One secret of effective octave work is watching the leading finger only; don't try to see both the thumb and little or fourth finger as they work. As the right hand moves up the keyboard, watch the little or fourth finger; as it moves down, watch the thumb. Reverse this process for the left hand. Retain the octave position in your fingers throughout without letting your wrist become rigid.

Since rhythm is such a vital force in music for dance, it might be wise to start with octaves in your left hand only. If you are a beginning accompanist, you will need a certain length of time just to become familiar enough with the format of the class to be able to play appropriate selections as the composer wrote them. After a while, you will have played at least one piece often enough to feel comfortable with it, and you can branch out technically within that piece. Let's take a waltz as an example. Example 82a is taken from the *Light Opera and Ballet Excerpts* Red Book.

When you are ready, you can start adding an octave on the "1" (the "OOM") of every bar, as in example 82b.

Then you can start augmenting the melody, being careful to retain the harmonies and inner voices, as in example 82c.

After a time, which depends on how consistent you are in practicing this approach, octave work will have become such a habit that your hands will automatically stretch into that octave span without a specific impulse from your brain, even when you are sight-reading a piece without octaves written into it.

Some philosophical bits I often repeat to myself are "less is more" and "economy of movement" and "simplicity is the key." These apply directly to octave execution. If I am trying to play octaves at ninety miles per hour, my movements need to be as direct and uncluttered as possible. My two outer fingers assume the necessary span; my hand moves up and down while the forearm guides its positioning; my wrist doesn't change height, nor does it remain rigid; and my hand doesn't splay out to one side or the other, except very slightly to accommodate the fourth finger on black notes. Ultimately, there is no tension involved, only the purest form of control.

As with everything else, this acquisition will take time, but you have to know that it *is* possible. When your forearms are cramped, your wrists feel sprained, and/or your fingers look like claws, you know something isn't right. It is usually plain, ordinary, unproductive tension. Send positive messages to the problem areas. Instead of saying, "My whatevers are killing me!" say, "I don't have to play with such tension." Yes, some tension will be involved at first; your muscles will hurt because they have probably never been called upon to work so hard. But your technique cannot develop fully with steel forearms and rigid wrists, any more than a dancer can dance to his fullest capacity with steel calves and rigid ankles.

Fingering

I am limiting a discussion of fingering to one of the smartest pieces of advice I ever heard. It is so basic that it is easy to forget. And it is a summing-up of how one acquires technique. Neal Kayan once told me I could use the most ridiculous, illogical fingering in the world as long as I *did it the same way every time.* Again, "Technique is a series of habits," and, finally at the age of thirty-four, I realized that I could play speedy, filigreed passages well if I just made a habit of consistent fingering. If you use a different fingering every time you play a passage, you are putting garbled information into your mental computer, and into your fingers. Getting the proper response from your fingers requires putting the proper information into the muscles and brain every time. If necessary, write the fingering you decide on above the notes; don't leave it to chance.

Pedaling

Please remember the basic inadequacy of any book such as this: the difficulty of verbalizing and explaining music. If words were an effective means of communicating the essence of music, we might not have music at all. What I am trying to pass on is truly effective only through a musical demonstration, but since that is impossible, words will have to suffice. Try these concepts out yourself; according to your current technical and awareness levels, choose which one(s) you can incorporate into your playing now, and retain a sense of what the more advanced concepts are aiming at.

The inadequacy of words is especially true in the area of pedaling. If you have had formal, classical piano training, you will use all the pedaling concepts you were taught. I have adopted additional techniques which are not part of classical schooling simply because the need for them never arises in music meant for listening only.

Unless otherwise noted, "the pedal" always means the right-hand or sustaining pedal throughout this book.

Reverse pedaling

I use reverse pedaling (for lack of a better term) in many areas of dance classes, and it can best be understood through hearing what it is and judging its effect on dancers.

Essentially, reverse pedaling is depressing the pedal in a fashion opposite to what feels normal. Observe where in the music you instinctively tap your foot when you hear a polka. If you were pedaling instead of tapping, you would be using the pedaling method we learned from our piano teachers: depressing the pedal on the first note of each bar. This method is adhered to when playing music that is legato in quality, such as pieces for pliés, ronds de jambe, and adagio/développé combinations.

In reverse pedaling, the pedal is released on each dancer's count, having been depressed on the preceding "and." This concept eliminates the heaviness that can creep (or lumber) into music for dance, especially loud, robust music. (If you have been accompanying dance for any length of time, you have probably heard the teacher reject something by saying, "That's too heavy." Reverse pedaling will often help to give the piece the necessary lightness without reducing its fullness or volume.)

Reverse pedaling is absolutely vital in all jumping steps. Both the sparkling quality of petit allegro and the airborne soaring of grand allegro are enhanced by using the pedal in this manner, and it subconsciously helps the dancers to achieve their goals. It is vital to remember that, no matter how a piece for jumping is notated, when the feet land on the ground, that beat must be staccato—not a brittle staccato, but what I call a lush staccato (one that took me many years to develop, and which I can't describe in words). Each of these landings needs air space afterward.

This pedaling concept is often used in non-jumping steps, also. The essence of and reason behind reverse pedaling is to provide contrasts in the music which reflect contrast of accents and qualities in the movement. You can use the pedal in an endless variety of ways to enhance the accents within any given piece.

The dégagé combination included with example 11 changes accents, which is reflected in the pedaling.

In example 41, notice the pedaling change in bar 7; this is done because the grand battement piqué is distinctly different in feeling from a regular grand battement, which goes up from and returns to fifth position. A grand battement piqué goes up from fifth position, comes down for a nanosecond to the tendu position and rises immediately to full height again, then closes to fifth position. The crucial point—from the tendu position back up again—should have the feeling of snatching one's hand away from a hot oven door. Since a leg is considerably heavier than a hand, it requires great strength to achieve the feeling of lightness, and a corresponding bouncing quality in the music (especially when it is a distinct change from what has preceded it) will lighten the load. If you can use your hands on the keyboard in the same way—with the hot-oven-door feeling—you will heighten the effect even more, as well as adding a new facet to your technique.

I feel that this concept of pedaling is extremely important. Many teachers have commented on my ability to produce huge volumes of sound when necessary, without ever sounding heavy. ('Twas not always thus!) It certainly isn't because I play the piano better than other accompanists, but it may be because I have learned to add octaves and to use the pedal effectively.

(I was recently asked for help by an accompanist who instantly heard and understood what a difference reverse pedaling makes. He was really excited about it and said, "I won't give away your secret." This is a misguided attitude that was prevalent in New York City in the sixties. Most accompanists never shared repertoire or concepts, for fear someone else might improve faster. I didn't agree with that attitude then, and I certainly don't now. There is enough work to go around, and I encourage all accompanists to share any helpful information with other accompanists in order to improve music in the classroom.)

It would require another book to demonstrate this reverse pedaling concept and how it is applied to each step. Pedaling has generally not been included in the musical examples because each movement combination requires its own unique execution of pedaling.

The sostenuto (middle) pedal

This pedal is ignored by most pianists. Every piano tuner and recording studio engineer I've met has been amazed at my concern over whether it functions properly. A good deal of piano literature benefits from its use, even though specific sostenuto pedal markings are not prevalent. The Impressionists in particular (Ravel, Debussy, etc.) took advantage of its wonderful possibilities.

The contribution to music for dance made by the use of the sostenuto pedal is in the areas of cleanliness and breadth of sound. It is generally used as a pedal-point sustaining the first note(s) of a bar in the lower register throughout either the whole bar or—if the harmony doesn't change—a number of bars.

Whenever I am lucky enough to play a piano with a sostenuto pedal, I use it in almost every piece I play that requires a legato feeling.

Example 62 is a beautiful, obscure piece by Rachmaninoff. It is an especially popular adagio (and also works well for musically slow pliés) and requires the use of the sostenuto pedal to consummate the composer's intent. (You could square it off with an improvised cadence at the end of measure 16, but the final four bars are too gorgeous to be cut.)

The soft (damper) pedal

A technically competent musician must be able to play very softly as well as very loudly. I have never liked the muffled quality that is usually produced by using the soft pedal. I also think it's cheating to have to use the soft pedal to play quietly, so I never use it.

How sensitive pedaling can help dancers breathe correctly

It is patently obvious to most observers of dance that proper breathing must play an essential role in such a physically demanding activity. Surprisingly enough, this basic necessity is often overlooked by teachers and dancers; both groups have been (or are) rarely taught when and from where to breathe. Breathing not only distributes oxygen throughout the body, it also makes the body lighter; through the intake of breath the upper torso lifts a bit off the hips and lightens the load the legs must support.

You can emphasize these benefits through a sensitive use of the pedal. You can enhance the effect of a rest at the end of a phrase by lifting the pedal completely (without interrupting the tempo). Or you can emphasize the approach of a particularly demanding movement phrase with a tasteful but unexpected break in the sound (again, stay in tempo).

You may wonder what the symbol ' is in several of the musical examples. It is the standard sign for breathing in both verbal and musical grammar, and it reflects an area in which dancers should inhale in order to more rewardingly fulfill their movements. No cambré or port de bras should be begun by either dancer or accompanist without a breath.

Even if only one person hears and responds to the help you are giving, it's worth the trouble.

~

One last comment on pedaling: When pianists come to difficult passages, we often unconsciously tread a little harder on the pedal than normal, in order to cover up our mistakes. That's cheating, too. With a little extra investment of brain power, we can make our fingers work properly and avoid the muddiness that comes from an overuse of the pedal.

Tone quality

Everyone seems to agree that, except for a few stylistic exceptions, a good musician must possess a beautiful tone. After acknowledging that basic premise, there is great disagreement as to how to produce it, especially on a percussive instrument like the piano. It would be easier to ignore any discussion of tone altogether but, since the sound of your music affects the quality of the dancers' movements, it is necessary to touch upon it.

The levels you will pass through during your never-ending technical improvement are especially obvious in the area of tone production. Your tone quality may suffer greatly during the period when you are mastering octaves, and you must remind yourself to really listen to yourself and to assess objectively what you hear. If you are called upon to play many hours in a row, you will go through periods of building the strength necessary to sustain your work and, again, your tone may suffer. You may even break some piano strings during this stage, but once your back has developed the proper support, you won't have to push so hard.

Aside from its inclusion in basic good musicianship, good tone quality is necessary for dancers to develop good movement quality. Harsh tone has a jarring effect and generally produces—often subconsciously—brittle movement.

I hesitate to offer any technical concepts concerning tone, but I would like to pass on three bits of information that have been extremely valuable to me.

The first is that it seems impossible to produce good tone with stiff wrists.

The second came from Neal Kayan. Put your fingers in a normal keyboard position on your thigh. Now draw the skin toward you, using only your fingertips. That feeling on the keys—especially in adagio passages requiring an exquisite, singing tone—is something I always try to produce in any passage that doesn't need a staccato feeling. Maestro Kayan likened this to drawing the sound out of the piano. He also warned me that my fingers might slip off the keys until I got the hang of it, but just an awareness of that problem seems to have prevented it from ever happening. (I think I started practicing the concept by positioning my fingers closer to the backboard than normal.) This concept has another benefit, too. You may find yourself in a dance studio confronted with a piano that has absurdly uneven action. You have a better chance of producing any tone at all on this "instrument" if your finger caresses a key than if it uses a single down-and-up action.

The third suggestion came also from Maestro Kayan. It may be an obvious component of good musicianship, but for me it was a revelation. He called it a "singing little finger," referring to how a finger (usually the little one) should caress each melodic note—especially when the melody is doubled in octaves—thereby preventing it from getting lost in a rich, lush, orchestral-sounding rendering.

In re-creating an orchestral sound on the piano, be aware of the rich variety of sonorities and timbres that are the personalities of orchestral instruments. While it is, of course, impossible to duplicate the particular qualities of each instrument on the piano, think about their individual sounds as you play. In my head, I hear the cello playing the melodies of many of my adagios, and an oboe sings a particularly mournful one.

Example 48, from *Raymonda*/"Pas de Dix" is a good piece to study, trying to re-create the orchestration by transferring the sound in your head through your fingertips. It is scored for violins, violas, and a quartet of French horns, and you can hear its full-bodied lushness on a recording or videotape of the ballet.

Memorization

Memorization is a very valuable tool for any musician, of course, and is especially so for a dance accompanist. One benefit was touched upon briefly in the section on organizing your music: memorization eliminates the need for carrying a pile of music around with you. But its prime asset is the fact that it frees your eyes to watch the class instead of the printed page.

After a certain period of time (which varies with everyone, depending on how many hours a day one spends at the piano), you have memorized quite a few pieces, even though you have never been tested—or tested yourself—to find out.

If you think you can't memorize, then look at it this way: Every time you play a piece, you are consciously or unconsciously reinforcing its pattern in the rhythmic-figure circuit of your mental computer. And some day you will be able not only to produce the pattern automatically, but also to understand it to the point where you will be able to apply it to another piece of music. This may be the same day that you compose or find a gorgeous melody that has a rhythmically unsuitable bass line, and you can't bear not to have it in your repertoire.

I found out how much I had memorized when I was asked to play an unscheduled private class for Violette Verdy and Patricia Wilde, two of Balanchine's most impressive ballerinas (and I do not use that term lightly). My music was at one end of Manhattan and I was at the other; I could have said no, but I wasn't about to pass up that opportunity, so I went. While I didn't do my best, I survived, and learned that most of my memory lapses were due to nerves, not lack of familiarization with the notes.[13]

I think many musicians and dancers lose track of (or, as in my case, never knew) how the body acquires technique. Constant repetition is the *only* way to develop a reliable technical basis that keeps going no matter what happens: an attack of nerves, a screaming child in the audience, a broken string, falling down, an unreliable partner, or stomach flu. My rapid technical improvement in New York was due not to practicing as one is taught to do in a music school but to the fact that I played the piano on an average of eight hours a day, seven days a week. It certainly couldn't be classified as the scales/arpeggios/concentrated-work-on-technique kind of practicing, but there is no doubt that keyboard familiarity, muscular habits, and the notes themselves were being consciously or subconsciously drummed into my being. (As a child, I practiced only because my teachers and my mother told me to, not because I understood the benefits I would reap. I didn't start to enjoy practicing until Neal Kayan cajoled me into it, and I astounded myself at the progress I made.)[14]

Consistent fingering is as vital to memorization as is the awareness of rhythmic patterns. And singing the melody in your head—or out loud—will help your fingers find the right notes.

We need to remember to trust our bodies to rise to the occasion in an emergency. Confidence—*not* arrogance—and an awareness of your capabilities at whatever level you find yourself will stand you in good stead.

Sightreading

Sightreading is the important first step in learning music, and if God didn't give you a lot of natural ability in this area, don't worry—and don't shun it. It is a craft that is part of music making, and it can be developed if you believe it can, and if you work at it. (And I speak from experience. I do not have natural sightreading ability, but it has developed into reasonable competence simply by my being forced to do it. And if I don't do it for a while, it goes away.)

You will eventually get to the point where you feel comfortable enough with the format of a dance class that you have a fairly good idea of what is liable to come next. When this happens, you will be able to explore the incredible richness and creativity of dance accompaniment that is not apparent in the beginning stages of trying to play within the confines—so they seem—of the teacher's needs. For instance, if you have just found a wonderful new music book, take it to your next basic dance class and try to play some new music from it for combinations whose meter and tempo you are fairly sure about (ronds de jambe, for instance, and dégagés). Very often the rhythmic computer in your head will take over when your left hand runs across some vagrant rhythmic figure that interrupts the flow.

A rule of thumb in sightreading—and in every aspect of dance accompaniment: Keep the left hand going, no matter what. The practice you have done of standard rhythmic patterns will stand you in good stead during sightreading.

In the course of sightreading a new piece, you may not be able to anticipate an uneven phrase. Don't just say to yourself, "Oh, now what do I do?" There are any number of solutions, such as a dominant-tonic cadence on "7" and "8" of an offending long phrase. Or if a phrase is too short, repeat as many counts of the melody as necessary to round out an 8- or 16-count phrase.

Cultivate the ability of reading one measure ahead while you are playing one measure behind.

Pianos you may meet

You will run across an endless assortment of pianos in unlimited degrees of condition. The worst I've ever used was in a public school in Winnipeg. It had thirteen keys missing and the pedals didn't work. During the half hour between warm-up and performance (a lecture-demonstration which also included difficult excerpts from *Raymonda*), I managed to tape the right-hand pedal together (I was extremely light-footed during that performance) and put black electrical tape on all the silent keys to help me avoid them. My use of octaves stood me in especially good stead that day; while the sound was very uneven, at least there were usually sounds, even when I hit an unworking note. The best piano I ever had was a brand new Hamburg Steinway for two years in its home town. It was the most incredible instrument I've ever played, including all the ones in the recording studios I've been in; it combined a perfectly even, not-too-easy, not-too-stiff action with a round, warm tone that was consistent throughout the registers. What a luxury.

Ninety-nine percent of the pianos you will play on will fall somewhere between these two extremes. If you have to play on a real turkey, just do the best you can. Complaining about it is absolutely useless, unless you truly feel you can change the situation. You are only complaining about a problem that the teacher is already acutely aware of, and you are producing negative energy in the process. Don't forget that good pianos are expensive, and good, durable pianos are very scarce. The constant use, occasional abuse, and fluctuations in humidity and temperature make durability a prime consideration in the choice of a classroom piano.

If you play on a grand piano, try to adjust to playing with the music rack folded down or removed altogether. The struts in the area behind the rack will support your music. Playing this way will allow you to see more of the class, and will give you no choice but to sit up straight.

If you play on an upright whose height prevents you from seeing the class, reposition it. Angle the piano to give you maximum visibility with minimum head turning. Or attach a mirror somewhere on the vertical surface.

Miscellaneous

While you are sorting out this mind-boggling amount of foreign data, don't lose track of the meaning behind the notes. As I have discussed before, good music is a primary factor in teaching dance students to move beyond mere technical feats. The same is true with a musician: Separating the feeling and meaning from the notes for a protracted length of time will often slow you down in the learning process.

During the learning process, work toward cultivating that very important ability of hearing music in your head—aural imagination. Eventually, you will have loaded hundreds of melodies into your mental computer, categorized more by quality than by name, and it will take just a rhythm, either spoken by the teacher or observed by you, to activate a perfect choice.

When I start to learn a new piece, I "mark" it—play it at a random but regular tempo and without dynamics—straight through a few times to get an idea of its intent, its scope, its personality, and where I may have to cut. I isolate the trouble spots and practice them as much as necessary, then reward myself with being able to play it through in a satisfying way. If you are like me, you may practice until perfect a piece at home and then find that it falls apart when you take it into the classroom for the first time. That seems to be normal—depressing, but normal. Remember that dancers are not as concerned with wrong notes as you are.

Anticipation is a magic word for any performing artist. It is a concept that almost defies verbalization, but it partly entails knowing that a trouble spot is coming up, and mustering the mental energy necessary for preventing the repetition of a bad habit. Do not allow yourself to make the same mistake twice.

Some accompanists have said that their technique deteriorates when they play many hours a day. This is hard for me to fathom, because I gained all my technique in the dance studio. It *may* be possible, but I feel that these accompanists' approach is misdirected. If you play many hours a day and are tired or bored, you have three choices: Change jobs, be unhappy, or use the time productively. Don't give in to boredom or fatigue. In either case, challenge yourself technically to counteract the situation. If you are tired, think, "What technical concept could I work on?" instead of, "Is this class never going to end?" Often, your involvement in a technical concept will give you a second wind—or a third or a seventh—and you will become re-involved in the class itself. Work on octaves or tone or reverse pedaling or consistent, impeccable fingering or whatever, and use the class as a practice session. There is not a pianist on earth who can say that his or her technique is as good as it could be.

If you have to resort to this approach, don't lose track of the students. They shouldn't have to suffer if your energy slackens.

If the class is *truly* boring and you have to play for that teacher for any length of time, speak to her outside of class. Say something like, "Is there any particular music you like?" or, "Maybe we could experiment with some different rhythms. I have a wonderful bolero (or whatever) that might be fun for changements (or whatever)." Boredom may have unconsciously affected your playing, and a dialogue like this may make the teacher realize that you need challenges as much as her students do. It will also show her that you care about what you and her students are doing.

Anyone who makes a lifetime career out of any occupation will be able to sustain her commitment, and continue to derive pleasure, only if she keeps improving her performance. This is as true—if not more so—for a dance accompanist as for a bank teller or an auto mechanic. So, improving your technique—broadening your means of communication—goes hand in hand with the development of your observational powers.

An overview of various dance classes

There are no hard and fast rules governing your choice of music in the classroom other than suitability and the teacher's requests, but you may find some of the following information helpful. Again, keep in mind your role as an educator; often, the only music education many dancers receive is what they absorb from the classroom accompanist.

Pre-ballet and children's classes

While music for dancers at every technical level should be an inspiration, music also serves as a pragmatic tool for beginners. Rank beginners, no matter how musical they may be, must often be shown how to use the music—how to order their movements into specific rhythmic patterns. Except for a few isolated instances, it is a mistake to allow even the tiniest tot to dance off the music without apprising him of the error. Lack of discipline in any art form promotes self-indulgence and overblown egos, and pre-ballet class is not too early to teach a bit of discipline to a budding dancer—indeed, to a budding person who has to function in society. For a professional dancer, being off the music in a performance is just as wrong as doing the wrong step (both actions look pretty much the same to 95 percent of the audience), so a youngster must start learning that immediately. (There is a big difference between intelligently applied discipline and rigid, repressive discipline.)

A pre-ballet class in the hands of a creative teacher can be one of the most enjoyable classes to play. Children are so open and unprogrammed that they are an absolute pleasure to watch as their natural movement is gradually channeled into the discipline of dance without losing the spontaneity and joy. The teacher of pre-ballet classes principally tries to instill in the students little more than the need for music in connection with basic steps, and how to use, react to, and enjoy it.

In both pre-ballet and children's classes, there will be a lot of hopping, skipping, jumping, and marching, all of which have specific rhythms and median tempos. (A child will skip faster than professional dancers not only because his legs are shorter, but also because professionals have increased their ballon—the airborne quality produced by strength in the leg muscles that deepens the demi-plié and heightens jumping movements.) Marches in all meters are suitable for walking and marching; miscellaneous 6/8s and non-coda 2/4s are suitable for hops, skips, jumps, polkas, and galops/chassés. (The musical form *galop* is totally unsuited to the dance step *galop.*) Tarantellas, among other forms, are suitable for running because of the rapid running eighth-note figure. The teacher will often make up a little dance using variations of the polka steps, for which I often substitute a rag for a change of pace. Selections from the traditional ballet repertoire, whenever suitable, are always a good choice; they combine eminently appropriate music with exposure to the musical history of dance. What I seldom use are pieces in a minor key and rhythmically or melodically complex pieces, unless specifically called for in an improvisation.

The teacher may do a number of creative games or improvisations with the children, such as Pretend You Are a Flower, or Jump Over the Fence. These situations are where you can be the most creative—and learn a fundamental of dance accompaniment: Look at a movement and translate it into music.

Tempo is even more vital than usual in pre-ballet, children's, and beginning classes. Advanced dancers and adult beginners may appreciate live music more than children, but it is much more important to have an accompanist for children's classes, so that the tempos can be meticulously attended to. Some elements of classical dance are not natural, and in the beginning stages of dance training, a perfect balance must be struck by which unnatural movement is made to become natural. Observe the tempo at which a child skips, then match it. (You will gradually learn to pick out the children in class who have a natural feeling for the marriage of music and dance; be sure to match their tempos instead of the poor child in the back corner who has one tin ear and two left feet.) But adhere strictly to the tempo the teacher sets for less natural-feeling movement, such as tendus or ronds de jambe. The rhythm should never be pounded out, but must be especially clear at these levels.

The less natural-feeling movements—the vocabulary of classical ballet—will be introduced gradually at different levels in a child's exposure to dance. In order to be learned correctly from the very first stage, they must be done slowly, but this does not necessarily restrict you to slow music. A teacher's understanding of the limitless possibilities of using music creatively is necessary here for maintaining an energetic and enjoyable musical atmosphere.

In most classes at these levels, there is a lot of time between combinations taken up by organizing, demonstrating, and explaining. Once you have gotten a general idea of how a class progresses, plan ahead and take in new music you have prepared, work on weak spots in your technique, and/or make yourself sightread. In short, take advantage of the extra time you have to think, which is not always available in more advanced classes.

Adult beginner class

The pace of these classes moves more quickly than the pace of young children's classes. In other words, there will be less time between combinations, but the steps and movements will still be done slowly, to ensure proper execution.

There are often a number of dance fans and balletomanes in adult beginner classes. Naturally they are incapable of executing the advanced technical vocabulary of professional dancers, but they are able to experience the same intense involvement of their bodies with the music. Technique is a means to the end of communication, and one can communicate and feel joy with a simple tendu if it is done with conviction and passion.

Selections from the traditional ballet repertoire are a good choice for these classes not only from the educational point of view, but also because those familiar strains will make them feel more as if they are really dancing. "Schmaltzy" and dynamically charged adagios are very suitable for adult beginners. Though their steps and movements may be very basic, they can express themselves through these movements.

One pitfall to avoid in children's and adult beginner classes is watching the students (as you must) and playing like they look. They may look plodding, mechanical, graceless, uninspired, or as if they are in great pain. (If you take some classes yourself, you will be able to understand better why they don't smile all the time while they are doing something that is supposed to be enjoyable.) To prevent your music from sounding like they look, watch the teacher's demonstration and try to emulate her flow of movement in your music. It is hard to recommend restricting such a natural, healthy action as laughing, but it is generally wise to resist the impulse to laugh at a beginner student's ungainly movements. Think how you would feel if the class laughed at you every time you either played something totally inappropriate or hit a wrong note.

This may be an appropriate place to mention the accompanist's reaction to the size and level of dance classes. Every class you play should be approached with maximum concentration and commitment. If a class is large, you may tend to get a bit nervous, and that extra measure of adrenaline pushes you a bit farther than you thought you could go. If a class is small, you owe it to the students and the teacher not to let down your energy. Each of them is reacting to your music in the same way that dancers in a large class do, and you must demand a certain consistency of dedication from yourself.

Intermediate, advanced, and professional classes

These levels of classes are where every conceivable form and style of music should be used. Some of the students may be preparing for a career on the stage, and if they aren't exposed to a wide variety of music in the classroom, they will be less prepared to deal with the musical demands that arise in rehearsal and performance situations. If they can't count and phrase a 9/8, how will they ever cope with the complexities of Stravinsky, Stockhausen, Webern, or John Cage? If they can't learn to coordinate their movements to the tempos you and the teacher establish, how will they manage the necessary responses to a conductor?

Since students at these levels have a broader range of technique, they should be able to use your music more expansively. The intelligent ones have solved many of the problems of getting to the right place at the right time; now they should be able to really put into practice the subtle art of "getting there is half the fun": using all the notes, hearing the phrasing and nuances, and *becoming* the music.

Point class

In point classes, women (rarely men) learn to dance in special shoes made of layers of satin and shellac (not wood or metal, as is commonly thought) that are designed to support the body on the tips of the toes.

The illusion of lightness projected by dancing on point is achieved through many years of building strength in the legs and feet—actually, in the entire body. This lightness must be reflected in the music you play for point class; music is often the students' only reminder that the blisters and aching feet are a means to an end.

A large number of female variations in the traditional ballets are written in 2/4, are pizzicato in nature, and require reverse pedaling (see page 169). These selections represent the lightness necessary for point class and are eminently suitable, but obviously an entire hour of pizzicato music in duple meter would deaden the ears and, consequently, the body. So gentle waltzes, boleros, minuets, and codas are also recommended, as well as light, breathing, singing adages.

Men's class

Men's class increases strength and stamina in preparation for dancing the demanding male variations in the traditional repertoire, as well as lifting and supporting female dancers in both the classical and contemporary repertoire. A great deal of strength is required for both women and men to achieve the deceptive look of ease associated with classical dancing, but men need an extra measure of strength primarily for one reason: lifting partners. The first section of most traditional pas de deux requires the man to lift, carry, and support the woman for an average of five minutes; then he must immediately dance his variation when his stamina has been severely taxed. And a lot of contemporary choreography contains a great deal of non-traditional partnering. Therefore, it is not surprising to occasionally find calisthenic exercises like push-ups in men's class.

Men's class needs rich, substantial music to foster a rich, substantial demiplié. You should be the full orchestra playing here, not just pizzicato strings, a harp, and solo wind instruments. There is a fine line between rich, substantial music and heavy, ponderous music. Volume depends more on how many notes you play at a given time than on how hard you depress the keys.

The steps the teacher gives will of course dictate your choice of music. Male variations from the traditional ballets are obviously suitable. Typical point class music (except for codas) is not suitable, nor are pieces like Schubert waltzes, which were written for intimacy, not grandeur.

Variations and repertoire classes

These classes are not described extensively, as they are self-explanatory. The teacher demonstrates the original choreography of a work and you play the corresponding music.

Classes for pas de deux, adagio, partnering, double work, and so on

The term *adagio* can often be misleading to a beginning accompanist. In technique class, adagio refers to slow, sustained dance movements and the quality of music that accompanies them. An adagio (or adage) can also mean a dance done by two people, not necessarily to slow music; and it can also be an isolated section of a complete dance or the first section of a traditional pas de deux (explained starting on page 209.)

Beginning adagio classes are designed mainly to help boys and girls overcome any initial inhibitions they might have about coming into close physical contact, as well as to familiarize them with the inherent problems of partnering. Basic combinations involving supported pirouettes (waltzes and mazurkas), promenades in attitude and arabesque (adagios and slow waltzes), and simple lifts (mazurkas and grand allegro waltzes) may be given. (These musical forms are normally used for the corresponding combinations; other forms are certainly possible.) In more advanced classes of this kind, students will work on more technically difficult combinations: The teacher may choreograph a short work to a piece of music she may ask you to choose; or the students may learn the adagio section from a traditional pas de deux.

Whatever the teacher's methods, she can be very creative, since she is not restricted to the barre-and-center format of technique classes. If she is confident in her use of music, she can use any piece of music in any style (as long as it is fairly classical in structure so that the students don't have to struggle with the music as well as with each other) and make it work for a beneficial combination for her students. The vocabulary of steps used in partnering class is a rather small fraction of the entire dance vocabulary, and a varied range of music will help her with the problems of making the same old steps seem fresh and new.

The importance of music takes on additional emphasis in adagio class. If musicality (or at least rhythmicality) is not observed, partnering can start to look more like wrestling. Men don't gracefully lift women into the air only by brute strength; split-second timing is required. If he gathers his strength as she pliés and they both go up together, the lift is accomplished smoothly. Music is the guiding force and link between the two partners; it tells them how much time each movement requires.

Theory class

Although such classes are not yet widespread, I am hopeful that their popularity will increase, as they have proven extremely beneficial to dance students, accompanists, and teachers. They are classes in which teachers and students talk about technical concepts of dance, such as how to go through the foot in a tendu; where the body weight must be placed to allow the use of the inside thigh muscle; and so forth. If a student either starts dancing after the age of fifteen or so, or has a body that is not ideal for classical dancing, these concepts must be fully understood intellectually before they can be properly executed physically. Students often don't ask questions during a normal technique class, since muscles cool down rapidly and lose their elasticity if they aren't kept moving. Theory class is more like a schoolroom than a dance classroom, in that a full technique class is rarely given. There is a lot of "show and tell" on the parts of both teachers and students; a twenty-minute discussion on perhaps one tendu en avant is not uncommon.

Your presence in a theory class is at the teacher's discretion, since music is not absolutely necessary (you could conceivably end up playing a total of ten minutes during one hour). If she wants you there, it is primarily because she realizes that, just by hearing one phrase of music, her students will be reminded that they are discussing dance, not calisthenics. Theory class also can be a very good situation for you to clear up things you don't understand, and to increase the students' awareness of the importance of your involvement in class.

Character class

Character class is so-called because dances of many national characters are taught, either in a pure form or "theatricalized" for the stage.

These classes can be difficult to play for in one respect: It is sometimes problematic to find a wide assortment of music. I hasten to add that, once this problem is surmounted, these classes can be more fun than any you will play for. By its very nature, all the music for these classes is high in energy, incomparably rhythmic, stylistically diverse, melodically captivating, lushly harmonic—*funky* is the best word I know to describe it.

In chapter 3, "Musical Forms for Dance," you will have noticed the inclusion of many musical forms which are indigenous to character class—polonaise, mazurka, tango, bolero, and so on. They are useful for both classical and character classes. All character dances have a country of origin: Hungarian czardas, Polish mazurka and polonaise, Austrian ländler, Italian tarantella, Bohemian polka, and so forth. The Spanish jota and Russian hopak were not included in chapter 3 because there aren't many of either form readily available. The jotas I know are in 3/8, the hopaks (also spelled gopak) I know are built like codas, and both forms are eminently suitable for both classical and character classes.

One purpose of character class is to prepare students for the character dances often found in the full-length classics. Excerpts from these ballets are often given in character class, enabling you to familiarize yourself with some standard repertoire. Even when the actual choreography is not given, character teachers will generally be very pleased with any of this repertoire in conjunction with their own combinations. The starting point of your basic character music repertoire will come from the following ballets: the three Tchaikovsky works *Nutcracker, Sleeping Beauty,* and *Swan Lake;* Rossini's *La Boutique Fantasque;* Delibes's *Coppélia;* and Meyerbeer's *Les Patineurs.*

Grieg's *Norwegian Dances* are useful, and there are a number of mazurkas in the *Light Compositions* Red Book.

Another purpose of character class is to encourage and develop more freedom of movement. Students can become overly concerned with turning out and pointing their feet (among other things) in classical dance. Because character dance focuses less on these technical requirements, it can go a long way in helping students recapture the joy of moving, which they will hopefully take back into their classical classes. The rich, sometimes exotic, music of character class helps students shed their inhibitions. I must say, though, that I have always felt that there should never be any difference in the quality, energy, and inspiration of "ballet" music versus "character" music.

Yet another purpose of character class is to sharpen a student's sense of rhythm. There is often a good deal of heel work and stamping in these classes (especially Spanish classes), and a student can easily hear when he is musically incorrect. Students in ballet classes are often so concerned with technique that they sometimes may neither hear nor feel nor see when they are musically incorrect.

The basic, often *pesante,* rhythms of character class will not only enrich your rhythmic awareness but also demand your utmost rhythmic accuracy.

Dancers, when out of control, often speed up their movements unconsciously, sloughing over and rushing through the difficult spots (as many musicians do). Lagging behind the music is often indicative of self-indulgence, or of trying to get a leg up that extra inch in arabesque, or of not having been made aware of the logic behind executing movements within a specified period of time. The first time I ever became aware of why accompanists shouldn't follow dancers was during a class taught by the late Yurek Lazowski, who was surely one of the world's finest teachers, both in terms of knowledge of his subject and of the ability to communicate it to his students. He was giving the following exercise (excuse the expression—if there ever was a class in which the word *exercise* did not exist, it was Mr. Lazowski's) in footwork:

Mr. Lazowski loved that piece and usually requested it, probably because its melody exactly translates the movement into sound. The students were getting faster and faster, and I was following them. What they were really doing was getting messier and messier, and I should have kept Mr. Lazowski's original tempo, forcing them to articulate properly instead of helping them to cheat.

Tap class

Your enjoyment of tap class will probably be directly related to your fondness for and your proficiency in the music used for it. If you enjoy pieces like "Tea for Two" and "Nola," you will love tap class.

In beginning tap classes, you will probably use old standards like the two just mentioned, as well as tunes like "Once in Love with Amy" and "Cecelia." Rags are also especially suitable, since their syncopation reflects much of tap dancing's greatest attraction.

Teachers of more advanced tap classes may branch out into some of the more complicated contemporary Broadway show tunes. Ray Bussey, formerly of the Joffrey and Harkness Ballets and one of the best tap dancers I have ever played for, used to set wonderful tap combinations to boleros and mazurkas; the abundance of melodic accents in a more classical style inspires unique combinations of tap dancing's "same old steps."

"Fake books" are invaluable for tap class. They are collections of popular songs and show tunes which include the melody line, lyrics, and the symbols for chord changes in the appropriate places. They are the main resource for music for tap class.

Workshops, lecture-demonstrations, visitors' day, and so on

You may be associated with a school or company that gives lecture-demonstrations or workshops for the public. In this case, you should take an active part in the selection of music. If you will be playing for the performances, choose music within your current technical capabilities, and allow for any degree of nerves you may suffer in the performance situation. When dancers miss entrances, forget steps, or fall down, the show usually goes on; but if the music falls apart, the action almost always comes to a screeching halt.

The main purposes of these casual performances are to educate the public and to build new audiences for dance. (Additionally, the benefit of performing experience for pre-professional dancers cannot be overrated.) Keep in mind that most of the potential audience knows practically nothing about dance, and many may be a bit suspicious of the art form. The choice of music may capture the audience's attention before the dancing does. Some of my "standard lecture-demonstration music" includes the following: Liszt's Hungarian Rhapsody no. 2 (made famous by a McDonald's breakfast jingle), a Joplin selection from *The Sting,* the Triumphal March from *Peter and the Wolf,* the Habañera from *Carmen,* and a rousing Sousa march.

All the above information applies also to visitors' day. My emphasis throughout this book on the necessity for insisting that students learn to dance with the music could be dismissed by some teachers as superfluous, since they feel none of their students would ever have a chance at a professional career. Dancing with the music is necessary for technical improvement and spiritual fulfillment, not just for aiming for a career in dance. Additionally, on visitors' day, the eyes of most parents are not very discerning when it comes to watching their little darlings show what they've learned, but they—just like an audience at the New York State Theater—can see when someone is off the music. Part of the charm of visitors' day is someone losing a shoe, another forgetting when to make his entrance, another waving at her grandmother, someone else being off the music, and yet another going the wrong way. These occurrences are usually not charming after the age of twelve or so, and are never charming on a professional stage.

Auditions

You may be called to play an audition for a company director who is hiring dancers. In most cases, auditions are just like normal classes. The reason they are mentioned here is because they are extremely nerve-wracking for the dancers, and you should be extra alert to read the teacher as accurately as you can.

Even if you are very experienced, choose your oldest, most reliable music so that you are in command of each combination musically, and so that the auditioner and auditionees know exactly what the rhythm is. An audition is not the place for you to try out new music or to make a pyrotechnic display. Your job in this case is to make this grueling ordeal as easy for the dancers as possible.

Be sure to ask whoever is contacting you for the job whether there will be any specific music required and, if necessary, ask them to send it to you.

The first class for a new teacher

One of the prime assets a dance accompanist needs to develop is flexibility. You should take advantage of every new accompanying opportunity that comes along, thereby broadening your exposure and increasing your understanding. Playing for a teacher you have never met has certain problems that can be minimized by about five minutes of well-directed conversation before the class begins. The trouble spots to be sorted out are usually the following:

- Does the teacher have a preference between 4- or 6-count preparations and two chords before each combination? If not, then you might say, "Then I'll play a 4- or 6-count preparation before every combination unless you tell me otherwise."
- Does the teacher know whether she demonstrates combinations faster than her students will execute them? If so, you will know that you will have to choose pieces whose median tempos are slightly slower than her verbalization. And you might also ask her to demonstrate four counts of the tempo she wants just before you begin each combination.
- Because pliés are usually the first, and often the longest, combination in class, it is helpful to know exactly what meter and tempo the teacher wants. If she says she wants a slow waltz (not knowing that she really wants a slow 3/4) and you end up having to play a lumberingly slow waltz, the class is off to a bad start. (If this does happen, turning the left hand into six harmonically suitable 8th notes instead of the waltz "OOM pah pah" makes it more bearable for all concerned.) You can solve this potential problem by asking, "Could you please demonstrate in tempo four counts of your plié combination?" (Beginning accompanists should also request this of the fondu combination, if she gives one.) It is wise to ask how many positions she does pliés in. Some teachers do them in three positions (first, second, and fifth), and others in four positions (first, second, fourth, and fifth)—and not necessarily in that order.
- Quite a few teachers change, or are unspecific about, the accents during the demonstration of a grand battement combination. You can solve this problem by asking, "Is the leg up on 'and' (medium-tempo 6/8 march) or on the count (other appropriate meter)?"
- Adagios are always a problem because of different qualities and varying ways of counting. You can solve this problem by playing one of your familiar ones before class and asking if it is acceptable. (I almost always play the theme from the second movement of Tchaikovsky's Piano Concerto no. 1; it is well-known, its median tempo is reasonably flexible, and it is hard to miscount.)
- Ask the teacher if she finishes her class with a révérence or a port de bras. If she does, ask her for the quality (adagio or bravura) and whether it is a specified length. (Since teachers are almost always at the front of the class during the révérence, you may not be able to hear her or see her in order to know when to stop playing.) It's a good idea to get the music out before class, or to know in your head what you will play for the révérence; it is a special time in the class, and you want to be fully prepared for it.

Potential areas of misunderstanding

The misunderstandings that occur through faulty communication with and from the teacher are especially frustrating for the beginning accompanist. You must remember that you will gradually be able to understand exactly what the teacher wants. (Well, maybe not always. I am writing this the day after playing some teachers' examinations. It has been a long time since I could not decipher a request from a dance teacher, and I was especially confused yesterday when a teacher asked me for "more accented music" for her plié combination. I personally cannot imagine accented music for pliés, but I try to please every teacher. Even after a protracted discussion after the class, I was still unable to understand what she meant. Her nonexistent English and my less-than-fluent German probably didn't help matters much.)

I think it will be helpful for less experienced accompanists to be aware of the usual trouble spots. One of my biggest frustrations as a beginner was knowing that I had a problem in a particular area, and being unable either to find a solution or to even formulate a question. Over the years I have sorted out a lot of my misunderstandings, and I hope this section will smooth the way a little bit for accompanists who are new to the field.

Tempo

Tempo, as usual, is number one on the list of misunderstandings in the classroom. Correct tempo is vital for the safety and correct development of the dancers, and for you, the accompanist, to be able to play what the teacher wants. For this reason I repeat ad nauseam that the teacher must either demonstrate in the correct tempo or establish it just before the dancers begin dancing. And if you are not experienced enough to be able to figure out when she wants the tempo she demonstrated and when not, ask.

The following are some standard tempo-altering devices that are commonly used in the dance studio.

Ritard

Ritard is an abbreviation of the word *ritardando.* There are differences between *ritardando, rallentando, ritenuto, allargando,* and all the other words that denote a slowing down; and I have heard that discussions over their various nuances cause fights between some conductors. To save time, facilitate reading, and avoid violence, I have chosen to use *ritard,* as either a verb or a noun. Most dance teachers, as well as many musicians, use it in this way.

A ritard is usually a gradual decrease in tempo. A tempo change from one bar to the next is not really a ritard, and is often preceded by a fermata.

As a general rule in the dance classroom, don't ritard unless you have a complete understanding and visual grasp of the movement that is being executed at the time—or unless, of course, the teacher asks you to do so. Beginning accompanists who are inexperienced in reading movement usually don't realize that seemingly static poses that have less visible movement to the untrained eye (such as arabesque, attitude, and balances) are, in truth, often the most difficult to sustain, especially when a ritard prolongs the sustaining.

As you become more experienced, you may find yourself wanting to ritard in the following situations:

- In plié combinations, when specific counts have not been given to change the feet from one position to the next, a slight ritard will allow the students enough time to finish the preceding movement properly, and to change the feet neatly.

- The same reason applies to stretching combinations, when the standing leg must often be adjusted from one body position to the next.

- A ritard for "music to balance by" was covered on page 151.

- When an adagio combination is done to both sides without a break in the music, the ritard before the second side serves two purposes: It gives the dancers an extra space to breathe and renew their energies; and many adagios start softly and build to a big climax, so the ritard gives you an extra space to diminuendo to the proper beginning dynamic level.

Ritards are often found within the main body of many pieces used for adagio combinations, and the teacher must be familiar with them before she starts choreographing her combination. If you have a new adagio with ritards in it, play it before class for the teacher, so she knows where the ritards are and can adjust her steps and movements to the proper technical level of her students. She might give a balance in arabesque to her advanced students during this ritard, and a lovely port de bras (with both feet on the floor) to her intermediate and beginning students. If the ritards are unsuitable for her movements in that particular case, choose another piece. (Ask her if she doesn't like it at all, or if it just isn't what she wants for that particular combination. If she doesn't like it at all, another teacher might adore it, so don't throw it away—along with all your hard work learning it.)

Ritards are sometimes used in barre combinations for changing from one side to the other without stopping the music. Almost without exception, you will be expected to resume the original tempo after the ritard is completed. This sounds easy, but most beginning accompanists have trouble with it. An awareness of the problem often solves it. (I do not advocate the use of these ritards on a regular basis. I have explained why on page 76 in the Teachers' chapter, since it is the teacher's decision to use them or not.)

Some teachers ask for a ritard in the pirouette section of a combination so that a dancer can accomplish more turns. This is generally unwise, since the most logical and dependable execution of pirouettes is accomplished through the use of rhythm: The head spots to the rhythm of the music, regardless of the tempo. Most musical dancers are thrown off by a ritard in a pirouette section because they rely completely on the impetus of the music to govern their movements. More logical—and more musical and more satisfying—solutions have been described in the section about the pirouette family, beginning on page 115.

While there may be instances to the contrary, a ritard is generally executed with the spaces of time between sounds growing longer as the ritard progresses. The proportion of this space enlargement depends completely on each situation, as does the length of the ritard—whether it begins (for instance) on count 13 or count 15. This is another situation in which your powers of observation and awareness of the teacher's needs must be turned to "high."

The execution of ritards is primarily dependent on three elements: proportion, instinct, and the dancers' needs. It would be nice to be able to let our musical instincts alone govern the length and breadth of a ritard, but—since the dancers' physical security and artistic interpretation are interdependent with the music—you must learn to compromise, when necessary, and to be reasonably consistent in your use of ritards. This is covered more fully in the tempo section of "In the rehearsal room." (See page 207.)

An important element in the execution of music is energy—the indefinable something that evokes an ongoing impetus and feeling of propulsion. It is easier, of course, to maintain this energy when the tempo is moving along at a regular pace. Be aware that a beginning accompanist may lose some of this impetus during ritards; aim toward maintaining the necessary support.

Your increasing awareness of the most suitable proportion of a ritard in each situation will allow you to couple instinct with consistency. Never lose track of the fact that you are a part of a whole; your worth depends not only on how well you play the piano but also on how much you can contribute to and interact with others.

Rubato

Rubato is the Italian word for stolen, and the Oxford Concise Dictionary of Music defines it thus: "A feature of performance in which strict time is for a while disregarded—what is 'robbed' from some note or notes being 'paid back' later. When this is done with genuine artistry and instinctive musical sensibility, the effect is to impart an admirable sense of freedom and spontaneity. Done badly, rubato becomes merely mechanical. The question of rubato in Chopin is particularly contentious, since its use in his music may be dangerously open to abuse. Accounts of his playing (and of Mozart's) suggest that he kept the left hand in strict time and added rubato to the right."

The use of rubato in the classroom is a very touchy subject. Its primary drawback to classroom suitability is its elasticity of tempo. (I find lamentably few musicians these days who execute rubato according to the last sentence in the previous paragraph.) If a dancer were allowed the luxury of learning through daily private lessons, its use might be more prevalent. But it is practically impossible to train—and to synchronize the movements of—more than one body to this elasticity. (One of the benefits of dancers working in groups is learning to move as one, as a corps de ballet or any ensemble of dancers is required to do.) And it should be remembered that it takes many hours of very expensive rehearsal time to get an orchestra to play with rubato.

I play very little Chopin in class, partly because so much of his music has suffered from overexposure and misguided execution, but mainly because much of the magic of his music lies in the use of rubato. His music does enjoy widespread exposure in the dance classroom; he was one of the few romantic master composers who used dance forms that are still part of the dance—and musical—vocabulary today: waltzes, mazurkas, and polonaises. (However, most Chopin mazurkas are stylistically and dynamically worlds apart from what most dance teachers think of as mazurkas.)

It is often difficult (and musically unsatisfying, to say the least) to play adagios without rubato or ritards. Creative teachers will usually be able to make use of your "most rubato" adage, as long as she can make sense of the phrases, and can hear the beginnings and ends of them.

Fermatas and accelerandos

Fermatas and accelerandos are not covered extensively in this section, as they are seldom used in the dance classroom. They are dealt with in more detail in the section "In the rehearsal room" (page 207).

A fermata 𝄐 is a hold—a device for stopping the action. Its use is rare in the classroom, and its length is governed totally by each situation in which one is used. Occasionally, I find myself playing for a teacher who yells, "Balance!" on the very last bar of the music. At that point, it is too late harmonically to go into my standard four-count addition, so I resort to a dominant-seventh fermata. This lends such a dramatic element of suspension that I wonder if it is possibly more effective than four or eight counts of additional music to balance by. If the teacher gives me no cue to relieve the tension, I "take a poll": I resolve the chord when the main body of the class starts returning to the finishing position, not when the first student falls out of the balance, or when the last one decides, "Well, that's enough of that."

Accelerandos are almost unheard of during the phrases of a classroom combination. The tempo of each combination almost always stays the same within each movement phrase. However, the teacher may want a change of tempo for the second execution of a combination. If there is a 4-count preparation before the faster section, begin the accelerando directly on the first count, and have the new tempo firmly in control by the fourth count. If there is no 4-count preparation, an accelerando is not involved; it is an immediate change of tempo.

Setting and changing tempos

Although a few teachers allow the accompanist to set the tempo, this is a dangerous practice. The reasons are obvious with a beginning accompanist. A more advanced accompanist will usually have a good general idea of the tempo of each combination, but only the teacher knows what particular thing she is aiming for in each combination, and the tempo is vital in this regard.

No accompanist, regardless of level or experience, should ever consider it a personal affront to change a tempo at the teacher's request. There is no such thing as an accompanist who can accurately judge every tempo every day. More often than not, I will say to teachers with whom I've never worked, "Please tell me right away if the tempo is not right." This immediately establishes open communication: It reminds the teacher that tempo is her responsibility, and it reminds me not to get uptight if she asks me to change it.

The most crucial section of every combination is the first four counts. If the tempo is wrong, the teacher will almost always adjust it during this time. A teacher will often do the first four counts of the combination with the students to see if the tempo is the one she wants, and you would be wise to start watching her while you are playing, so that you can use her visual and oral cues to make any necessary adjustments. This is especially helpful in classes where teachers demonstrate in faster tempos than what they will ultimately want.

Accompanists eventually learn to change tempo on a moment's notice, although it is always helpful for the teacher to give every accompanist—and her students!—at least four counts of warning. When communication is well established between teacher and accompanist, just a glance will suffice to indicate that a tempo change is forthcoming.

Under no circumstances should a student, dancer, ballerina, premier danseur, prima donna, or diva ask the accompanist to change the tempo. When this occurs, my standard remark is, "Ask the teacher. It's her class, not mine." ("And not yours, either," I mutter to myself.)

Grand allegro combinations are often executed with the women's group(s) going first and the men's group(s) next, with no break in the music. The men often require a slower tempo, and a 4-count preparation in the new tempo between the groups is clearer for all concerned.

There is a certain thought process that I use when teachers, choreographers, ballet masters, conductors, or directors say, "Just a hair faster (or slower), please." (It is really true that a hair's difference in tempo to a dancer can make a vast difference in his execution and overall performance.) It often takes a while to learn how each person measures a hair; some actually mean a whole hank. But for those who truly mean a hair, I tell myself, "the same tempo but faster (or slower)." I know it sounds oxymoronic, but it works for me.

Marking

Marking a combination can sometimes contribute to a misunderstanding about tempo.

Dance teachers usually mark combinations because they are out of shape. The term "out of shape" refers not to the teacher's figure, but to her muscles. Without a daily class, it is impossible to retain the strength and muscle tone necessary to execute correctly many of classical dance's steps and movements. So the teacher resorts to marking: demonstrating physically watered-down versions of the combinations with either her body or her hands.

She also marks to save time. It would probably require five hours to teach a class in which the teacher demonstrated every combination all the way through in the proper tempo. So, once she has established for you (and for the students) the proper tempo, she may mark the rest of the demonstration much more quickly. This is especially true for (but not restricted to) inherently slower combinations, such as pliés, ronds de jambe, and adagios. A beginning accompanist needs to start to practice retaining the tempo of those first eight or so counts (before she starts to mark) while deciding what to play, since that tempo is a major factor in the decision. As you become more experienced, you will also be able, through the inflections in her voice, to pick up any deviation from the way she normally phrases combinations (such as a rogue 9-count phrase), and to intuit when it is almost time to start—even though your conscious mind is involved in deciding what to play.

It is conceivable—and absolutely understandable—for an accompanist at any level to lose that first tempo. If that is the case, ask the teacher to clarify it for you just before you begin a combination.

If the teacher wants to mark a combination with the music for the students after the demonstration, I always play more softly than usual, so the teacher can be heard clearly. (The dynamic level of both her voice and my playing during a mark is decidedly different from when the students are doing a combination.)

It is not uncommon for even experienced accompanists sometimes to be unsure about a teacher's request. If you are 95 percent sure that you know what she wants, and she asks you, "Is that clear?" you can save time by saying, "Let's mark it with music and see." Having her re-demonstrate the combination is time consuming, and marking is always helpful for everyone concerned.

Adagios

Adagios are the worst troublemakers in the communication process between teacher and accompanist. Tempo is the biggest problem, primarily for the reasons described above in the marking section. Very few teachers are still able to demonstrate an adagio in the tempo in which they want their students to dance, so they give the accompanist a false impression of tempo during the demonstration. And most dance teachers don't realize how vital it is for us to know an adagio's median tempo before we choose a piece, so—either as an afterthought just before beginning or during the first few counts of the execution—they yell, "Slower!"

Overall mood and quality, which touch upon the areas of style and dynamics, can be misunderstood, too. So it is highly recommended that the teacher ask the accompanist to play an adagio before she sets it, so she can either choreograph her movements to the accompanist's selection or ask him for a different one.

Probably the greatest misunderstanding about adages is that a teacher often says, "I want a really slow adagio" that will include an 8-count développé. The students will *dance* it really slowly, but if we *play* a really slow adagio, it will do the students in. A medium-tempo gentle waltz, such as example 23, would be appropriate for this request. (A really slow adagio works with a 4- or 2-count développé.) If you are a new accompanist, you may want to discuss this with a teacher: Play a medium-tempo gentle waltz, then a "normal" adagio (such as example 52), and then ask her how her legs feel after doing the same combination to each piece. (If necessary, refer back to the detailed discussion on adagio tempos on page 37.)

I have played for several teachers over the years who have asked me in the center for the same adage that I played at the barre or for stretching. It took me decades to figure out why they would ask for something so boring. Finally

I realized that they had choreographed their center adage combinations to what I played at the barre. After the light dawned, I learned to ask, "Do you really want the same music, or may I play something similar in the same meter and tempo?"

If a teacher asks me to play an adagio before she sets one, I usually ask two questions: "What size—gentle, medium, or huge?" and "Does it have to be square?" About one-fourth of the adagios in my repertoire are not in convenient 16- or 32-count phrases. It's not so much that I *won't* cut them down to fit, as much as it is that I *can't;* their musical phrases are so right the way the composers wrote them that they can't be valid statements if I alter them. (My exception to this rule is Rachmaninoff's 18th Paganini Variation, described on page 138.)

The quality of any given adagio combination is not always apparent, even to advanced accompanists, especially if the teacher verbalizes it as she would a grocery list. It is possible to execute the same adagio combination to both the hush of a *Gymnopédie* by Satie and the somber grandeur of a section of Rachmaninoff's Prelude in g minor (op. 23, no. 5). The choreography of the adagio would be exactly the same, but there should be a vastly different quality of movement, according to the music. You must listen carefully to the way the teacher verbalizes her demonstrations. If in doubt, ask.

If you love adagios as much as I do, the following personal experience may be of help to you.

I went back to New York City to play and teach for Marjorie Mussman during the summer of 1978. Since I hadn't played for her for many years, I made at home a cassette of all my "unusual" adagios (including their names and composers for later identification) and sent it on ahead to her. Our schedules were so hectic that summer that we could never have found enough time to cover as much ground as this tape did. These unusual adagios (a "usual" or "normal" adagio is a fairly slow three of thirty-two counts) come in every conceivable meter and tempo, as well as in a variety of qualities and unconventional phrasing. She familiarized herself with the tempo, phrasing, and dynamics of each piece, and, with her students, we were able to more fully explore adagio movement than if I had been restricted to normal adagios.

I am certainly not alone in believing that the adagio in the center is a very special time during the class. (I think of it as the heart of the class.) Regardless of the level of your experience, you and the teacher(s) for whom you play regularly might want to make use of an adagio cassette in order to provide a wider variety of adagio music. Person-to-person communication is, of course, the best, but if time constraints dictate it, this is a reasonable substitute.

“Ands”

There will probably be many accompanists who deal with “ands” very easily, but they were such a big problem area for me for so long that I felt they should be mentioned here. If I had realized (or been told) that it is essentially a mathematical problem, I could have solved it sooner.

“Ands” is a convenient label to describe certain combinations in which steps go out on “and” and in on the count. These combinations are usually tendus, dégagés, and grands battements, and the following discussion applies to all three in exactly the same way.

Using tendus as an example, tendus going out on the count almost always come in on the next count, not on the next “and.”

But when tendus go out on the “and,” they never come in on the next “and” but on the next count.

This produces twice as many tendus twice as fast as in the first example, and the music will need to have the corresponding accents. The musical excerpt in both examples works well for both ways of executing tendus because of its melodic structure.

On the other hand, example 12 works only for tendus that go out on the count. Even though there are notes on each “and,” the piece is more of a lilting polka; its personality suffers and it becomes very heavy when it is slowed down, which it must be in order to accommodate most “and” combinations.

Pieces in duple meter with a dotted melodic rhythm are always reliable “ands” for tendus and dégagés. Many codas work well, too, but I play them only for dégagés, because that’s usually when dancers start to come alive at the barre. The more driving and energetic rhythmic structure of a coda seems to intrude upon the dancers’ concentration on warming up their feet and legs during tendus.

Almost all 6/8 marches have a melodic structure with appropriate “ands” and a rhythmic structure full enough to support the proper workable tempo for "and" grands battements. For some reason, they make the legs feel lighter than most 4/4 marches. (Remember: They are counted just like 4/4 marches.) Ever since I discovered the reliability of 6/8 marches for "and" grands battements, I have tended to fall into the rut of using them exclusively, and I have to remind myself every once in a while to play the few 4/4 marches that work for "ands," such as examples 34a and 80 or the triumphant, martial theme from Tchaikovsky's Violin Concerto.

"That's too heavy"

At one time or another almost every accompanist has heard a teacher comment, "That's too heavy." "Heavy" is the best teachers can do to verbally describe the sound of music that beats dancers into the ground instead of helping them into the air. They can't speak in musical, theoretical terms any better than you can discuss the theoretical intricacies of dance, so your request for clarification will usually be met with frustration on both your parts.

"Heavy" can be a description of either the music you have chosen or the way you play it. One of the following remedies will usually solve the problem.

- Your pedaling is misplaced. Try reversing your normal pedaling so that different beats of the music are emphasized.
- You misread, or were probably misinformed about, the tempo or meter or both. In all cases, choose another piece whose inherent tempo matches the teacher's needs. In the case of adagios, choose another one or slow down your choice with arpeggiation. In the case of non-adagios, choose a piece that has fewer notes in it, especially in the left hand. For example, a polka has half as many notes in the left hand as a coda, but both can often be played at the same tempo. A change in meter can also relieve heaviness (for example, from a fast 3/4 to a rag or polka).
- You are playing a few notes harshly and loudly, instead of more notes with more volume. Work on your octaves.
- Someone has exhorted you to play "louder! fuller!" so you are playing every note of every bar at triple forte. Take the previous tip to heart, and remember that one does not play every note loudly in any loud piece.

Miscellaneous

The following situation illustrates the need for your constant alertness in class. The teacher is giving a correction or demonstrating a combination, and you are hunting through your music for a particular piece or (hopefully not) putting together your shopping list. The magic "and" jolts you out of your reverie, and you react like Pavlov's dogs by playing a preparation without looking at the class. But this "and" is only part of her dialogue to the students, and you are left with egg on your face. When this happens often enough, you will see the necessity of being tuned in at all times to the teacher, if only to prevent further embarrassment.

The following are two instances in which a beginning accompanist may become confused by what the teacher says.

- A teacher may say, "Now we are going to do dégagés," and she will set the following combination: "tendu, lift, tendu, close." This is a beginner form of dégagé; the entire step—one dégagé—is accomplished in four counts to a fairly brisk piece of music. (See example 66 section A.)

Then she may say, "Now we are going to do faster dégagés," and she will set the following combination: "four dégagés with the leg out on 'and' and in on '1.'" Do not be misled into thinking your music will go faster; one dégagé is now being executed in one count to a considerably slower piece. The music is entirely different from the first example. (See example 39.)

This concept is applicable to many steps in dance. They are learned in a very slow body tempo (but the music doesn't always have to be slow), or are broken down into parts, as in the foregoing dégagé example. Grands battements are usually taught in exactly the same way. And ronds de jambe à terre at the beginning level are usually broken down into four parts: tendu front, tendu side, tendu back, and close in first, third, or fifth position. You would not play "tendu music," however; the smoothness and roundness of a rond de jambe à terre must be evident from the beginning, so a medium-slow legato waltz would be appropriate.

- A teacher will often ask for a waltz for a grand allegro combination, and the accents in the movements she demonstrates—or even the words she says—will suggest a duple meter. You might ask, "May I play a two?" If she says no, don't argue; go to her after class and ask why, so that you can understand why she wanted a waltz, and so that she can understand why you're confused. (Mr. Brunson used to count every grand battement demonstration in three, so I would always play a waltz, and he would always stop and say, "No, I want a march." After about the fourth time, I went to him after class and said, "If you always want a march, why do you always count a 3/4?" He said, "I don't know why, but let's just say that, no matter what I count, I usually want a march." "Usually," of course, is the key word here; I ended up playing 6/8 or 4/4 marches for his grands battements unless they included grands battements en balançoire or en cloche, which almost always demand a 3/4.)

These two situations illustrate what can happen with many groups of steps. How much leeway you have in changing the choice of music depends on the relationship you and the teacher cultivate together, and on your degree of experience.

In the rehearsal room

There is a different thrust to the work in a rehearsal studio as opposed to a classroom. A professional dancer's prime focus in rehearsal is to learn steps set to music by a choreographer for eventual performance on stage. While the perfection of technique is a never-ending process, professional dancers generally seem to leave that all-important aspect to their daily company class. In rehearsal, they direct their mental and physical energies toward the assimilation of specific steps and movement phrases to specific counts and musical phrases, which eventually become "ballets" or "pieces" or "works" or "happenings" or who knows what else.

Being a company pianist can involve some or all of the following functions: playing for company class and pre-performance warm-ups; playing for rehearsals; running the tape recorder for rehearsals and/or performances; bringing coffee to a bunch of exhausted people; calling lighting cues from the score during performance; cutting and splicing performance tapes; organizing, maintaining, and distributing the music library and orchestra parts; maintaining emotional equilibrium and a steady tempo in the midst of chaos; playing with the orchestra as a soloist or part of the ensemble; and being the Rock of Gibraltar. If you are auditioning for a job as company pianist, it would be wise for you to ask how many of these duties you will be expected to fulfill.

Company class and pre-performance warm-up

Whether it is the director, ballet master or mistress, régisseur (why doesn't anybody say régisseuse?), or company teacher who teaches these classes, each person may have a distinctly different approach from another, as well as from one day to the next.

If the company teacher also teaches in an affiliated school, she may be very demanding with the students in the school, pushing them to unbelievable limits, and then come into company class and be downright cajoling, soothing, and gentle with the company members. If this is the case, she is aware that the company members have a rigorous performing or rehearsal schedule ahead of them (or may have just finished one). On the other hand, if the company is in a rehearsal period in which there is not an overwhelming number of works to be prepared, she may go back to the methods she uses at the school and push the dancers harder than usual.

If she doesn't tell you what period she's in, very often her voice will let you know. The atmosphere of any dance class can often be discerned by how the teacher says, "First position" (or whatever she says) as the class begins.

Some teachers foster a very casual atmosphere, treating company class as nothing but a warm-up for the dancers' muscles. (Maybe this is why the use of the word *training* instead of *company class* has become so prevalent in Europe. It is another word I would instantly abolish. Football players do training; dancers try to make art.) Others always demand the utmost mental concentration and physical energy from the dancers every day, regardless of their schedule. The ideal balance seems to be the teacher who respects exhausted dancers' needs to nurse their bodies, while maintaining an energetic, well-paced class with a positive, disciplined atmosphere for the dancers who are feeling good.

Although professional dancers are expected to work on their technique in daily class, they are often too tired to resist the temptation of treating company class as simply a warm-up. Therefore, music should be a prime source of inspiration, especially in company class. Be extra diligent about bringing in new music to spark dancers' desire to work. If you don't have much contact with whoever is teaching company class, you might follow the suggestion on page 195 and make a tape of your unusual adagios so the teacher can be fully familiar with them. (A lush, soaring adagio will revitalize almost every dancer's waning will to work.) When rehearsal schedules are tight, company class is usually the first thing to be reduced in length, and a company teacher will try to get as much work as possible into a shorter period of time. So there should be no moments wasted trying to sort out an unusual number of phrases or an odd meter.

Some teachers always want the pre-performance warm-up to be highly charged musically, to get the dancers' adrenaline going; others feel the dancers need to be soothed and not have their thoughts of the upcoming performance intruded upon. It is best to establish this ahead of time, so that no teacher-accompanist misunderstandings interfere with the dancers' concentration.

It can be difficult being the only pianist for a company, because this usually means that you are the sole source of musical inspiration for daily company class. You must develop a very large repertoire to keep the dancers—and yourself—constantly interested and inspired. Exploring all the musical choices for each particular combination will also help: sometimes a barcarolle for an adagio, sometimes a tango for tendus or dégagés, sometimes a moderato two for ronds de jambe à terre, stop time during a frappé combination, and so on. You will have to play unusual meters for the teacher before or after class, so she can think up appropriate combinations: a polacca or allegro 9/8 for dégagés or petit allegro, a polonaise for grands battements, and so on.[15]

Playing for rehearsal

Rehearsals can be either boring or fascinating, depending on one's approach and attitude. I have always been an incurable people watcher and, over the years, have become an insatiable dancer watcher, so rehearsals for me are as fascinating—if not quite as much fun—as playing for class. I really enjoy watching the different ways in which choreographers and dancers work and move, how they approach difficult passages, and how they turn occasional tentative lurches into smooth movement phrases.

Your involvement in a new (for you) production will be most rewarding if:

- you get the score a reasonable amount of time before the rehearsals begin, so you can be thoroughly familiar with it. If the choreographer is creating a new piece, you can perfect the musical execution at the same time that the dancers learn the steps; if it is a piece already in the repertoire, you'll need to have it closer to performance level by the first rehearsal;
- you are present at a meeting with the choreographer and the conductor to establish tempos, so there won't be any discrepancy between the choreographer's needs, the conductor's expectations, and your inclinations (most choreographers learn the hard way that, if their pieces are to be performed to live music, the fewer tempo changes they insist upon, the better their chances are of having reliable musical performances);
- you are with the choreographer in every rehearsal of that piece, so you can mark the music and know exactly where he finishes each day;
- you play the stage rehearsals, being thoroughly familiar with the tempos by that time; and
- you are asked to be the liaison between the choreographer/director and the conductor during orchestral rehearsals, which usually involves sitting behind the conductor and within earshot of the choreographer/director and relaying information from one to the other. This avoids a lot of shouting, and you can also probably translate dance problems into musical solutions for the conductor and vice versa. You can also tell the conductor where the choreographer/director wants to start in the score after a stop. Be sure that the rehearsal numbers in your score are the same as the conductor's.

You will be expected to be just as alert in rehearsal as you are when playing for class, although in a different way. There is a lot of stopping and starting in many rehearsals, and it is important to make a mental note of where you stop playing each time. Even after a break during which the choreographer is setting steps, you must know exactly where he is musically and be ready for that almighty "and." Since there is often much more conversation going on in a rehearsal than in a technique class, you must be extra tuned in to hear that "and." You will gradually acquire the ability to identify the choreographer's voice (as well as that of anyone leading a rehearsal or teaching a class), even when he speaks softly to you amid absolute cacophony.

The primary musical difference between class and rehearsal is that in rehearsal you are playing a piece of music that will eventually be performed onstage according to the composer's wishes. Phrasing, dynamics, and ritards are observed as faithfully as if you were playing a Beethoven sonata. Tempos should be as consistent as possible from day to day. That should not imply that you are less observant in these areas in class; it just means that the final musical product you are rehearsing will be ultimately performed with less daily fluctuation in tempo and dynamics than combinations in technique class, whose needs often demand different adjustments.

Think of yourself as the conductor's—and even the composer's—representative; try to play the music the way the dancers will end up hearing it, not the way you personally think it should be played, or at the tempo that the dancers want. And if this is a problem, discuss it with the conductor and the choreographer.

It is imperative that the piano be placed in such a way that you have an uninterrupted sight line to the choreographer and dancers, or—at the very least—you see them with your peripheral vision.

Even if you see a dancer fall in rehearsal, keep playing until told to stop. Falls are not unheard of onstage, and it is imperative that the "faller" and everyone else learn to keep going, no matter what happens.

The choreographer

Let it be stressed how appreciative teachers, dancers, choreographers, directors, ballet masters, régisseurs—in fact all knowledgeable people in the dance world—are of competent, professional accompanists. (If you are good-natured and easy to work with on top of being good at your job, they will treasure you.) In the rehearsal situation, a choreographer (assuming he has any shred of musical awareness) will treat you like his right-hand person, and will be most grateful for your cooperation and attentiveness.

Although there is usually a great deal of give and take between a choreographer and accompanist, and although the atmosphere in a rehearsal studio is often more relaxed than in a classroom, it is still not wise to argue about tempos (or anything else) in the middle of a rehearsal. He is still the boss, just as the teacher is in the classroom. Yes, the music has a right to be expressed as the composer would have wished, but arguing about things will only strain your relationship and create an atmosphere of tension in the entire room. You can either have a quiet tête-à-tête at the piano, or wait until after the rehearsal to solve your problems together.

The choreographer may want to go over each passage several times, stopping at the end of a maxi-phrase until the dancers are fairly sure of it. After a number of times, he will want you to continue on into the next phrase, so he will be reminded of what comes next. As you become more experienced, you will become better at judging when to stop playing, and when to continue, during the choreographer's creating process.

If a choreographer asks you how many counts there are in a particular phrase, be sure you know how he is counting before you answer. You may be counting bars, and he may be counting counts.

It is impossible to discuss all pieces of music that are problematic, but I would like to mention the Waltz of the Snowflakes from *Nutcracker* here, because it drives some inexperienced choreographers and accompanists crazy (and I am speaking from experience). Maybe Tchaikovsky was in a perverse mood the day he labeled it a waltz. There *are* waltz sections in it (the G major sections), but mostly it is counted in sixes. If a choreographer tries to set it or an accompanist tries to play it thinking in the traditional "OOM pah pah" waltz rhythm, it will go against the actual flow of the music. Two bars equal six counts.

When a choreographer says, "Let's go from the beginning," there may be instances when it is judicious to ask, "From the beginning of this section or from the very beginning?"

Choreographers (and all people in charge of rehearsal) generally expect you to play four or six counts before the dancers will begin—for the same reason you play introductions in technique class.

"I'm ready when you are" is often a very helpful thing to say to a choreographer, who may not always be certain how quick you are to be ready to play after a stop in the action, or who may be musing over the next choreographic phrase. That gives him the freedom to start when he chooses; teachers and choreographers, and no one else, choose the pace at which they run their classes and rehearsals.

The conductor

Conductors are bombarded from all sides. The choreographer tells him it's too slow, the dancers tell him it's too fast, the curtain doesn't go up on cue, and the orchestra would rather be playing a Brahms symphony. This is the conductor's lot and if you meet one who seems a bit too temperamental, he may have reason to be, but these facts do not excuse his behavior. It is often just as true for some conductors as for some pianists that they will be hired more often because they are easy to work with. This does *not* necessarily mean that they are better.

In czarist Russia, so the story goes, conductors were required to follow the tempos of each royal personage's favorite ballerina; if a conductor's errant tempo disturbed the performance of one of these ladies, he was never heard of again. This attitude held over into the glory days of Soviet ballet, and is still present in the attitudes of some Russian dancers. (More than once has a Russian dancer roared at me in the classroom during his variation, "SLOWER!" I try very hard to be accommodating to dancers, but I find it the height of rudeness for a dancer whom I have never met before not only to expect me to intuit his personal tempo, but to speak to *anyone* in such a rude manner. The last one who did this in the studio was nicknamed The Hurler by my daughter. Not only was he rude, but he was also a very poor excuse for a classical dancer.)

The point I am trying to make is that there should be a mutual respect between dance people and music people.

A sensitive dance conductor is able to reconcile the needs of the dancers with the wishes of both the composer and the choreographer, as well as—at the same time—keep a large number of musicians together. A conductor like this will often sit in on beginning rehearsals, sizing up the choreographer or the music or both. As performance time approaches, he will probably conduct you during rehearsals. Then you have to become the follower, not the leader that you have been for a considerable period of time. As tempting as it may be (since you have become so used to it during this period), don't watch the dancers and adjust to their tempos. That is now the conductor's job, as he will have to do it in the pit.

It is also important for you to maintain, as much as possible, the tempos that the conductor demands from the orchestra, even if they don't agree with your musical taste. Don't forget that one of your jobs is to help dancers, and it doesn't do them any good to dance to one set of tempos in the studio and another on stage.

Most conductors establish new tempos within a piece by relating it to the tempo immediately preceding it: "a fraction slower," or "two hairs faster," than the one before. Therefore, it is important for him to be present at run-throughs—no stopping for any reason, just like onstage—so he can solidify the correct tempos in his arms and mind.

If you have never worked with a conductor before, by all means tell him. I didn't tell the first conductor I ever worked with that I had never even *seen* a conductor up close before. (Most of them are not the frightening creatures we are led to believe.) I could have spared him and the company a lot of wasted time, and myself a lot of embarrassment, if I had just spent ten minutes with him before the rehearsal. In those ten minutes, I could have learned enough to get myself started. The most important thing would have been that the time between his upbeat and downbeat defines the tempo.

Most new company members are not aware of how different dancing to live music is from dancing to taped music. If they have performed often to taped music, they will be confused about why the conductor is not as consistent in his tempos as the tape. If you sense that the conductor you are working with is either above speaking to a young dancer about this or unable to do so in non-intimidating (versus holier-than-thou or gruff) terms, add this helpful service to the list of duties for company pianists.

(To any conductors who are reading this: May I respectfully request that you keep your voice reasonably quiet if you have to speak during rehearsal? To be perfectly frank, I have seen all too many conductors come into rehearsal and behave as if they owned the place: speaking loudly while their colleague is playing and the dancers are dancing, and, often, talking about things that have absolutely nothing to do with the business at hand. When I see this happen, I often have the feeling that they would never do this during a chorus rehearsal. There is a general lack of respect for dance in the world of the performing arts, and I think it's time we tried to change it a little bit—or at least show a bit of respect to our colleagues.)

The photographer

Why, you are wondering, is this person mentioning a photographer in a book about dance accompaniment? Because I wanted to offer a helpful hint to photographers—professional and amateur—who are dissatisfied with what they see on their film. If they would keep the rhythmic pulse of the music in their heads as they take pictures, they would have much more success. Most choreographers relate their movements to the musical impulses, and very often the most interesting or expressive movements will be found on the rhythm's odd-numbered beats. It is not always possible—for example, during a stage rehearsal—to yell, "One, two three, JUMP!" to get the picture you want; using the music's impulses will usually fill the bill.

Catchwords

Catchwords are like signposts in the rehearsal process. Since a choreographer will rarely, if ever, say he wants to start at a particular bar, these catchwords will be his, your, and the dancers' common points of reference.

He may say, "the trio section," in which case you have to know whether he means the trio section in the music or the section for three dancers. He may say, "the repeat section," in which case you must understand each other very well, as there are a number of repeat sections in, for example, the Waltz of the Flowers from *Nutcracker.* He may say, "We'll go from the monsters"—where the monsters enter. Or "from Dartmouth," because a phrase of the music reminds him of the cheerleading song from that college. However he labels them, it is important that you write the label in the music exactly where that section begins.

Every rehearsal pianist must be equipped with a pencil with an eraser. Writing with pen is not a good idea because a choreographer may change his mind several times before he finally decides on a movement phrase, and because the score, if on rental, will have to be returned with all marks erased. Always keep a good pencil in your pocket or purse, or tie one to the piano so it will always be there.

Tempo

During private practice of the music you are working on, a metronome is a very handy thing, especially if you are not familiar with the music. However, remember that dancers, choreographers, and conductors—and pianists—are not metronomic. The tempo will vary slightly from rehearsal to rehearsal, and from performance to performance—again, according to the proportion of tempo that is defined on page 8. However, in the area of music for performance, the proportion will be decidedly smaller. The proportion is geared directly to the physical momentum that dancers build up as they move. This is why the correct median tempos must be established at the very first rehearsal; the choreographer should already know the music's thrust, flow, and momentum so he can begin to create his movements accordingly.

Your sense of time will be put to the strictest test in the rehearsal studio, because choreographers generally expect you to be responsible for the tempos. Sometimes you can summon up the proper tempo from one day to the next by playing a difficult passage and calling upon your muscle memory to remember whether the proper tempo feels comfortable or frantic. Or an adagio tempo may be recalled by the phrase, "slower (or faster) than you think." Sometimes, during a stop for corrections, I will keep my foot tapping in the tempo I want to keep. If I am asked to speed up or slow down a tempo, I find it easier to keep the erroneous tempo in my head as I begin and adjust it from that, rather than trying to re-create the new tempo out of thin air. By all means, it is better to use a metronome to establish a tempo, rather than run the risk of serious injury to the dancers by miscalculating. (And the metronome can be an indisputable bond between choreographer and pianist.) But gradually wean yourself away from its use, and cultivate your own innate sense of time.

While the choreographer is working on a particularly difficult movement phrase, he will often ask you to slow down the music until the dancers have it in their minds and bodies. It is not easy to hold onto the original tempo in your head while you are playing passages much more slowly, but it will come with practice—like everything else.

While dancers are learning a new piece, especially if it is to unusual music, you may notice them counting like mad. If they are still moving their lips two weeks before the premiere, it might be wise to remind them that the audience may become more fascinated with the movements of their lips than of their bodies, and that they should try to confine their counting to inside their heads. Sniffing is a helpful, almost inaudible, way of keeping track of the pulse, if needs be.

Ritards, accelerandos, and fermatas

These tempo directions are executed relatively loosely in the classroom compared to their execution in the rehearsal studio. In the classroom, they are employed to serve the needs of the dancers first. A ritard helps an advanced dancer remember that an arabesque doesn't park in position but continues to grow and extend into space, or helps a beginning dancer to find his balance by giving him an extra second or two. In rehearsal, these directions are employed to serve the music first, as they are as integral a part of the music as the notes themselves. In the classroom, we often play ritards that are not written on the printed page; in rehearsal, this is almost never done, except in pas de deux, as we shall see.

The proportions of these tempo changes must be as consistent as possible from day to day because the dancers must time their movements accordingly. For instance, there may be a four-bar ritard section in which sixteen dancers are asked to move into a different formation. If you are inconsistent in the proportion of that ritard, they may charge like a herd of frightened gazelles to get to their places one day, and the next they may have so much time that they get there too soon and have to park in an unchoreographed, static pose waiting for the "a tempo."

Fermatas are often encountered in music for dance performances. If a group of dancers is dealing with a fermata, you have more control in deciding the length of it, since it is more logical for a group of dancers to take the cue from one pianist than vice versa. If the fermata occurs during a section for a soloist, he may be balancing on that fermata, in which case you take the cue to resume from him (within reasonable musical proportions and taste). Many dancers want to know how many counts each fermata is held. Although this practice takes some of the spontaneity out of a performance, it also eliminates guesswork if a conductor is involved. It seems to go against a pianist's grain to do so, but you can count in whatever tempo you are in (even if a ritard or accelerando directly precedes a fermata) and often come up with the number of counts the fermata is held.

Problems

You may eventually run into problems with a few dancers regarding tempo. Some dancers are extremely musical; they can adjust to any reasonable tempo. Others are not so musical, but are aware that they occasionally have problems in this area, and solve them by friendly discussion with the accompanist and the ballet master or the choreographer (or both). Then there are the dancers who are either unmusical or merely rhythmical; they are so insecure about their own capabilities and self-image that they lash out at another person and blame him for their own inadequacies. That other person is usually the accompanist, because the music directly affects their performance—and also because the accompanist is usually the low man on the artistic-staff totem pole, and traditionally is expected not to open his mouth.

If this situation arises, you will be hurt or angry, and will find it difficult to deal with. If you did, indeed, misjudge the tempo, apologize and say, "Sorry, let's try it again." If you have reason to believe you are correct, say so politely; politeness might take the wind out of their stormy sails and get them to behave civilly and professionally. "I really think this is the tempo I played yesterday," is just about all you can say without flying off the handle and bringing yourself down to their level of emotional histrionics. Most competent ballet masters will not allow outbursts of unproductive temper in their rehearsals. When necessary, they run their rehearsals with as firm a hand as teachers should run their classes. (Democracy is generally absent from the world of dance, and especially from the world of ballet.) Situations such as this never get to such an unproductive point if the ballet master, who can usually sense an erroneous tempo faster than a pianist, starts clapping the correct tempo.

If you are unsure of the tempos, it is advisable to go to the ballet master before the rehearsal begins and ask, "I'm not really sure of the tempos, so could you please help me out if I go astray?" Dancers often seem to forget that a conductor will never be able to hit exactly the same tempo night after night (and especially when there are a number of days or even months between performances), so *it is beneficial for them to adjust to reasonable fluctuations in tempos during rehearsals.* The stock remark for anyone in charge of a rehearsal in which a dancer complains about the tempo is, "It may be like that onstage. Are you going to stop during the performance?"

Marking scores

There are many symbols and abbreviations used in marking dance scores; they look like secret codes to all but the most experienced company pianist. It is wise not to make up your own symbols unless they absolutely cannot be misinterpreted, as another pianist may be playing from your score at some point. Example 51 shows many of these markings and their meanings (they are there for information only, and *not* to be observed during the playing of this piece!).

There are three ways for stage action to get started:

- the dancer(s) enter(s) in silence and the pianist/orchestra comes in on a visual cue;

- the pianist/orchestra begins and the dancer(s) enter(s) on a particular note; or
- the dancer(s) offstage and the pianist/orchestra start(s) at the same time (normally possible only with a TV monitor).

Each of these ways must be worked out beforehand. Eye contact before each is vital (eye contact for the third way means for the conductor to look directly into the videocamera in the pit as a signal that he is ready to start). This communication between dancer(s) and pianist/conductor must be set up in the rehearsal studio, so each can familiarize himself with the timing. Onstage the dancer will use the same process with the conductor; he will not wait for the ballet master's "and." Be sure to mark on your scores how each section begins.

The grand pas de deux

There are many grands pas de deux (usually abbreviated to, simply, pas de deux) excerpted from full-length traditional ballets that are included in company repertoires. Some of the most well-known are from *Don Quixote* (Minkus); *Le Corsaire* (Adam); *Les Sylphides* (Chopin); *Spring Waters* (Rachmaninoff); the Peasant and Grand pas de deux from *Giselle* (Adam); and those from the three Tchaikovsky ballets: White Swan and Black Swan from *Swan Lake;* the Bluebird and Wedding pas de deux from *Sleeping Beauty;* and the Snow and Grand pas de deux from *Nutcracker.*

Pas de deux means "step for two," and its standard format is:

Entrée/Adagio	for a male and female dancer, usually to slow music;
Variation I	for the man, almost always musically robust;
Variation II	for the woman, almost always contrastingly delicate;
Coda	for both, usually including solos for each and the finale together, always loud and "finale-ish," and almost always in an allegro 2/4 meter.

Some pas de deux, such as the Snow, *Spring Waters,* and *Les Sylphides,* were written without variations or coda. Others, such as the grand pas de deux from *Giselle,* are often performed without variations or coda, either because the coda was usually choreographed for the entire ensemble, or because the inherently tragic character of the pas de deux within the context of the story precludes exhibitions of pyrotechnical feats.

These standard pas de deux, like the ballets from which they are excerpted, have assumed very definite musical traditions over the years, in that each has its own ritards, accelerandos, fermatas, and peculiarities of execution. If you haven't had much experience with this literature, you must prepare yourself before the first rehearsal in one of two ways (preferably both):

- Ask either a pianist who knows the pas de deux, or one or both of the principal dancers involved, to help you with tempos, and to point out any stylistic or dynamic changes you may have to make;
- Listen to and watch the pas de deux on video, absorbing its orchestral scope and playing along with it, if possible—or listen to it on tape, keeping in mind that tempos on commercial tapes are often faster and fairly unrealistic in terms of the dancers' execution.

If you have never rehearsed a pas de deux before, or if you have never rehearsed a particular one, say so before the rehearsal begins, so that the ballet master and the dancers involved are aware that they will be expected to help you with tempos. In the first few rehearsals, it is best for them to demonstrate the tempos they need before each section of the pas de deux; demonstrating all the tempos for you before the whole piece starts is unrealistic.

In variations and especially in codas, there is often a distinct diVerence of tempo between one maxi-phrase and the next. This is because each dancer is executing tour de force steps that vary in tempo according to the steps' qualities and who is executing them. In codas, because Dancer A is often finishing her last phrase of movement just as Dancer B begins his, there is often no ritard down or accelerando up to a new tempo. In the adagio section and variations, however, there are usually very definite tempo transitions reflected by ritards and accelerandos, which lead the dancers into the new tempos.

As performance time approaches, the pas de deux couple will want to run the piece at least once a day straight through without stopping, no matter what happens. This develops not only the physical stamina necessary to get through the piece, but also the emotional stamina—the knowledge that they can still make a valid artistic statement even though a pirouette didn't work, or one of them fell down, or they forgot a step.

Generally, dancers rehearsing a pas de deux are given a good deal of leeway in tempo discussions. They are always experienced professionals, usually principal dancers (on a higher level than soloists or corps de ballet members), and the virtuoso steps they are required to perform necessitate the appropriate tempos for their particular bodies and ways of moving. Be aware that the tempos of all sections of a pas de deux can change between the time it is set on the dancers and the time it is performed. Until they have the steps and movements in their muscle memory, they may not dance full-out, and they should not expect you to intuit from day to day their particular tempos any more than you should expect them to be consistent in their tempos until the movements have become well-embedded in their brains and muscles.

If you are experiencing a larger-than-usual volume of tempo complaints, you might try this comment; it always gets a chuckle, and it makes astute people think: "Would you like me to play too fast or too slow today?"

Rehearsal with tape/CD

Although this function may seem to be outside the realm of this book, it is included because occasionally (and quite often in Europe) you will be called upon to run the tape recorder or CD player for rehearsal.

Some pianists resent being put into the position of what they call a "mere mechanic." Personally I never mind it too much because I can dancer-watch even more enjoyably than when playing for a rehearsal. But I do feel that the ballet master or assistant can do a much better job than a pianist, since they are more likely to know exactly where to stop or start. If you have to do it, these guidelines will help you to get started, and to learn how to deal with the mechanical music maker.

There can be many reasons for running rehearsals with tape as opposed to live music. Some of them are:

- the music is unplayable; it may be atonal, arrhythmic, or just plain non-music (tape collages of sirens, ocean waves, or mosquitoes buzzing against a screen);
- no piano reduction exists, as with many symphonic works, or—if it does—it is hand-written, often illegible, and/or an unrealistic reproduction of what the dancers will hear coming out of the pit;
- the company performs to tape either all the time or on tour.

Some pianists mark the score with the catchwords and the corresponding number on the tape counter. I prefer to do it by attaching tape numbers to visual cues or catchwords, because it seems easier to find what I need in a list of ten catchwords rather than sorting through 483 bars of music. (I have little notebooks set aside for only these notes.) If the music is atonal or arrhythmic, it rarely bears any resemblance to visually recognizable phrases. Even if it is tonal music in a standard form, you have to know it quite well to be able to find a new phrase quickly within the musical notation. I might add, though, that if there is a score, I write in as much of the choreography as possible, for accuracy during a future restaging of the piece.

The ideal situation for the beginning operator of a tape recorder is to sit in on a rehearsal and ask someone to call out each catchword as it occurs. Write down these catchwords, leaving a margin down the left side of the paper for the numbers, which you will fill in during the next rehearsal. If this is impossible, and you are just thrown cold into a rehearsal, listen for new maxi-phrases of music and write down an approximation of the movement (or a soloist's entrance or a group's exit) and the corresponding number on the tape counter. Your mind may become boggled at the beginning (mine certainly did) by watching the movement, checking the number, and writing, but you'll get used to it. You probably won't know the names of each movement the dancers execute, but your observations may be quite graphic anyway, and the point is for everyone to understand one another. "Diagonal line," "corps swoops," "Titoyo's fan kick," "quiet section," and "Ronald's entrance" are all self-explanatory and understood by all.

Use the dancers' or choreographer's catchwords whenever possible; everyone will be speaking the same language, you won't have to analyze the steps on top of everything else, and their terms are often more original and accurate than those we think up.

Use the numbers that correspond to the beginnings of musical maxi-phrases; a dancer can't acclimate himself to the middle of a phrase.

Now comes the really mechanical part. Find the beginning of the first note of the music and at that point set the tape counter to zero. Then when you press "start" the music will begin instantly. This is necessary because sometimes a ballet starts musically when a dancer jumps into the air, and you must be able to make the first note of the music coordinate exactly with that jump.

Do not reset the tape counter to zero in later sections of the music, as this can lead to confusion in the tape-counter numbers you write on your list. Keep a single zero for an entire tape.

Get into the habit as soon as possible of reducing the volume completely before pressing "stop"; that way you will avoid the possibility of scaring everyone to death by a triple forte chord when you press "start" again. This will also eliminate any white noise or hiss from the speakers; if you aren't sitting directly under the speakers, you won't hear it, but it will annoy a lot of other people.

When it is time to resume after a break in the action, you should position the tape in such a way as to give the dancers a lead-in—a phrase for them to get their bearings in the music (a direct counterpart to introductions in class). It is not always possible to precisely calculate on a piece of tape exactly where a preparation will start, so it is better for the dancers to have too much music than too little to get themselves oriented.

You may encounter problems if your company has more than one studio and a different brand of tape recorder in each one. Different machines run at different speeds, and different-sized reels often change the speed of revolution, too. So a dancer is *not* always crazy when he says, "The tape is faster (or slower) today." If the same machine's numbers are completely out of synch with those that you have previously written, someone may have changed the receiving reels in your absence. The size of the receiving reel greatly affects the numbers.

Example 83 is a reproduction of a page from my tape recorder notes that might be helpful. It is taken from the notebooks I kept during my association with Martin Schläpfer's company in Bern.

If your organization is currently shopping around for a new tape recorder, an elapsed- or real-time counter, which counts the music in minutes and seconds, is by far the most practical and accurate. Even better: using CDs for rehearsals and performances produces the ultimate in accuracy and convenience.

If the company has begun rehearsing to one version of a piece and the choreographer decides to change to another version (because he likes it slower or faster, because he hears different instruments more clearly in a particular section, or whatever), either destroy, hide, or recycle the first version. I know that sounds too logical to mention, but I have worked in companies with three versions of the same piece, creating chaos for the dancers, frustration for the choreographer, and a lot of wasted time for everyone.

It is essential to have the music instantly available to the choreographer or ballet master during rehearsal, exactly as live music is. Therefore, you must be conscientious in your duties, not involved in the newspaper, crossword puzzles, or casual conversation with passersby.

~

If you are responsible for the physical preparation or maintenance of the tapes (taping from the master record, CD, or tape; splicing; etc.), here are a few points that may help you.

If you are the person who inserts the leaders between movements or at musical pauses, meet with the choreographer to find out whether he wants (a) to have the same length of pause every time there is a musical stop, or (b) to have the tape started with a visual cue, which also allows for applause. In the case of the former, it is wise to leave blank tape for the length of the pause, because colored or white leaders cause some tape machines to stop. In the case of the latter, make a short leader and put the end of it right next to where the music begins on the tape, not just anywhere. For consistency in performance, you want to know that the music will begin right after the leader. If you keep the leader short, you will always have enough time to advance the receiving reel manually, so you won't run the risk of starting the music too soon by pressing "start" to advance the leader. If two tapes are being made at the same time, the leaders should all be the same length so the tape-counter numbers will be the same.

When splicing in a leader, be sure not to cut off the reverberations of the last note of the previous music.

Tactfully help the choreographer to understand, if he doesn't already, the theatrical value of the right length of silence between musical sections. If there is the right amount of time, the audience and the dancers will have a moment to breathe.

~

Playing the tape for performance is exactly the same as playing it for a run-through in rehearsal. You will have made meticulous, succinct notes concerning visual cues and leaders (it is very unwise to leave these cues to chance and not write them down), and you will have discussed the possibility of an encore with the choreographer and included it at the end of both the rehearsal and performance tapes. (It is too risky to rewind the tape to find the last section for an encore unless it is very clearly marked with a special leader.)

Be prepared on tour for the occasional ornery tape machine that will not stop when you expect it to.

The music librarian

This function, as described at the beginning of the section, is self-explanatory. It may also include contacting publishers concerning the availability of scores and parts, ascertaining whether a particular piece of music is in the public domain, and securing copyrights. You may be asked to distribute parts to music stands before performances and to collect them afterward, making sure they travel with all company materials (scenery, costumes, etc.). You should always keep your rehearsal scores and tapes, as well as class music, with you in case of delay.

Calling cues

If the stage manager doesn't read music, it makes sense for a musician to call certain technical cues from a score in order to ensure a consistent level on the technical side of the performance (light cues on time, curtain going up and down at the proper moments, scenery changes, etc.). Since most lighting boards are computerized these days, this process involves sitting with the choreographer during stage, technical, and lighting rehearsals and writing each progressive cue number over the corresponding bar in the score where each action occurs.

The gray areas

Dancers are an emotional breed. I will never be convinced that they are all a bunch of narcissistic, egomaniacal, irresponsible, stupid children, as some would lead us to believe. I have known too many wonderful dancers who have none of those qualities. But they *are* emotional. An unemotional dancer is like a pianist who plays nothing but scales and arpeggios. If either makes it to the stage, he rarely lasts long.

Professional dancers shouldn't be coddled; they should be treated with respect for the impressive things they achieve physically and emotionally on stage. Every performing artist lays himself bare on a stage, but dancers run the added risk of permanent, serious injury every time they dance. A sprained ankle can set a career back for several months, and a more serious injury can put an immediate end to a career that may have only just begun.

Maintaining your composure (without sacrificing your principles) and avoiding the prima donna role will benefit yourself and the rest of your colleagues. If you are at all tuned in to dancers, and if you are reasonably competent in your work and reasonably easy to get along with, there is not a company on earth that won't treat you immediately as one of the family. There seems to be a stronger bond among professionals in the dance world than in any other.

The working conditions—especially the daily company class—of a professional dancer cannot help but breed insecurity and competition (healthy or unhealthy, depending on the individual and—often—on the artistic staff's influence and attitude). Dancing is the only art form whose participants are required to refine and strengthen their technique as a group for at least an hour every day before beginning their creative work. "Oh, she's so turned-out" and "My body could never do that" and "I'm just not a turner" and "I can't jump as high as he can"—these are all common complaints from not only students but also professionals. We as pianists are not as constantly bombarded with our failings as dancers are and, especially, are not confronted with our shortcomings in front of our colleagues on a daily basis. Nor do we spend the rest of our careers taking orders from ballet masters and directors and teachers and conductors and choreographers in every area: technical execution, emotional projection, timing, costume, hairstyle, attitude, diet, and so on. And we don't have to fight for parts in the way dancers do. If we play our prepared pieces well enough, we will usually find places in the recital. A dancer can be absolutely brilliant, but if he is not the right "type" (height, weight, hair color, body shape—even personality), he won't get the part—or even the job.

The lot of a dancer will become apparent to you sooner or later. The point of mentioning it now is to help you understand the need of empathizing with highly trained professionals—to understand what they are about, what they have been through, and what they have to deal with every day. Hence the recommendation that you bring them coffee if they need it (pianists usually have more free time and are less exhausted than dancers; besides, we don't have to change out of our wet practice clothes to go out, and then put them back on when we return). Give them a few words of encouragement if they are warranted. "You did such beautiful pirouettes today" or "That's a nice hairdo" in the midst of a "Don't lift your arm so high" day may earn you a friend for life.

Checklist

While sorting out the technical verbiage within this book, you may have lost track of some of the essence and essentials of dance accompaniment. This art form, like all others, should be executed so seamlessly and organically that its deceptive ease covers up all the theories, concepts, hard work, and practicing.

In the introduction I mentioned that there are no infallible rules in dance accompaniment, but here are a few strong recommendations:

- dedication to the teacher's wishes and needs
- musical support of the dancers' movements
- being visually tuned in to the action as much as possible
- augmentation with octaves when needed
- the use of reverse pedaling to reduce heaviness and provide contrast
- effective organization of your music
- stylistic and rhythmic diversity

The following suggestions may help you in your approach to accompaniment:

- Watch videos and listen to music for dance performance, and work toward producing orchestral fullness on the piano.
- Start thinking of music in eight-, sixteen-, and thirty-two-count phrases.
- When choosing what to play, determine first the meter, then the tempo, then the quality, then the accents.
- Make a checklist of concepts you want to work on.
- Practice the standard rhythmic structures so you can produce them automatically in a variety of keys.
- Watch and take class.
- Take a few minutes after every class and rehearsal to analyze your mistakes, so you can work on them at a later date.

No one acquires the skills of effective, inspiring accompaniment for dance overnight. As is true with everything else in life, our development as an accompanist is a never-ending *process*—a continuing period of growth in which we question whether a particular concept was better today than yesterday, and in which we search for new ways to motivate dancers, thereby motivating ourselves and contributing to our own personal and musical growth.

Afterword

Music and dance are inextricably linked. Music is often referred to as the motivating force behind dance. However, dance teachers and accompanists are a fortunate few who see both art forms as motivating catalysts for their own creative energies.

In the final analysis, the accompanist and teacher receive as much as they give.

~ *Musical Examples*

The following musical examples were put together by a beginning computer person—the author. Some of the desired functions were either inconsistent, such as dots, dashes, and straight lines for 8va markings; or were not possible by me, such as consistent note values in polyphonic writing.

Sometimes sixteenth notes more accurately reflect the note values, but eighth notes are easier to read.

Some of the examples may have different note values than what their composers wrote because I preferred ease of reading to a perfect re-creation.

Rather than presenting watered-down versions of the musical examples to accommodate less technically advanced accompanists, I have chosen to present full, substantial (where appropriate) renderings which demonstrate the support helpful to—and appreciated by—most dancers at every level. If necessary, an accompanist can eliminate the octaves (preferably only in the right hand) until he is farther along technically.

I decided not to include all the titles and composers of the pieces, because I couldn't remember all the names. Naturally I could have used only pieces whose names I remember, but I preferred to be able to choose exactly the right piece for each situation.

Since teachers, not accompanists, do most of the naming of pieces in class, each title usually reflects the words a teacher would use to ask for that particular piece. If it is not obvious from the title whether an example is a two, a three, or a six, it will be clarified. (I am assuming that everyone knows a waltz is a three; therefore, this information is omitted.) Teachers: If you are confident that you understand the difference between a waltz and a 6/8, by all means call 6/8s by their rightful name. Remember, though, that it prevents an accompanist from choosing another kind of three that might work better.

Because the examples had to stay in numerical order, it was not possible to organize them according to the recommendations in the repertoire section; it would have required too much wasted space. Photocopy, cut, and paste!

When more than one page number appears, the first number is the primary reference in the text.

Remember:

- The symbol - takes the same amount of time as each of the words in a sentence but is silent.
- The counting in each example reflects its own unique way of counting the melody; the way to count each general form is included in chapter 3.
- Pedaling is mostly omitted because of the unique demands of each combination's accents.
- If there is a choice of counting, as in example 19, the instinctive counting of a musical teacher and the choreography of a combination will be the deciding factors.

I have never—not even in the smallest Dolly Dinkle dancing school—heard a teacher who teaches a ballet class exclusively in one language. Therefore, in the examples with combinations included, you will find both English and French words.

The following abbreviations are used in the musical examples:

CM	changement
GB	grand battement
pos	position
rdj	rond de jambe à terre
rdjel	rond de jambe en l'air
str.	straighten
2. x 8va	play the repeat an octave higher
2. x w/oct.	play the repeat with octaves

♩ = 142

Medium-tempo waltz

Ex. 1
p.10

5 - & 6 - & 7 - & 8 - &

1 & uh 2 & 3 - & 4 - &

1.

5 & uh 6 & uh 7 - & 8 & uh

2.
8
&
uh
3

1.
2.

Ex. 2
pp. 12, 7

3
3
3
3

♩ = 66
Habañera or tango: a two
Ex. 3
pp. 17, 7
5 &6 &
7 &8 &
1 & - uh 2 &
3 & - uh 4 &
5 - & uh6 &
7 &8 &

=66
Non-habañera or tango
Ex. 3a
p. 17

= 84
Rag: a two
Ex. 4
p. 17
5 - & - 6 & - uh
7 - & - 8 - & -
1 - & - 2 - & -
3 - & - 4 & - uh
5 - & - 6 - & uh
7 - & - 8 - & uh
8vb

8vb
8vb
8vb
8vb
8vb
8vb
8vb
8vb

8vb
8va
8vb

♩ = 176
Polka: a two
Ex. 5
pp. 18, 117, 141
5. position
5 & 6 & 7 & 8 - & uh
p r e p a r a t i o n
1 & uh 2 & 3 & 4 &
plié C---------M C--M C--------M str. plié C---
5 & uh 6 & 7 & 8 &
M C---M C-------M str. plié glis---sade je-----té glis------sade je-----té glis-----
sade assemblé C--------M str. plié
1.
2. x 8va
2.
16va...
1.

2.
8va
8vb

= 110
Coda: a two
Ex. 6
pp. 18, 136
5 - & - 6 - & - 7 - & - 8 - & uh
!/5 - & - 2/6 - & - 3/7 - & uh 4/8 - & -
8vb
8vb
8vb

8vb
8vb
8vb
8vb

8va

=108
Coda: a two
Ex. 7
p. 18
5 - & - 6 - & - 7 - & - 8 - - &
1 - & - 2 - & - 3 - - & 4 - - &
8vb
5 - - & 6 - - & 7 - - & 8 - & -
8vb
1.
2. x w/oct. 8va

2.
8vb
8vb
8vb
8vb
8vb
1.
2.
8va

♩=116
Czardas-friska or coda: a two
Ex. 8
p. 19
1 - 2 & 3 & 4 & 5 - 6 - 7 - 8 -
1 - 2 &uh 3 & 4 - 5 - 6 & 7 & 8 -
2. x w/oct. 8vb

8vb
8va
8vb
8va
8va

8vb
8va
8vb

♩ = 68
Moderato two
2 slow, 3 fast ronds de jambe à terre
Ex. 9
pp. 19, 105
1. position
5 - and uh 6 - and - 7 - and - 8 - and uh 1 - and uh
p r e p a r a t i o n tendu front
2 - and uh 3 - and - 4 - and - 5 - and uh 6 - and uh
tendu side tendu back first position rdj en dehors rdj
7 - and - 8 - and -
rdj rdj rdj hold tendu front; execute the previous 8 counts en dedans
8vb

8vb
8vb

= 128
Grand allegro two
Ex. 10
p. 19
5- &-6-&-
7 - &- 8-& uh
1- &- 2- &uh
3- & -4- &-
5 - & - 6 -& -
7 - & -8- & -
2. x 8va
8vb

8vb
8vb
8va
8vb
8vb
8vb
8vb
8va
8vb

♩=104
Light "and": a two
Ex. 11
pp. 19, 169
5. position 5 - & - 6 - & - 7 - & - 8 - & -
p r e p a r a t i o n
1 - & - 2 - & - 3 - & - 4 - & -
dégagé 5. pos. dégagé 5. pos. dégagé 5. pos.
5 - & - 6 - & - 7 - & - 8 - & -
out in out in out in
1.
2.
6 - & - 7 - & - 8 - & - Fine
dégagé
close and close and close
8va

8vb
8vb
8va
D. S. al Fine

♩ = 104
Light, fast two
Ex. 12
pp. 19, 108, 196
5 & 6 & 7 & 8 & uh 1 & 2 & uh 3 & 4 & uh
5. pos. p r e p a r a t i o n dégagé side rd------jel 5. pos. rd------jel 5. pos. rd-----
5 & 6 & 7 & 8 & uh
jel rd-----jel rd---------jel 5. pos.
8va
1.
2.

♩=88
Sarabande: a three
Ex. 13
p. 20
1 - 2 - 3 & 4 - 5 & 6 & 1 &2 - 3 & 4 & 5 - 6 -
2 &2 - 3 & 4 - 5 & 6 -
1.
2.

♩ = 78
Polonaise: a grandiose six
Ex. 14
p. 20
1 - & uh 2 & 3 & 4 - 5 - 6 & 1 - & uh 2 - 3 &
4 - & uh 5 - 6 & 2 & uh 2 & 3 & 4 & uh 5 - 6 &
8va
8vb

♩ = 86

Polacca: a bouncy six

Ex. 15
p. 20

♩ = 88
Bolero: a bouncy six
Ex. 16
pp. 21, 65, 157
1 & 2 & 3 &
4 & 5 & 6 &
1 & 2 & 3 &
4 & 5 & 6 &
2 & 2 & 3 &
4 & 5 & 6 &

8va
8va
8va
8vb
8vb
8va
8va
8va
8vb
8va
8va
16va
8vb

♩ = 96 **Minuet: a three** **Ex. 17**
p. 22

♩ = 138
Ländler: a three
Ex. 18
p. 22
5 2 3 6 2 3 7 2 3 8 2 3 &
1 2 3 2 2 3 3 2 3 4 2 3
tr
5 2 3 6 2 3 7 2 3 8 2 3
1.
2.
8 2 3

1.
2.
tr
tr
tr
tr

tr
tr
1.
2.

1.
2.
8vb

♩=112
Mazurka: a three
Ex. 19
pp. 23, 220
8va
5 & 2 3
6 & 2 3
7 2 3
1 2 3
8 2 3 &
4 5 6 &
1 & 2 & 3 &
1 & 2 & 3 &
2 & 2 3 &
4 & 5 6 &
3 & 2 & 3 &
2 & 2 & 3 &
4 2 3 &
4 5 6 &
5 & 2 & 3 &
6 & 2 3 &
7 & 2 & 3 &
8 2 3
8vb
8vb
8vb

16va
8vb

♩ = 120 **Mazurka: a three** **Ex. 20 p. 23**

♩ = 116 **Mazurka: a three** **Ex. 21 p. 23**

8vb
8vb
8vb
8vb
8vb
8vb
8vb
8va
8vb

8vb

♩ = 100
Slow waltz
Ex. 22
p. 24
5 - & 6 - & 7 - & 8 & uh
1 - & 2 - & 3 - & 4 - &
5 - & 6 - & 7 - & 8 & uh
1.
2.
7 - & 8 & uh

1.
2.

♩ = 132
Medium-tempo waltz
Ex. 23
pp. 24, 194
5 - & 6 - & 7 - & 8 & uh
1 - & 2 - & 3 - & 4 - &
5 - & 6 - & 7 - & 8 - uh
1.
8va
tr
8va

2.
1.
8va

2.
8vb
8vb
8va

♩=176
Spanish waltz
Ex. 24
p. 24
5 & - 6 & uh 7 & - 8 & uh
1 & uh 2 & uh 3 & uh 4 & uh 5 & uh
6 & uh 7 & uh 8 & uh

1.
2.
8vb

8vb
8vb
8vb
8va
8va
8vb
8vb
8vb

8va
8va
8vb

♩ = 206
Fast waltz
Ex. 25
p. 25
5 - & 6 - & 7 - & 8 & uh
1 - & 2 - & 3 - & 4 - &
8va
5 - & 6 - & 7 - & 8 - &
8va

8vb
8vb

8va
8va
8va

8va
8va
8vb
8vb
8vb

8va

♩ = 176 **Moderato big waltz** **Ex. 26 p. 26**

2.
8va
Fine
8vb
8vb
8vb

D. C. al Fine

♩ = 184
Medium-tempo grand allegro waltz
Ex. 27
p. 26
5 & uh 6 & uh 7 - & 8 & uh
1 & uh 2 & uh 3 & uh 4 & uh
5 - & 6 - & 7 - & 8 & uh
2. x 8va
8vb

8va
16va
8vb

𝅗𝅥 = 196 **Fast big waltz** **Ex. 28 p. 26**

2
7 & uh 8 - &
8vb
8vb
8vb
8vb
8vb
8vb

8vb
8va

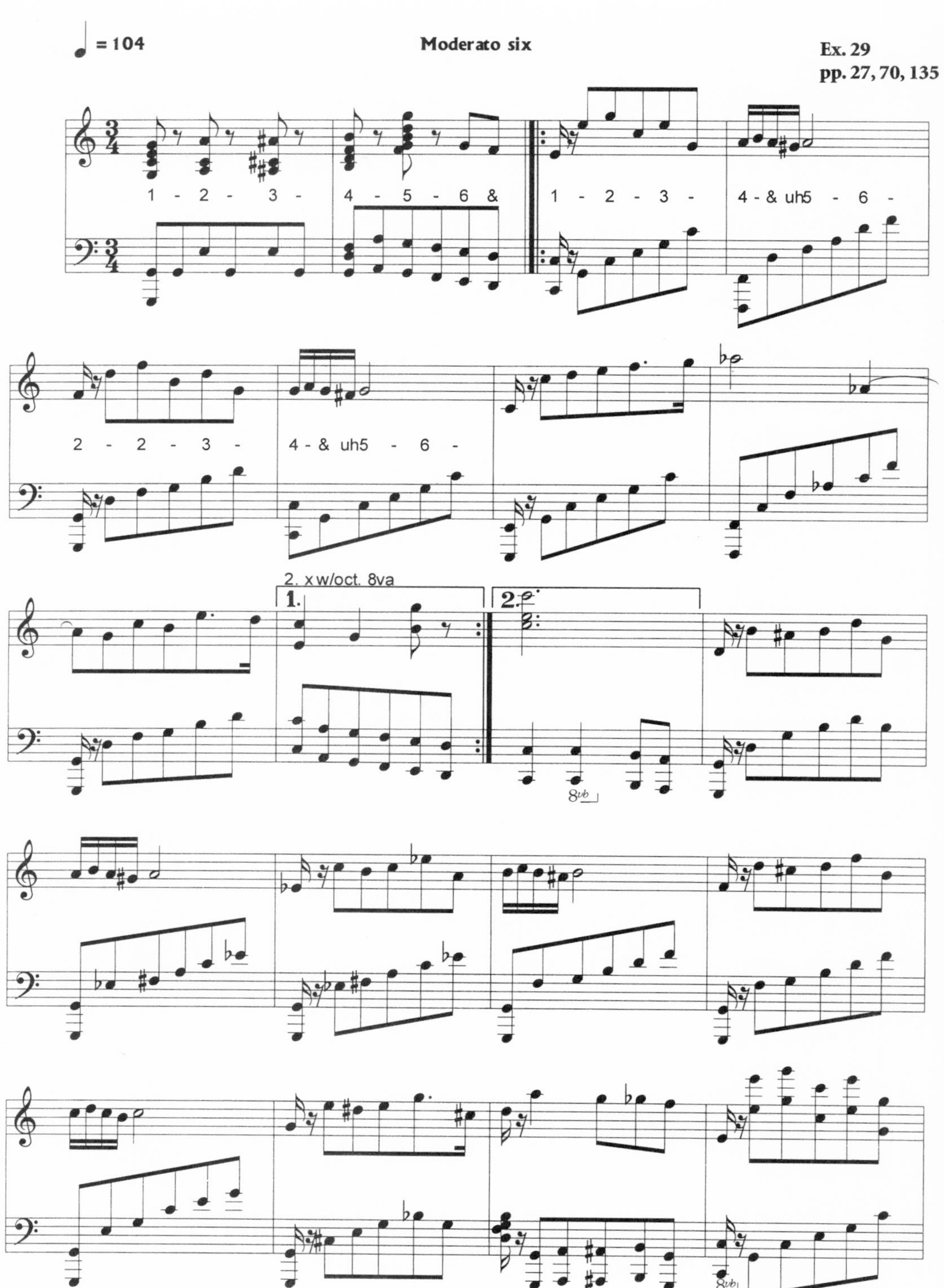

♩ = 104
Moderato six
Ex. 29
pp. 27, 70, 135
1 - 2 - 3 -
4 - 5 - 6 &
1 - 2 - 3 -
4 - & uh5 - 6 -
2 - 2 - 3 -
4 - & uh5 - 6 -
2. x w/oct. 8va
1.
2.
8vb
8vb

8vb

♪ = 148
Medium-tempo 3/8 or waltz
Ex. 30
p. 27
5 - &
6 & -
7 - &
8 & uh
8vb
1 2 3
2 2 3
3 & 2 3
4 - -
5 2 3
6 2 3
7 &2 3
8 - &
3
3
8vb
8vb

8vb
8vb
8vb
8vb
8vb
8vb
3
8vb
8vb

8vb
8vb
8va
1.
either Da Capo, if needed
8vb
2.
or finish
8vb
8vb

= 172
Medium-tempo big waltz
Ex. 31
pp. 27, 26
5 & -
6 & uh
7 & uh
8 & uh
1 & -
2 & uh
3 & -
4 & uh
5 & -
6 & uh
7 & -
8 & uh
8va
1.
2.
to Coda
3
3
1.

2.
D.C. al Segno
Coda
8vb
1.
2. x 8va
2.
8vb

♪ = 180
Fast big 3/8 or three
Ex. 32
p. 28
5 - 2 - 3 -
6 - 2 - 3 -
7 - 2 - 3 -
8 - 2 - 3 -
1 - 2 - 3 -
2 - 2 - 3 -
3 - 2 - 3 -
4 - 2 - 3 -
5 - 2 - 3 -
6 - 2 - 3 -
7 - 2 - 3 -
8 - 2 - 3 -
1.
8vb

2.
8vb
8va
8va
8va

8va
8vb
l. h.
l. h.
l. h.
l. h.
l. h.
8vb
8vb
l. h.
l. h.
l. h.
l. h.
simile

♪ =236
Fast, bouncy three
Ex. 33
p. 28
5 - &
6 - &
7 - &
8 - &
1 - &
2 - &
3 - &
4 - &
5 - &
6 - &
7 - &
8 - &
1.

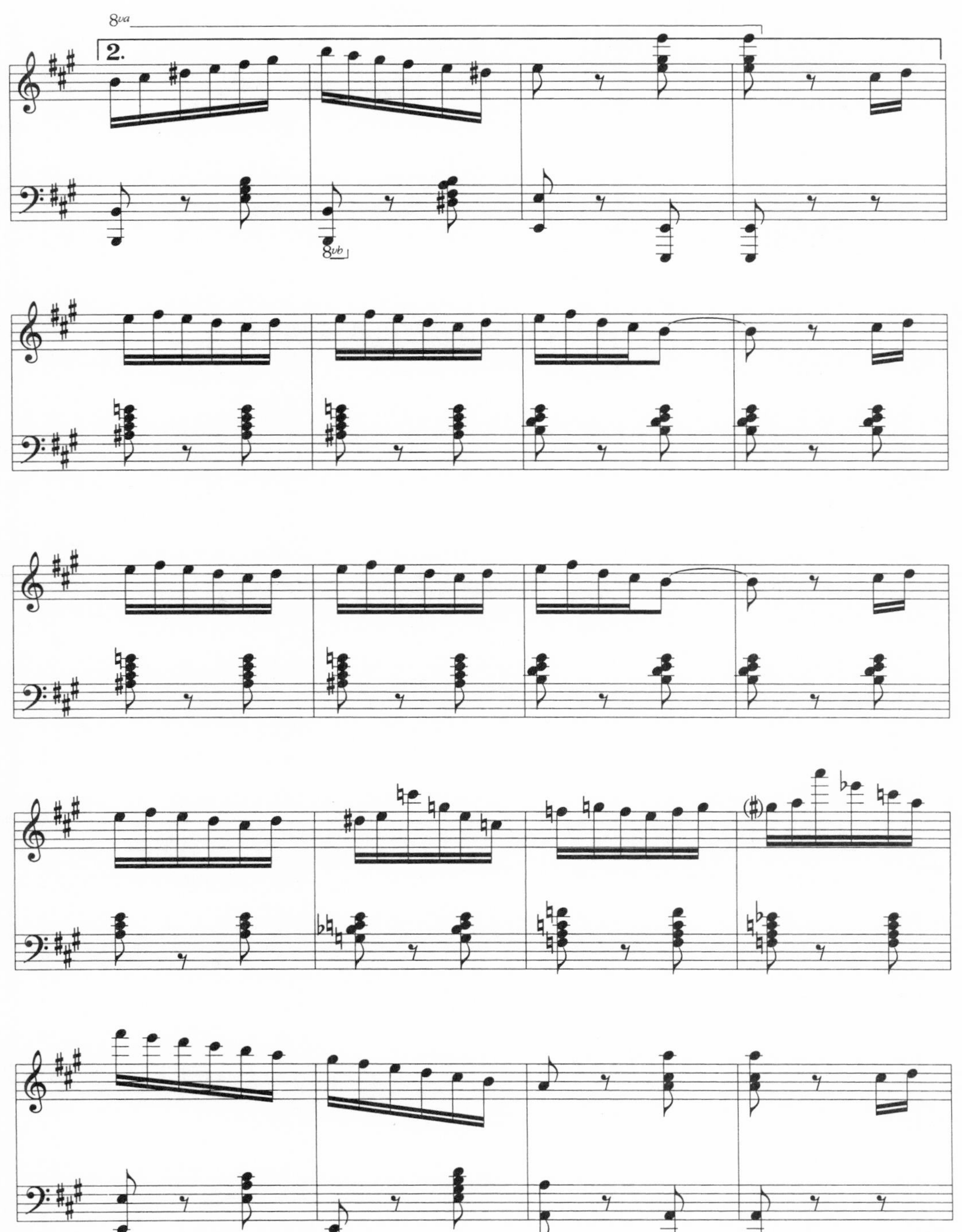
8va
2.
8vb

♩=112
Heroic czardas-lassú: a two
Ex. 34a
pp. 29, 197
5 - & - 6 - & -uh 7 - & - 8 - & -
1 - & - 2 - & uh 3 - & uh 4 - & uh
5 - & - 6 - & - 7 - & - 8- & -
8vb
8va
1.
2.

8vb

♩ = 104
Sensuous czardas-lassú: a two
Ex. 34b
p. 29
5 - & - 6 - & uh 7 - & - 8 - & -
1 - & uh 2 - & - 3 - & - 4 - & -
5 - & uh 6 - & uh 7 - & - 8 - & -

=112
March: a two
Ex. 35
pp. 29, 18
5 & 6 & 7 & 8 & uh 1 & uh2 & uh 3 & uh4 & uh
5 & uh6 & uh 7 - 8 & uh
8va
16va

♩ = 118
Gavotte: a two
Ex. 36
p. 30
5 & 6 & 7 & 8 & 1 & 2 & 3 & 4 & 5 & 6 &
7 & 8 &
8vb

♩ = 126 **Stop-time in two** **Ex. 37 p. 30**

8vb
8va

♩ = 116
March: a two
Ex. 38
p. 30
5 & uh6 &
7 & 8 &
1 & uh2 &
3 & 4 & uh
5 & uh6 &
7 & 8 &
8vb
8va
3

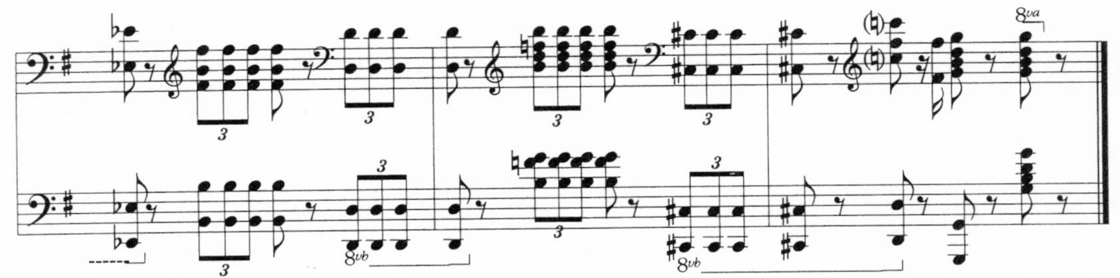
8va
8vb
8vb

♩=112
"And": a two
Ex. 39
pp. 30, 118, 198
5. position 5 & 6 & 7 & 8 & 1 & 2 & 3 & 4 &
p r e p a r a t i o n plié CM CM CM plié CM CM CM plié
5 & 6 & 7 & 8 &

♩. = 44
Barcarolle: a three
5 &uh 6 - & 7 &uh 8 - & 1 &uh 2 - & 3 - & 4 - &
5 &uh 6 - & 7 - & 8 - &
8vb
8va
8va
8vb

♩. = 102
6/8 march: a two
Ex. 41
pp. 31, 18, 169
5. pos.
5 - - & - -
6 - - & - -
7 - - & - uh
8 - - & - -
p r e p a r a t i o n
GB up
1 - - & - -
close GB up
2 - - & - -
close GB up
3 - - & - -
piqué up
4 - - & - -
close GB up
5 - - & - -
close GB up
6 - - & - -
close GB up
7 - - & - -
piqué up
8 - - & - -
close GB up
2. x 8va
8vb

8va
16va
8va
8va
8vb

♩. = 60
Grand allegro waltz
Ex. 42
p. 32
5 - & 6 - &
7 & uh 8 & uh
1 - & 2 & uh
3 - & 4 & uh
5 & - 6 & -
7 & - 8 & uh
8vb
8vb

8va
8va
8vb

♩. =58 **Medium-tempo grand allegro: 3/8 or three** **Ex. 43 p. 32**

8va
8vb
8va
3
3
8vb

♩. = 96
Tarantella: a three
Ex. 44
p. 33
5 - & 6 - & 7 - & 8 & uh 1 - & 2 - & 3 - & 4 - &
5 - & 6 - & 7 - & 8 - &
8va
1.
2.

8vb
8va
8vb
8va

♩. =92
Light, bouncy 6/8 or three
Ex. 45
pp. 33, 117
5 - & 6 - &
7 - & 8 & uh
1 - & 2 - &
3 - & 4 - &
5 & uh 6 - &
7 & uh 8 & uh
8vb

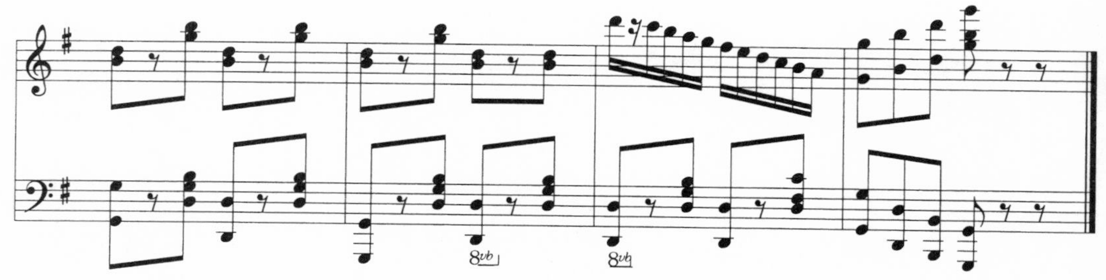
8vb
8vb

♩. = 78
Bouncy 6/8 or three
Ex. 46
p. 33
5 - & 6 - &
7 - & 8 &uh
1 - & 2 & uh
3 - & 4 - &
5 - & 6 & uh
7 - - 8 & uh
1.
2. x w/oct. 8va
2.
8vb

tr
tr
tr

♩. =90
Medium-tempo three
Ex. 47
p. 33
5 - & 6 - &
7 - & 8 & uh
1 - & 2 - &
3 - & 4 - &
5 - & 6 - &
7 - & 8 - &
8va
8vb

8va
8va
8va
8va
1. D.S. al Fine
2. 16va.....
8vb

♩. = 62
Medium-tempo 6/8 or three
Ex. 48
pp. 34, 173
5 - & 6 - & 7 - & 8 & uh 1 &uh 2 & uh 3 &uh 4 & uh 5 &uh 6 & uh
7 &uh 8 & uh

8vb

♩. =92
Allegro 9/8: a six
Ex. 49
pp. 34, 65
1 - & 2 - & 3 - &
4 - & 5 - & 6 & uh
1 - & 2 - & 3 - &
4 - & 5 - & 6 - &
1.
2 - & 2 - & 3 - &
4 - & 5 - & 6 & uh
8vb
2.
8va
8vb
8va
8va
8va
16va
8vb

♩. =96 **Fast three** **Ex. 50 p. 34**

♩=68
Moderato two
Ex. 51
pp. 37, 208
5 - & uh 6 - & - 7 - & - 8 - & -
1 - & uh 2 - & uh 3 - & - 4 - & - uh
5 - & - uh 6 - - & 7 - & - 8 - & -

1. watch 2. accel. 3. rit.

♩ = 100

Adagio in three

Ex. 52
pp. 38, 39, 112, 194

2.
8vb
8vb
8vb
8va

♩=86
Adage in three
Ex. 53
pp. 38, 158
5 - &
6 - &
7 - &
8 - &
1 - &
2 - &
3 & uh
4 - &
5 & uh
6 - &
7 - &
8 & uh
8va

♩. = 80
Adage in phrases of 6: a six
Ex. 54
pp. 38, 154
4-count introduction
5 - - 2 - - 3 - -
6 - - 2 - - 3 - -
7 & uh 2 & uh 3 & uh
8 - - 2 - 3 – &
2-bar/6-count introduction
1 - - 2 & uh 3 & uh
4 - - 5 - - 6 - &
1 - - 2 - & 3 - &
4 - & 5 - & 6 - &
2 - - 2 & uh 3 & uh
4 & uh 5 - & 6 - &

8va
8vb

= 72
Adagio in phrases of 6: a six
Ex. 55
p. 38
1 - 2 - 3 & 4 - 5 - 6 -
1 - 2 - 3 & 4 &5 - 6 -
2 - 2 - 3 & 4 &5 - 6 -
1.

2.
6
6
8va
8va

= 98
Adagio in three
Ex. 56
p. 39
5 & uh
6 & uh
7 - &
8 & uh
8vb
1 - &
2 - &
3 - &
4 & uh
5 - &
6 & uh
7 - &
8 - &
tr
1.
2.
8va

♩ = 72
Moderato two
Ex. 57
p. 39
5 - & uh 6 - & -
7 - & - 8 - & uh
1 - - & 2 - & uh
3 - - & 4 - & uh
5 - & uh 6 - & uh
7 - - & 8 - & uh
8vb

=68
12/8 adagio: a two
Ex. 58
p. 39
5 - - & uh6 - - & - -
7 - - & - - 8 - - & - uh
1 - - & - - 2 - - & uh
3 - - & - - 4 - - & uh
5 - - & uh 6 - - &
7 - - & - - 8 - - & uh

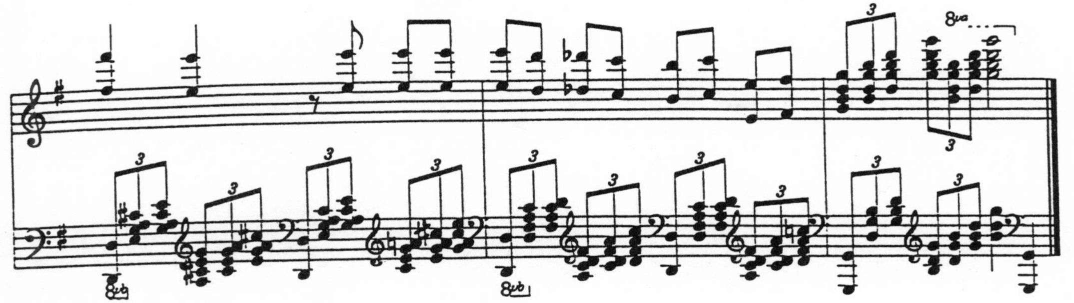
8va
8vb
8vb
3

♩ =62 **4/4 Adagio: a two** **Ex. 59 p. 39**

Very slow 4/4 adage: a two

Ex. 60
pp. 39, 7

♩. = 44
Adagio in three
Ex. 61
pp. 40
5 - & 6 - & 7 - & 8 - & 1 & uh 2 - &
3 - - 4 - - 5 & uh 6 - & 7 - - 8 - &
8vb
8va

8vb
8vb
8va

♩. = 76

Adage in phrases of 6: a six

Ex. 62
pp. 40, 171

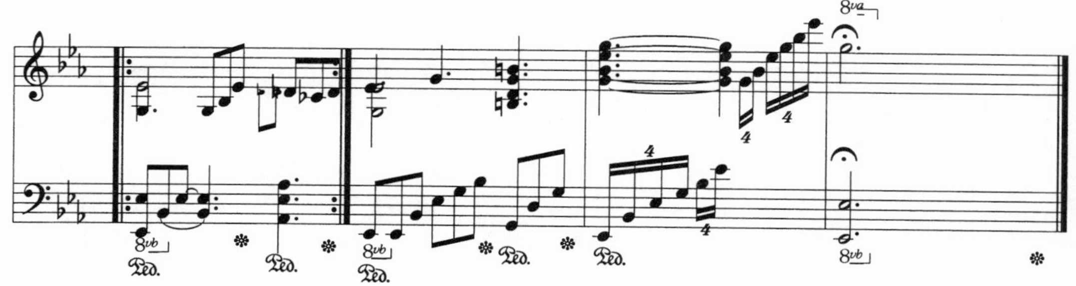
8va
4
4
4
4
8vb
Ped.
Ped.
8vb
Ped.
Ped.
Ped.
8vb

♩. = 74
12/8 adage: a two
Ex. 63
p. 41
5 - - & - uh6 - - & - -
7 - - & - - 8 - - & - uh
1 - - & - - 2 - - & - -
3 - - - - & 4 - - & - -
5 - - & - - 6 - - & - -
7 - - - - & 8 - - & - -
1.
2.

♩. = 60
12/8 adagio: a two
Ex. 64
pp. 41, 156
5 - - & - uh 6 - - & - - 7 - - & - - 8 - - & - uh 1 - - & - - 2 - - & uh
3 - - & - - 4 - - & uh 5 - - & - - 6 - - & - uh 7 - - & - - 8 - - & uh
1.
2.

A: ♩ = 192
B: ♩ = 184
Medium-tempo waltz
Mr. Brunson's plié combination
Ex. 65
pp. 103, 102, 112, 146, 149
1. pos., bras bas
A
5 - & 6 - & 7 & uh 8 - &
arms 1. position
arms 2. position
1 & uh 2 - & 3 - & 4 - &
demi-plié
straighten
5 & uh 6 - & 7 & uh 8 & uh
demi-plié
straighten
grand plié
8vb
8vb
straighten
inhale, non-barre arm to high 5th

cambré forward
8vb
8va
straighten up
arms 1. position
arms high 5th
8vb
8va
arms 2. position
tendu to 2. position
1) demi-plié
2) cambré to the barre
straighten

1) demi-plié
straighten
2) straighten up
1) grand plié
2) arms to 1. position, relevé for more advanced students
1.
2. x 8va
1) straighten
inhale
2) arms to 2. position
8vb
2. 8va
tendu to 4. position
1) demi-plié
straighten
2) cambré back
1)
demi-plié
straighten
2)
straighten up

1) grand plié
2) arms to 1. position
arms to 3. position
1.
2. x 8va
1) straighten
2) arms to 1. position
inhale, non-barre arm to high 5th
2. 8va
arms to 2. position, tendu to 5. position
demi-plié
straighten
demi-plié
straighten
grand plié
8vb

straighten
mf
8va
8vb
inhale
B
circular port de bras en dedans
circular port de bras en dehors

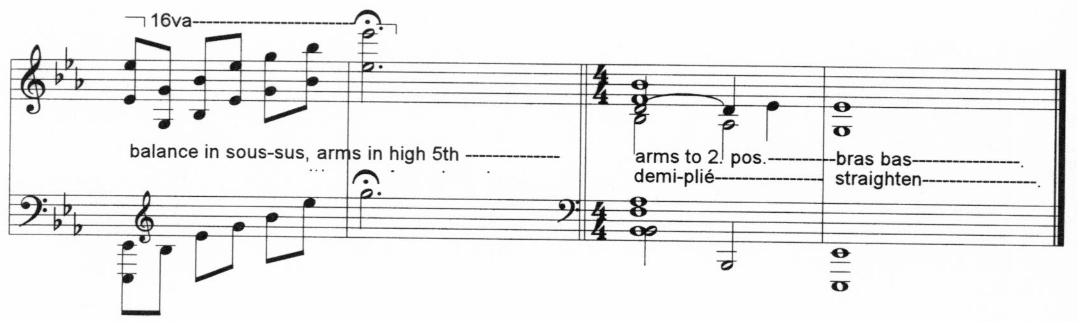
16va
balance in sous-sus, arms in high 5th
arms to 2. pos.
bras bas
demi-plié
straighten

A: ♩ = 84
B: 𝅗𝅥 = 122
Medium-tempo and fast twos
Ex. 66
pp. 104, 198
5. pos.
A
5 & 6 & 7 & 8 &
p r e p a r a t i o n
1 & 2 & 3 & 4 &
tendu frt. lift tendu close
5 & 6 & 7 & 8 &
dégagé 5. dégagé 5.
repeat the previous 8 counts to the side
repeat to the back
repeat to the side
B
8 dégagés à la seconde
balance in coupé or passé
1,3

2.
passé
4.
passé
8va
8vb

♩ = 108
Coda: a two
Ex. 67
p. 107
5 - & -
6 - & -
7 - & -
8 - - &
1 & uh
2 & uh
3 - & -
4 - & uh
5 & uh
1.
6 & uh
7 - & uh
2. x w/oct. 8va
8 - & uh
2.
6 & uh
7 - & uh
8 - & -
8vb

1.
2.
8vb
8vb
8vb
8vb
8vb
8vb
8vb
8vb

8vb
8vb
2. x 8va

8vb
8vb

♪ = 150
Medium-tempo two
Ex. 68
p. 107
5 - & uh 6 - & uh
7 - & - 8 - & uh
1 - & uh 2 - & uh
3 - & uh 4 - & uh
8vb
5 - & uh 6 - & uh
tr
7 - & - 8 - & -
1.
8vb
tr
2.
8vb

8va

Ex. 69
p. 108

2.
8va
8vb
8vb

=108
Medium-tempo two
Ex. 70
p. 108
5 - &uh6 - & uh
7 - & - 8 - & -
1- &uh2 - & -
3 - &uh4 - - -
5 - &uh6 - &uh
7 - & - 8 - & -

=182
Medium-tempo 3/8 or three
Ex. 71
p. 110
8va
5 - & 6 - & 7 & uh 8 & uh
1 - & 2 - & 3 - & 4 - &
5 - & 6 - & 7 - & 8 - &
8vb
2. x 8va

A: ♩=112
B: 𝅗𝅥=138
Medium-tempo two plus mazurka
Ex. 72
pp. 115, 149, 410
A
5 & 6 &
7 & 8 &
1 & 2 &
3 & 4 &
5 & 6 &
7 & 8 &
8vb
1.
2.

5. pos.
B
1 & 2 3
tendu side
2 & 2 3
plié 4. pos.
3 & 2 3
pir. STOP in passé
4 & 2 3
plié 5. pos.
5 &2 3
tendu 2. position
6 & 2 3
plié 4. position
7 & 2 3
pir. pir. STOP in passé
2. x w/oct. 8va
8 & 2 3
plié 5. pos.

♩ = 126 **Slow-ish waltz in 3 phrases of 8** **Ex. 73**
p. 137

1.
2.
3
8vb
8vb

♩ = 69
Adage in uneven phrases of 6: a six
Ex. 74
pp. 138, 102
1 - - 2 - - 3 - -
4 - - 5 - - 6 - & uh
1 - - 2 - - 3 - -
4 - - 5 & 6 - & uh
2 - - 2 & 3 & uh
4 - - 5 - - 6 - & uh
8va
8vb

8vb
8vb
8vb
8vb

A ♩ = 96
B ♩ = 140
C ♩ = 182
Slow, medium-tempo, and fast waltzes
Mr. Brunson's rdj à terre combination
Ex. 75
pp. 138, 105
8va
5. pos., arms bras bas
A
5 - & 6 & uh 7 & uh 8 & uh
arms to 1. position
arms to 2. position
1 - & 2 & uh 3 - & 4 & uh
passé
plié 5. pos. back
passé
plié 5. pos. front
8vb
5 - & 6 - & 7 - & 8 - &
tendu front
tendu side
tendu back
slowly thru 1. pos.
4 ronds de jambe à terre en dehors
tendu front
tendu back thru 1. pos.
1.
coupé back
plié in 5. pos.
the previous 16 counts en dedans

2.
coupé front
5. pos.
B
1) relevé lent, standing leg in plié
2) slowly into passé, straighten standing leg
lift the knee
5. pos. back
reverse the previous
8 counts
inhale
mf
8va
C ff circular port de bras en dedans
8vb
inhale
circular port de bras en dehors
8va

8va
8vb
rise to sous-sus---------
mp
arms to 2. pos.-----
demi-plié-------------
p
bras bas.
straighten.

♩ = 86 **Petit allegro with 3-3-2 phrasing instead of 4-4** **Ex. 76 p. 141**

♩ = 112 **Coda: a two** **Ex. 77 p. 143**

8vb
8vb
8va
8vb
8vb
(♯)
(♯)

8va
8vb
8vb
8vb
8vb
8vb
8vb
1.
8vb
8vb
8vb

8va
2.
8vb
8vb

=112
Coda: a two
Ex. 78
p. 143
5 - - &
6 - - &
7 - & -
8 - - &
1 - - &
2 - - &
3 - & uh
4 - - &
5 - - &
6 - - &
7 - & uh
8 - - &
2. x 8va
sim.
8 - - &
3

8va
8vb
8vb
1.
2.

♩ = 112

Stop-time coda: a two

Ex. 78a
p. 143

8va
8vb

= 104

Slow waltz

Ex. 79
p. 146

2.
16va

♩ = 108
March: a two
Ex. 80
pp. 156, 109, 197
5 & 6 &
7 & 8 &
1 & 2 &
3 & 4 &
5 & 6 &
7 & 8 &
8vb
8va

♩ =114 **Coda: a two** **Ex. 81**
p. 166

1.
2.
8va
8va
8va
8vb
8va
8vb

8va
8vb
8va

♩ = 112
Simple slow-ish waltz
Ex. 82a
p. 167

♩ = 112
Slow-ish waltz with additional octaves
Ex. 82b
p. 167
8vb
8vb
8vb

♩ = 112
Slow-ish waltz with additional harmony
Ex. 82c
p. 167
5 - & 6 - & 7 - & 8 & uh
1 - & 2 & uh 3 - & 4 & uh
8vb
8vb
5 - & 6 & uh 7 - & 8 &
8vb
8vb
8va
8vb

Ex. 83
p. 212

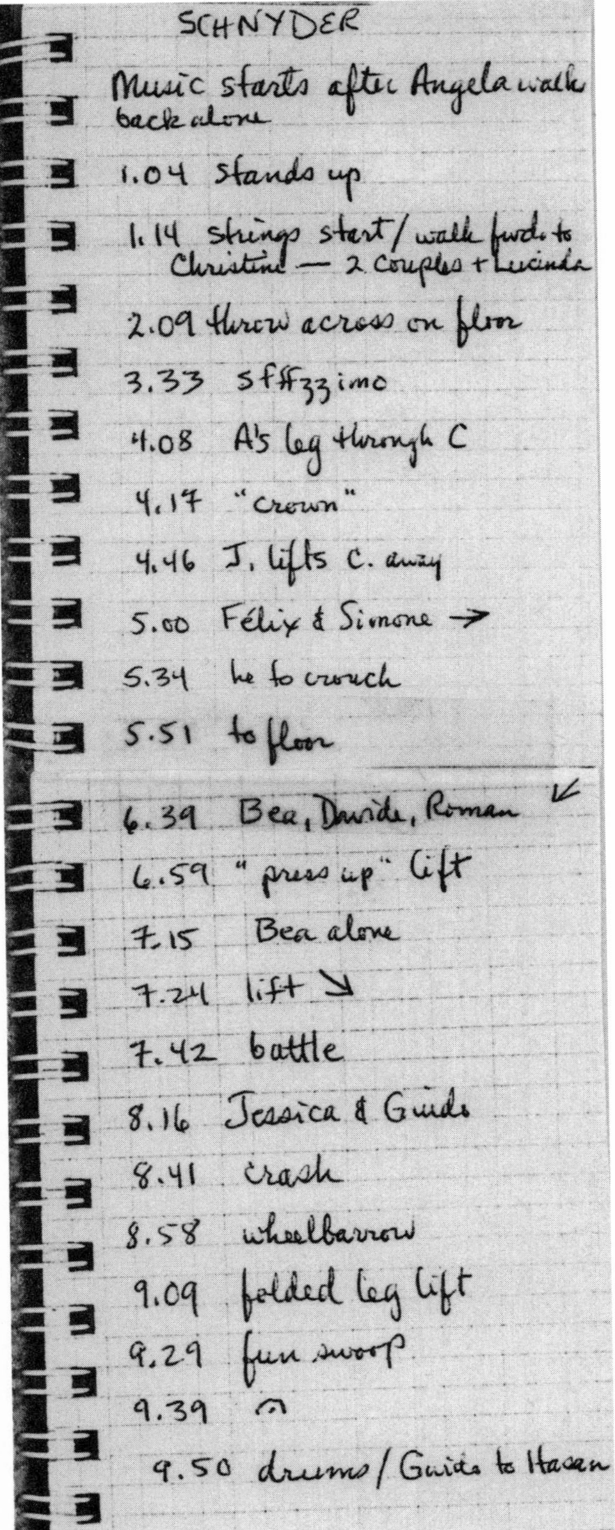
SCHNYDER

Music starts after Angela walk back alone

1.04 Stands up

1.14 strings start / walk fwd. to Christine — 2 couples + Lucinda

2.09 throw across on floor

3.33 sffffzzimo

4.08 A's leg through C

4.17 "crown"

4.46 J. lifts C. away

5.00 Félix & Simone →

5.34 he to crouch

5.51 to floor

6.39 Bea, Davide, Roman ↙

6.59 "press up" lift

7.15 Bea alone

7.24 lift ↘

7.42 battle

8.16 Jessica & Guido

8.41 crash

8.58 wheelbarrow

9.09 folded leg lift

9.29 fun swoop

9.39 𝄐

9.50 drums / Guido to Hasan

Glossary

This section will list all the dance steps, movements, and positions mentioned in this book, as well as a few musical terms. The brief descriptions are geared to accompanists who are unfamiliar with the vocabulary of classical dance. "Proper" alphabetization has not been followed, because someone unfamiliar with the French language will look for a term according to what he hears ("en dedans"), not according to the key word ("dedans, en").

Included also in this section are terms used throughout the book which may be unfamiliar to all readers, and which have not been defined in the text mostly because of space constraints. (Unfamiliar terms which have been defined in the text will be found in the index.) Terms marked with an asterisk can be preceded by the word *battement.*

For more complete information on the terminology of classical ballet, the following are recommended:

- Gretchen Ward Warren's *Classical Ballet Technique* is a beautifully arranged dictionary of the classical ballet vocabulary with accompanying photographs.
- The title of Gail Grant's *Technical Manual and Dictionary of Classical Ballet* is self-explanatory; the book is small and succinct.

à la seconde: (a) in second position or to the side; (b) an abbreviation of (grande) pirouette à la seconde.

Alberti bass: a pattern of 8th- or 16th-note broken chords in the left hand.

arabesque: one of the most fundamental positions in ballet. The dancer stands on one leg and raises the other behind him, either with the toe poised on the floor or lifted into the air. The arms in arabesque may be arranged in any number of positions.

arabesque penchée: an arabesque in which the upper body bends toward the floor while the raised leg extends higher.

arabesque piquée: an arabesque accomplished with the standing leg reaching its vertical position sharply, usually without bending the knee.

assemblé: a jumping movement in which the legs are brought tightly together into fifth position in the air. It may be used in petit, medium, and grand allegro movement.

attitude: a fundamental position in ballet. The working leg is raised and bent at—ideally—a horizontal angle of 90°. It may be executed to the front, side, or back.

balancé (not to be confused with the English word *balance*): a three-part step that feels like a waltz.

Balanchine, George (1904–1983): Russian-born American choreographer, founder of the New York City Ballet.

**balançoire (en):* an abbreviated term for grands battements en balançoire.

ballerina: a term, greatly abused these days, that should be reserved only for female dancers of the highest caliber.

ballet master/mistress: the person responsible for rehearsing a company's repertoire and for teaching company class.

ballon: a noun referring to the lightness and bounce associated with jumping.

ballonné: a jumping step in which one leg kicks out in the air and sharply bends in again upon landing.

ballotté: a jumping step in which the legs thrust alternately to the front and to the back.

bar: the amount of music contained between 2 vertical lines (bar lines) in a piece of music. A bar can contain any number of counts, depending on the time signature/meter.

barre: (a) the first part of a standard ballet class; (b) the wooden rail usually used for balance during this part of the class.

battement: there are at least twenty different kinds of battement steps and movements (battement frappé, battement fondu, grand battement, etc.), most of which are abbreviated in the dance studio by eliminating the word *battement.* Its literal meaning, "beating," is fairly irrelevant, as it has little to do with how most of these steps are executed.

battement piqué: a movement, often included in dégagé and grand battement combinations, in which the pointed toes of the working leg tap the floor sharply and immediately rebound upward. This term is used interchangeably with battement pointé.

battement pointé: see *battement piqué.*

batterie: the family of jumping steps in which the legs are quickly and repeatedly crossed and uncrossed (beaten) in the air, which gives the illusion of weaving.

beat (musical): dance teachers seem to shy away from the word *beat,* fortunately, because it would be easy for them to confuse a beat with a count. A beat is the basic rhythmic unit of a piece. In 4/4 time there are 4 beats and 2 counts in a bar (the bottom 4 means each beat is a quarter note); in 6/8 time there are 6 beats and 2 counts in a bar (the 8 means each beat is an eighth note).

beaten: the English adjective that describes batterie.

Bournonville, Auguste (1805–1879): Danish dancer, choreographer, and teacher.

bras: arms (as in *port de bras*).

brisé: a small (usually), beaten, jumping step.

cabriole: a jumping step in which one leg is thrust into the air and the other lifts to beat against it in the air.

cambré: a bending of the body from the waist if bending to the side or to the back, or from the hip joints if bending forward.

Cecchetti, Enrico (1850–1928): Italian dancer, ballet master, and founder of a well-known ballet-teaching method.

center (or *centre practice*): the second part of a standard ballet class, done without the aid of a barre.

chaînés: the common colloquial term for tours chaînés déboulés: a series of small, compact, lightning-speed (when executed by an advanced dancer) turns.

changement: a small (usually) jumping step in which the feet change from one fifth position to the other in the air.

chassé: a jumping, traveling step similar to a skip.

choreographer: the person who invents and puts together dances.

**cloche (en):* an abbreviated term for *(grands) battements en cloche.*

contretemps: a syncopated jumping step.

corps de ballet (or *corps*): (a) a group of dancers moving together in formation, often in unison, such as the swans in *Swan Lake;* (b) a term of rank which refers to the dancers lowest in the (chiefly American) hierarchy of a ballet company.

count: a dance teacher's counts are the numbers she uses to form phrases of movement during her classroom demonstrations. These counts do not always correspond to a musician's counts.

coupé: (a) a movement, usually jumped, in which the weight is changed from one foot to the other through fifth position; (b) an incorrect but common term for the position of the foot with the toe held pointed at the opposite ankle.

Cunningham, Merce: American modern dancer, choreographer, and teacher.

déboulés: see *chaînés.*

**dégagé:* an extension of the tendu, in which the leg brushes to the front, side, or back with the toes pointing slightly off the floor.

dégagé family: refers to three steps (dégagé, jeté, glissé) sharing an almost identical form and quality.

demi-plié: a bending of the knee(s) in which the heel(s) stay(s) on the floor.

demi-pointe: on the balls of the feet.

derrière: behind—a location.

devant: in front—a location.

*développé: a movement in which the working leg is drawn up the standing leg into passé, extends to the front, side, or back, then returns to the starting position. It is a fundamental movement in adagio combinations, and is sometimes—with a different quality—included in grand battement combinations.

échappé: a quick movement—either jumped or not—in which both legs are thrust apart.

emboîtés: a series of small, quick jumping steps—often turned—in which the feet alternate the coupé position. (There are also different forms of emboîtés.)

en arrière: traveling backward.

en avant: traveling forward.

en croix: to the front, to the side, to the back, and again to the side.

en dedans: toward the inside—that is, movement initiated from the back that circles inward around toward the front of the body.

en dehors: toward the outside—that is, movement initiated from the front that circles outward around toward the back of the body.

en manège: describes the execution of a series of movements, usually turns or jumps, in a circle.

enchaînement: the French and British term for combination—a phrase of dance movement.

entrechat quatre: one of several jumping steps in which the legs seem to braid themselves by beating (from 2 to 10 times) and crossing each other.

fermata: a symbol over a note or notes that means to hold the note or notes for an unspecified length of time.

Fokine, Michel (1880–1942): Russian-born international choreographer associated with Serge Diaghilev's Ballets Russes.

*fondu: a movement in which both legs bend, then straighten as the working leg extends outward.

fouetté: a term referring to two very different types of movement: (a) a virtuoso series of turns (properly called fouettés rond de jambe en tournant) involving repeated relevés on one leg while the other whips in and out from passé; (b) a turning movement of the torso (sometimes called battement fouetté sauté when jumped), either en dedans or en dehors, during which the extended working leg stays in the same location on the floor or in the air. The body may execute a quarter, half, or full turn during this movement.

*frappé: a step in which the working foot touches the standing leg's ankle and is thrust out to the front, to the side, or to the back.

full-out: dancing with 100-percent energy while executing all steps to one's fullest capacity.

glissade: a preparatory, traveling, and/or linking step with a gliding feeling.

glissade précipitée: a small, fast glissade—like a musician's grace note.

**glissé:* see *dégagé.*

Graham, Martha (1893–1991): American modern dancer, choreographer, and teacher.

grand battement: a big kick, as high as possible, to the front, side, or back.

grand battement piqué: see *battement piqué.*

grande pirouette à la seconde: a virtuoso movement for (usually) male dancers in which the body turns, either as quickly as possible or in a regular rhythm, while one leg is extended to the side at 90°.

grand jeté: a soaring leap in which the legs are spread wide apart in the air.

grand jeté en tournant: a soaring leap initiated by a grand battement to the front, after which the body makes a half turn in the air and lands in arabesque.

grand pas de deux: a virtuoso duet, often excerpted from one of the nineteenth-century traditional ballets, whose structure is described on page 209.

grand plié: a bending of both knees in which the heels come off the floor, except in second position.

grand rond de jambe en l'air: a (usually) adagio movement in which the working leg extends to the front (ideally at 90°) and circles around to the side and back (en dehors), or extends to the back and circles around to the side and front (en dedans).

grands battements en balançoire: a series of big kicks, swinging from front to back.

grands battements en cloche: a series of kicks to the front and back qualitatively the same as and visually very similar to grands battements en balançoire. They can also be done in a completely different quality: very quickly and compactly with the working foot two inches off the floor.

**jeté:* (a) an adjective that can be applied to many movements, such as rond de jambe jeté; (b) another term for the step dégagé; (c) a small jumping step and—of course—a large one, as in grand jeté.

Limón, José (1908–1972): Mexican-born American modern dancer, choreographer, and teacher.

manège: an incorrect but common usage of the term *en manège.*

measure: see *bar.*

MM (Maelzel metronome): the term used to denote the speed at which a composer recommends his piece to be played. (Johann N. Maelzel established a metronome factory in Paris in 1816.)

pas: a step.

pas de basque: a three-part traveling step executed either gliding along the floor or jumped.

pas de bourrée: a three-part linking step, often done quickly in one count, with countless variations.

pas de chat: a jumping step during which both legs, one followed quickly by the other, are lifted underneath the body with the knees bent.

pas de deux/trois/quatre (etc.): a dance for two/three/four (etc.) people.

passé: a term often used, incorrectly, for the retiré movement.

penchée: a common abbreviation of the term *arabesque penchée.*

pesante: weighty

Petipa, Marius (1819–1910): French-born Russian choreographer of *Sleeping Beauty* and *Swan Lake,* among others.

petit battement battu: one pointed foot beats quickly against the ankle or instep of the standing leg.

petit battement serré: qualitatively the same as *petit battement battu.*

**piqué:* (a) stepping quickly with one leg, either onto pointe or demi-pointe, in any direction; (b) see also *battement piqué.*

piqué turn: a turn executed while stepping directly onto pointe or demi-pointe with one leg, usually done in a series diagonally across the floor or in a circle.

pirouette: a turn.

pirouette à la seconde: a common abbreviation for *grande pirouette à la seconde.*

placement: the specialized posture a dancer develops that allows him to maintain balance and to perform strenuous movements without injury.

plié: a bending of the knees—the most basic and important movement in every form of dance.

**pointé:* see *battement piqué.*

pol-bo-min: a group of musical forms sharing the same tempo and meter, and that include polonaises, boleros, minuets, and allegro 9/8s.

port de bras: (a) correctly, arm movements; (b) colloquially, often, movement of the upper body in coordination with movements of the arms.

précipitée: see *glissade précipitée.*

premier danseur: the term (mostly obsolete) for a male dancer at the same level as a ballerina.

principal: a member of the highest of the three levels in the (chiefly American) hierarchy of a ballet company.

promenade: a movement in which a dancer holds a position (often arabesque or attitude) standing on one leg while being led around in a circle by a partner. Promenades can also be done without a partner by moving the standing heel in tiny increments in a circle.

RAD: Royal Academy of Dancing, an English-based ballet training organization.

régisseur: see *ballet master/mistress.*

relevé: a rise or a slight jump from flat feet either to the balls of the feet or onto point.

relevé lent: a phrase of adagio movement in which the working leg extends without bending to the front, side, or back, and then returns to the starting position.

**retiré:* a movement or position in the shape of a triangle, with the pointed toes of the working leg placed at the knee of the standing leg. It is the first part of a développé, as well as the position in which many pirouettes are executed.

révérence: the bow, often in combination with a series of ports de bras, with which class concludes.

Robbins, Jerome (1918–1998): dancer and classical, neo-classical, and Broadway choreographer.

rond de jambe: a circular movement of the working leg done either on the floor (à terre) or in the air (en l'air).

sauté: (n.) a small, usually simple jump; (adj.) jumped, as in *échappé sauté.*

side practice: another term for the barre—the first part of a typical ballet class.

sissonne: a petit- and medium-allegro (occasionally, grand-allegro) jumping step with many variations.

soloist: a member of the middle level of the (chiefly American) hierarchy of a ballet company.

soutenu turn: a simple—usually single—turn with both feet on the floor.

spotting: the technique of focusing the eyes on the same single spot during each revolution of turns in succession or multiple pirouettes. This prevents dizziness.

stop time: a device whereby the musician stops the sound—but not the pulse—for an arbitrary number of counts (rarely more than four). If you've ever seen Ray Bolger dancing to "Once in Love with Amy," you've experienced stop time.

stride piano: the most prevalent rhythmic pattern in both music for the dance classroom and American popular songs. It originated in ragtime, and consists of an octave on each primary beat followed by a chord or chords. (True stride piano uses a tenth instead of an octave; I feel the tenth sounds too unclassical unless, of course, you're playing a popular song.)

sur le cou-de-pied: a position of the pointed working foot placed against the ankle of the standing leg.

temps de cuisse: a syncopated jumping step.

temps levé: a simple hopping movement from one leg to the same leg.

temps lié: a phrase of adagio movement necessitating a never-ending plié.

**tendu:* a simple (but not easy) movement in which one leg stretches to the front, side, or back with the pointed toes always remaining on the floor.

terre-à-terre: an adjective describing a ground-hugging movement or dancer.

tombé: a preparatory step in which the body falls forward, sideways, or backward.

tour: a turn.

tour en l'air: part of the classical vocabulary for male dancers: one or two turns in the air during which the feet do a changement.

tour jeté: a common colloquialism for *grand jeté en tournant.*

traditional ballet: one of several ballets, listed on page 127, that form the backbone of the classical repertoire. Verdi's *Aida,* Beethoven's Fifth Symphony, Ibsen's *A Doll's House,* Michelangelo's *Pietà,* and Leonardo's *Mona Lisa* are among their counterparts in other artistic fields.

turn-out: a basic principle of ballet technique that refers to the outward rotation of the legs starting in the hip sockets and ending in the feet.

Vaganova, Agrippina (1879–1951): Russian dancer and teacher.

variation: a solo dance.

Notes

Chapter 2. Essential Elements of Music for Dance

1. I have purposely chosen not to discuss compound meter. It can be a very confusing concept to anyone without an understanding of basic music theory. It is sad but true that so few dance professionals today are given even the rudiments of music—the art form so inextricably linked with dance. So the most one can hope for is that all teachers learn to count duple and triple meters clearly.

In Recommended Reading you will find information on a very fine book about music theory written specifically for dancers, *The Muncey Music Book*, by Anthony Twiner. It explains meter clearly and simply, and goes a long way to illuminate the divine logic of music.

Chapter 4. For Dance Teachers

1. A case in point: one of my employers gave sixty-four *changements* during the first class back after a three-week Christmas break. When I asked her about it, she said, "No, I couldn't have done that. I would never have been so stupid!"

Chapter 5. For Accompanists

1. Notes to teachers: most of the teachers I play for demonstrate tendus with demi-pliés as if they were speaking and dancing a march: with no elasticity in the demi-plié whatsoever. When I ask them about it, they are always very intent on the sharpness of the tendu and seem to ignore the quality of the equally important plié. Only rarely do I dare to get into a discussion of the merits of going through the foot at a slow tempo, then melting into the demi-plié—and of course the subsequent tendu combinations emphasize the sharpness of the tendu (while still going through the foot). I have often felt that maybe this obliviousness to the normal quality of a demi-plié has developed because (chicken or egg?) accompanists play what they hear teachers demonstrate, and teachers demonstrate according to what they know the accompanist will play, *and* without realizing that they are ignoring a vital part of the combination.

Additionally, if you are a teacher who believes in multitudes of tendus and dégagés at the barre, you must vary the tempi and rhythms of these combinations. Demonstrating them all in duple meter at almost the same tempo and in similar quality—an all-too-prevalent practice—implies they are time-fillers instead of individual combinations with varying qualities and intentions.

2. Note to teachers: Don't ascribe two counts to a demi-plié in a fondu combination. Pieces with the appropriate quality for fondus are almost never counted in this way.

3. Note to teachers: Please be sure your accompanist hears this. Teachers often tack on a cambré—or a balance—as an afterthought and accompanists aren't prepared for it, which means they can't help the students get into it or maintain it productively.

4. Notes to teachers: You may understandably wonder how an advanced student can learn to do more pirouettes and still retain his relationship to the music when most standard musical forms don't seem to allow for more than three pirouettes. It took many years of observation before I figured this out. I had seen many dancers do exquisite multiple pirouettes. Francesca Corkle and Mark Morris will remain forever implanted in my mind's eye in this regard; their attention to form, substance, and musicality permeates every aspect of their dancing to an extraordinary degree, no less so than during the execution of one of the most obvious technical "tricks": pirouettes. But it was Jerry Schwender who was responsible for my conscious understanding of how it could be accomplished. (I'm sure Mark and Francesca did pirouettes in exactly the same way, but I wasn't yet experienced enough to analyze how they did them.)

Jerry was one of the cleanest and most musical dancers I ever saw—noteworthy in his concentrated approach to his work—and his pirouettes were not only flawless and perfectly musical, but they were also always at his command.

In a pirouette combination done to a waltz, most dancers will accomplish three pirouettes in the following manner:

Jerry, instead of trying to squeeze four or five pirouettes into the same amount of time, would take off sooner and execute four, five, or six gorgeous pirouettes that corresponded exactly to the music, like this:

It can take many years for a dancer to realize that two controlled, musical, perfectly placed pirouettes are much more impressive to an audience than fourteen whizzing turns in the gorilla position. Sadly, many dancers never seem to realize this.

Another tip—this one from Armin Wild. In order to emphasize the "up-ness" of a pirouette's finishing position, he choreographs a "hold" (in passé on demi-pointe) as part of elementary and intermediate pirouette combinations, as in example 72. The third beat of the third bar is what the students are aiming for. This not only gives the students a specific goal to aim for physically, it also forces them to count and listen meticulously.

And yet another tip, which I have heard emphasized by every good teacher I have played for: "sitting" in any demi-plié is counterproductive, and especially so in pirouette preparations. A never-ending plié must precede even a single pirouette, even if that means that the movement before the demi-plié has to be held longer.

5. How well any grand allegro step is executed depends on how well the preparatory step is executed. And, as any good dancer or teacher will tell you, proper execution depends on musical awareness; working with, instead of going against, the music facilitates the movement. For example, arabesque piquée, chassé, grand jeté is a favorite beginning to some grand allegro combinations. The arabesque piquée must be done either on the "7" before the "1" or on the "1" itself, not on the "8." Additionally, I hope teachers will choose to have their dancers in the air on the odd-numbered counts of a grand allegro combination. Pushing off from the floor on these counts has become so prevalent these days that it has begun to look normal, but if you see a dancer at the height of his jump on these counts, you will immediately see how much more impressive and expressive it is.

6. Note to teachers: There are dancers who absolutely cannot be off the music in "à la secondes" or "fouettés" (as they are often called colloquially). Much of their accuracy is due to getting the preparation steps in exactly the right place musically. You may have to tell less fortunate dancers that it's usually better to continue at their own tempi off the music than to struggle to get back on. It's hard for me to say that, but for performance purposes, it's necessary; continuing off the music takes less brain power than breaking the momentum and trying to find the right beat, which would be very obvious to an audience. On the other hand, allowing a dancer to be consistently off the music is a dangerous practice.

7. Note to teachers: Some teachers acknowledge only the accompanist during the *révérence.* I feel very strongly that students should show their appreciation equally to the teacher and to the accompanist.

8. Notes to teachers: Teachers often request bows to be done in two counts, which usually look like hiccups because they are so fast. (Teachers can bow gracefully in two counts; students can rarely manage it, unless they are following the movements of their teacher.) Four counts works much better. Before a révérence is one time I feel that an introduction is unnecessary, especially if it is an 8-count révérence; the introduction would be half the length of the combination. A protracted "a-a-a-and," looking at the accompanist so he can pointedly play a single-note "and," is very effective and more in keeping with the mood at the end of class.

If the length of your révérence/port de bras changes from class to class, you must let the pianist know each time how long it will be. Finishing too soon—or playing longer than needed—in the middle of class is bad enough, but it is horrible for us to have stopped when the class is still involved in this special moment, or to be starting a new phrase while the class is clapping, and to have to dribble off into silence. We're the ones who end up looking like idiots; we are totally dependent on you to give us information to avoid this situation.

9. You have turned to this note certainly because of that strange word *or.* In the late nineteenth century, choreographers as well as dancers at the diva level began to snitch a variation from one ballet and put it into another, or sometimes they would even take a whole section from one ballet and put it into another. This mix-and-match process produced some ballet scores (the five listed) written by more than one of the listed composers, who were among the most well-known ballet composers of their day—through the end of the nineteenth century. I have no idea how the composers reacted to this thievery, but the practice continues today. For instance, on one videotape of *Coppélia*, Mikhail Baryshnikov dances a variation that is originally from *La Source* (example 43). Throughout the text, I have occasionally written information like *Don Quixote* (Minkus). I did that because it didn't make sense to write *Don Quixote* (Minkus, among others), and also because Minkus wrote the majority of the music in *Don Quixote.*

10. For me, sixes in every tempo are in a separate category; if I will be playing for a particular teacher for more than a few classes, I play her a bolero and an allegro 9/8 before class and ask her if she would like to use one for a petit allegro combination.

11. Mr. Brunson demanded more from his accompanists than any teacher I have ever played for, especially in the areas of speed, stamina, orchestralike fullness, and dynamic shading. Watching him teach made one realize instantly how far a teacher can push students *and* accompanists without pushing them over the brink out of control. He insisted that the music duplicate the ultimate personality of each step, whether it was being executed by an adult beginner or a seasoned professional.

12. During the preparation of this book for publication in Switzerland, a colleague of mine—a very experienced accompanist—told me that he has recently found that sitting low at the keyboard has improved his technique tremendously. He sits so low that he sawed off the bottoms of the piano stool legs. I am going to experiment with it, mainly because sitting so low prevents one from slouching. This colleague's information made me question the validity of this entire section, and I toyed with the idea of omitting it. But I decided that both approaches should be mentioned; one or the other may prove helpful to the reader. (Six months later: it definitely does *not* work for me.)

13. It was during this Verdy-Wilde class that I first became aware of how choosing a piece of music that does not correspond to what the teacher has counted can completely change the thrust of a combination. Until that time, most teachers had always accepted whatever I played, even if it was not what they had requested. I am quick to point out that they did this *not* because I was so good, but because they didn't want to lose time haggling over music. And if I didn't play what they requested, it was because I didn't have it in my repertoire. Ms. Wilde was the first person who ever said it straight out: "That's not what I wanted, but I don't want to waste time." I realized that, with the billions of pieces of music floating around in the universe, there would certainly be at least one of whatever I needed to satisfy the request of any teacher. And by this time I had taken enough dance classes myself to be able to see what the combination was and to remember it so I could work on the music outside of class.

14. Not to belabor the point, but I would like to quote from what I think of as the dancer's bible, *Dance Technique and Injury Prevention* by Justin Howse and Shirley Hancock: "Co-ordination training develops pre-programmed automatic multi-mus-

cular patterns. These are known as engrams. Constant, exact repetition or practice will produce an engram, a condition where individual muscles or movements are not consciously considered. . . . These automatic engrams can only be developed by voluntary repetition of the precise programme. This must be followed accurately otherwise the input of information will vary each time and the engram cannot be developed. It follows that initially the pattern must be slow enough to be accurate."

15. I have seen many teachers turn a blind eye to musicality (and the lack thereof) in company class, possibly out of sympathy for the dancers' workload and having other things to think about. I am the first person to also sympathize with professional dancers, but allowing them to be constantly unmusical is to do them a great disservice. They cannot afford to be unmusical onstage. And valuable rehearsal time is wasted correcting musicality that should be firmly anchored—habitual—in the daily class. *And musicality is as much a part of technique as turn-out is.*

References

Kennedy, Michael. *The Concise Oxford Dictionary of Music.* Ed. Joyce Bourne. 4th ed. Oxford: Oxford University Press, 1996.

Howse, Justin, and Shirley Hancock. *Dance Technique and Injury Prevention.* 2d. ed. New York: Theatre Arts Books/Routledge, 1992.

Koegler, Horst. *Concise Oxford Dictionary of Ballet.* 2d ed. Oxford: Oxford University Press, 1982.

Recommended Reading

Grant, Gail. *Technical Manual and Dictionary of Classical Ballet.* 3d rev. ed. New York: Dover, 1982.

Soares, Janet Mansfield. *Louis Horst: Musician in a Dancer's World.* Durham, N.C.: Duke University Press, 1992.

Teck, Katherine. *Music for the Dance: Reflections on a Collaborative Art.* Westport, Conn.: Greenwood Press, 1989.

———. *Movement to Music: Musicians in the Dance Studio.* Westport, Conn.: Greenwood Press, 1990.

———. *Ear Training for the Body: A Dancer's Guide to Music.* Pennington, N.J.: Princeton Book Company, 1994.

Twiner, Anthony. *The Muncey Music Book.* London: Dance Books, 1986 (distributed in the U.S.A. by Princeton Book Co., P.O. Box 57, Pennington, N.J. 08534).

Warren, Gretchen Ward. *Classical Ballet Technique.* Gainesville: University Press of Florida, 1989.

Index

All steps and movements used throughout the text are defined in the glossary. Those appearing in the index are there mainly to assist an accompanist in his search for appropriate music. Any term not found in the index is in either the table of contents or the glossary.

Harriet Cavalli was born in Rochester, New York, and studied at the New England Conservatory of Music in Boston. After four years of playing the Cecchetti syllabus and for tap and open classes in the Boston area, she moved to New York City with her family in 1962. Her close association with Perry Brunson began at this time at the Ballet Russe School of Dance; she was his accompanist for a large part of his teaching career, and he was also her first and most influential ballet teacher.

From 1962 until 1970 Ms. Cavalli worked for most of the major dance institutions in New York, such as the Joffrey and Harkness Ballets and American Ballet Theatre, among others. From 1971 to 1974 she was with the Royal Winnipeg Ballet; from 1974 to 1979 she worked for the First Chamber Dance Company in Seattle as both executive administrator and music director of the company, as well as continuing her association with Mr. Brunson in the Trainee Program; and from 1979 to 1983 she was with John Neumeier at the Hamburg (Germany) State Opera, and in Switzerland with Riccardo Duse (Bern) and Oscar Araiz (Geneva).

From 1983 until 1986 she was principal accompanist and teacher of dance history and music for dancers at the Cornish College of the Arts in Seattle. She was arranger and soloist for Mark Morris's *Canonic 3/4 Studies.* Returning to Europe, she was with Uwe Scholz and the Zurich Opera Ballet (1986–1988), Heinz Spoerli and the Basel Ballet (1988–1991), and François Klaus and Martin Schläpfer and the Bern Ballet (1991–1999). She currently works with Mr. Schläpfer's BallettMainz at the Mainz State Theater in Germany.

Ms. Cavalli has made numerous records, cassettes, and CDs for ballet classes, the latest of which were with Mr. Schläpfer. They may be ordered by e-mail at harrietshakti@yahoo.com. She specializes in teaching music for dance teachers and for dancers, as well as training pianists in the art of dance accompaniment, and has given numerous seminars in Europe and the United States on these topics. She has given regular lessons in ballet to professional dancers over the years. And having played for more than 400 dance teachers has given her unique insight into the communication process between the two protagonists in the dance classroom.

The German version of this book, *Tanz und Musik,* appeared in 1998 through the sponsorship and support of the Swiss Ballet Teachers' Association.

Ms. Cavalli has studied ballet with Perry Brunson, Maria Swoboda, Flemming Halby, Donna Silva, and Martin Schläpfer.